Leadership Coaching
for the Workplace

Leadership Coaching
for the Workplace

TIMOTHY BENTLEY

ESTHER KOHN-BENTLEY

Irwin Publishing Ltd.
Toronto/Vancouver, Canada

ISBN 0-7725-2887-X

National Library of Canada Cataloguing in Publication Data is available from the National Library of Canada.

Designer: Sonya V. Thursby/OPUS HOUSE INCORPORATED
Typesetting: J. Lynn Campbell/OPUS HOUSE INCORPORATED
Production Editor: Jennifer Howse
Cover: Tom Szuba/MASTERFILE

Published by
Irwin Publishing Ltd.
325 Humber College Blvd.
Toronto, ON M9W 7C3

We acknowledge for their financial support of our publishing program the Canada Council, the Ontario Arts Council, and the Government of Canada through the Book Publishing Industry Development Program (BPIDP).

Printed and bound in Canada
1 2 3 4 5   05 04 03 02 01

> Contents

> List of Figures

As a practitioner and researcher in the field of organizational change, I am profoundly aware of the gap between theory and practice. Despite shared visions, company philosophies and collaborative change rhetoric, many leaders are still unable to deal with the basic interpersonal processes of the workplace.

Within learning organizations, the key to change ultimately lies in each individual's ability to bring a whole, aware, vulnerable, genuine, congruent, and integrated self to the workplace—in a phrase, to bring one's emotional maturity. As organizations include a critical mass of individuals who are consciously and continuously developing this aspect of themselves, the basic quality of working life will change for everyone.

Until recently, bureaucratic and hierarchically structured organizations—our legacy from the industrial age—have prevailed as models for the workplace. Although they have often been held responsible for much of the coercive, disempowering impact of organizational life, they have also shielded workers from having to interact in genuine ways. In a sense, the rigidities of hierarchy have been protective—one could always seek direction from the *Policies and Procedures Manual* or blame the job description, the manager, or the system for problems unskilfully dealt with and unresolved.

Increasingly, organizational members can no longer shelter in such systemic protection. Flattened structures, re-engineered work processes, increased use of teams, and the changing demands on managers are only a few of the shifts heralding a completely new set of relational challenges for today's worker. More permeable boundaries and flexible work structures force employees into interactions demanding a level of authenticity not previously imagined in the workplace. Organizations are asking people to deal with one another directly and openly, to manage their differences skillfully, and to maintain solid working relationships in the face of seemingly intractable conflicts. Rifts caused by value differences, lack of cross-cultural understanding or appreciation, historic pain reasserting itself in the present, knee-jerk reactions to authority, and entrenched positions on any number of issues are the ingredients of today's dysfunctional workplace.

Within this context, Timothy Bentley and Esther Kohn-Bentley have written a remarkable book to address the challenge of facilitating individual development for organizational change. They note, "Coaching provides a peerless opportunity to nurture the most benevolent forces within the organization, and to encourage the most humane instincts of its leaders."

In presenting their concept of coaching as a "Deep Learning Process," the authors offer a tangible approach for both the aspiring and the experienced professional coach for developing leadership in the workplace. At first glance, their book seems to be a step-by-step guide to coaching; but on careful reading, one realizes that the book reveals the intricacies of a field of practice that can seem deceptively straightforward. The authors explore basic principles and beliefs underlying the field—compassion, integrity, respect for the client, and respect for oneself as the coach and for the coaching relationship—in all of its richness and complexity. With its emphasis on a client-centred, whole-person, action orientation within the workplace systems, the content of this book reflects the values of adult education, as well as those of organizational change and learning.

Despite the authors' disclaimer that "it is impossible to adequately define the work whether in a few words or in the pages of an entire book," they have indeed managed to provide a clear and detailed portrait of coaching as both an art and a science, while skillfully interspersing philosophy with practice. Concrete, practical, and theoretically sound suggestions are artfully interwoven with narrative case examples from the authors' extensive experience in a wide variety of coaching situations. Whether we are hearing about one coachee's challenges in dealing with a difficult manager, another's attempts to transform her leadership style from authoritarian to collaborative, or an individual's efforts to cope with rapid technological change, one has the clear impression that years of well-honed wisdom are imbedded in these narratives.

This book is knit together with gentle humour, illustrative experiences, and personal anecdotes to aid the digestion of serious content and complex ideas. Also, the recurrent coach and coachee dialogues provide the rare experience of watching a master at work, with the sense that you are actually sitting in the same room.

The initial chapters address the emergent coaching profession in the context of its historic and theoretical roots, examining its development with many disciplinary influences. The authors welcome and legitimize the input of a variety of professional approaches, making it accessible to anyone whose career interests have led to coaching. But it does not leave one with the impression that this is a field for amateurs. Rather, it promotes a cautious entry level matching one's skills, while providing support for the continuous development of those skills through reflective practice. In this way, the authors gracefully manage the tension between advocating specific values and approaches, outlined in lucid detail, with a framework endorsing differences in style, experience, application, and intention.

To promote the ongoing development of the reader, the book is replete with resources in the form of specific instruments such as a competency self-assessment questionnaire for coaches, a listing of sources for further training and accreditation in the field, and a substantial annotated bibliography and resources for further study.

The book is full of heart—as well as brain, courage, and spirit. In the Oz of organizational life, it provides clear direction for coaching professionals to develop themselves and their clients as whole people at work. It will become a classic in the field of coaching, and a touchstone in the area of organizational change and leadership.

Marilyn Laiken, Ph.D.
Professor of Adult Education,
Workplace Learning and Change
The Ontario Institute for Studies in Education
at the University of Toronto

This book has bubbled up out of our excitement about our work. Over the past two decades we have watched coaching change people's lives for the better, watched as they became confident, capable, and immensely more self-aware. We've also seen the coaching process stimulate the development of workplaces that encourage the creativity and productivity of those who work within them.

Yet little has been written to clarify why, how, and when coaching actually works.

Reflecting on our own practice recently, we realize that we have been following principles and procedures we have never written down, developing a body of wisdom so familiar that we practise it habitually. It seems time to gather and to distill those factors that make our work effective and to share them with others. Many of these factors are identified under the title "The Deep Learning Process," and they underlie much of this book.

These pages are addressed to those whose work is based on helping people to develop themselves. We include those who are formally coaches, those who are consultants, counsellors, and therapists, and those who make referrals to any of these groups. We also include executives, supervisors, and managers, specialists in human resources, organizational development, and training, as well as teachers and students of management.

Whatever your role, you will find valuable new insights and well-tested old truths in these pages. We have introduced plenty of examples of good coaching, not to mention a few of horrible coaching, with the hope that the principles of coaching will leap off the page and help you to reflect productively about your own practice and relationships both in and out of the workplace.

This text is designed to paint a comprehensive picture of the person of the coach and the practice of coaching, demonstrating how you can move your work to a deeper level as you develop an increasingly sophisticated style of coaching. And it offers guidance to help ensure that the changes made by those with whom you work are not merely cosmetically pleasing but profound and sustainable.

Some Caution

Enthusiastic though we may be about the impact this book may have, we must add the caution that reading can never substitute for good training or experience. The value of this book is in providing general guidance only. No text can adequately instruct the reader in how to practise coaching in specific circumstances. Nor is it intended to provide legal advice, not even in Chapter Five where an example of a contract is shown; the relevant law varies widely from jurisdiction to jurisdiction.

Furthermore, nothing written here should induce you to ignore your own intuition, wisdom, or good sense. Do not follow any suggestion unless you are fully confident that it is right for you and for your coachee in the unique situation you are facing.

Because confidentiality is a central pillar of the coaching process, all identifying data, including names, have been changed to protect the anonymity of our real-life clients. As well, sometimes the individuals in the case examples are composites of two or more real people.

We have decided to use the rather ungraceful term "coachee" rather than "client" throughout, to avoid confusion between the individual being coached and the person or organization that hired the coach—the latter is often referred to as the "client."

We have alternated the use of male and female pronouns from chapter to chapter to recognize that the coach and the coachee may realistically be either male or female. Finally, we recognize that the term "direct report" may be unfamiliar to some readers. It refers to any person who reports directly to a given manager.

Acknowledgements

Others have contributed more to this book than we can adequately acknowledge. Above all, our unnamed coachees have honoured us with their trust, inspired us with their courage, and literally taught us how to coach.

Among our formal teachers, those who first introduced us to the principles of deep learning include Dr. Helen Morley, Donald Gillies, Ronald Owston, Ann Bartram, Jane Sutherland, and Dr. Alisa Hornung.

Our students of advanced coaching, along with participants in innumerable professional workshops, keep on asking tough questions that bring our intuitive reactions into the light of day and force us to examine them.

Special appreciation is due to Professor Marilyn Laiken for many years of warm encouragement in this work and for writing the Foreword.

Thelma Barer-Stein, as agent and developmental editor, has guided this process with keen attention and a valuable sense of direction.

Melinda Sinclair provided mini-reviews of several books in the Resources section, critiqued parts of the manuscript, and encouraged us to explore our ideas in the forum of the Adler School for Professional Coaching.

Fellow members of the Coaching Guild—Sheila Goldgrab, Peter Johnson, Rosemary Russell, Ellen Samiec, Brenda Saunders, and Melinda Sinclair—provided us with much stimulation and support.

Pat Archer, a brilliant therapist and coach, encouraged us with keen interest and enduring care.

The CEO of Leading Edge Seminars, Michael Kerman, always provided generous quantities of intelligence, friendship, and emotional support.

Our talented staff at Panoramic Feedback kept 360-degree feedback instruments travelling securely in cyberspace, despite our being distracted by the writing process.

We thank our children, Trisha, Andrew, and Aaron, daughter-in-law Nili, and grandson Artie, and our dear parents Alice, Mala, and Leon, for their love, support, and forbearance during those times we neglected them in the race to finish this manuscript.

Our friends have been remarkably kind, encouraging, and supportive. Where would we be without your sustaining affection?

Timothy Bentley and Esther Kohn-Bentley

PART 1

How Coaching Supports Deep Change

PART 1

HOW COACHING SUPPORTS DEEP CHANGE

> ## Chapter 1: Developing Leadership for a New Age

The advent of leadership coaching in the workplace stands out from the tumultuous landscape of the past decade like a rare and luminous landmark. New technologies and new enterprises have transformed the way we work by decreasing our sense of power and increasing our anxiety.

It is no coincidence that the coaching movement has emerged in parallel with these changes. It offers a powerful method that transforms our traditional resistance to change, harnessing our powers to learn new survival skills. Through coaching, we are becoming again masters of our environment. It is little wonder that the demand for fine coaches has outstripped the supply.

This book provides a detailed map of the practice of coaching for everyone who has a stake in this force for human progress. Its contribution is to present leadership coaching from a perspective—the Deep Learning Process—that increases both the depth and staying power of the changes that result.

Coaching Serves the Business Revolution

Leadership coaching was born and is now a part of our corporate consciousness simply because there was and is no other choice. It answers many demands posed by the revolution in our workplace: to shift our thinking from maintenance to innovation, to vastly improve our people skills, and to develop an entrepreneurial approach to employment. In addition, leadership coaching provides guidance when traditional structures, such as job specifications, are evaporating. In the end, it helps us to understand what we are truly good at and how we can use these abilities to strengthen the organizational culture; it also addresses our fears of radical change.

Coaching provides in-depth solutions to those needs as no classroom and no seminar can. In fact, no conventional form of learning has shown a comparable capability to help people to make profound and difficult changes in the way they approach their work, and to make those changes last.

Most urgently of all, workplace coaching is a response to the intense need for renewal in the ranks of our senior leaders and managers, casting fresh light on the emerging science of management. It accelerates the growth in effectiveness of supervisors, and the impact of these personal transformations ripples outward. The benefits are often dramatic, affecting all levels of management and employees, improving teamwork, productivity, and the quality of work life in a multitude of workplaces.

Now that organizations have begun to adopt a coaching perspective as part of their culture, they find themselves moving closer to the grail of sustainable growth by protecting their investment in human capital, and by refreshing those who carry irreplaceable knowledge and specialized skills. Leadership coaching increases the likelihood that valued senior managers will remain productive and loyal, and at a modest cost compared to recruiting and training their replacements.

Today's coaching is an up-to-date spin on a venerable tradition. It is based on an ancient form of learning—one person helping another to learn, with individualized encouragement, guidance, instruction, and inspiration. Throughout history, monarchs and other world leaders have shared the credit for their success with mentors, sages, and confidants. Now it is the turn of leadership coaching.

The Value of Coaching Skills

This book offers a step-by-step guide to the leadership coaching process that will help you function more effectively, whether you work within an organization as an executive or manager, coach people as part of a broader area of responsibility—such as Human Resources, Succession Planning, or Organization Development—or provide support to the workplace as an external consultant. If you provide coaching as your full-time occupation, or if, as an administrator, you need to know more about how coaching can help to develop your people, you will find valuable information here. And if you expect to use coaching skills more in your work or to become a full-time coach, this will be your handbook.

Have you ever wondered what differentiates an extraordinary coach from one who simply hangs out a shingle or just fills a position? Have you ever watched someone coached into excellence and then tumble back into mediocrity? Here is an opportunity to learn the characteristics that distinguish a fine coach, to understand how personal change may be only temporary, and what you can do about it. Have you observed that the most profound need for people to change within an organization has gone largely untouched? These pages will help to point you toward practical solutions.

Because coaching is practised in many professions and formats, there is no single definition that can fully capture its meaning. This is how we see leadership coaching:

1. It is a confidential team relationship between a skilled guide (the coach) and a learner (the coachee).
2. The learner has a strong need (sometimes recognized initially only by others) to develop new abilities or to make personal changes.
3. The coachee benefits from the leverage of a one-to-one relationship in which she or he is regarded as an equal.
4. The coach brings special skills to the team, encouraging learning that is life-changing and long-lasting.

A BRITTLE SUPERVISOR BECOMES FLEXIBLE

The story of a supervisor we'll call Daryl exemplifies how leadership coaching can encourage significant personal change even though at first, change appears impossible to outsiders, and even when the coachee is initially unaware that coaching could be of value.

Daryl had many years of experience as a successful and respected supervisor of researchers in a leading hospital. But with the advent of new technology, the executive committee decided that the need for him to supervise others had diminished, and determined that it would be more cost-effective for Daryl to dedicate his energy and intelligence to directing research in leading-edge fields vital to the hospital's prestige.

The complicating factor was that Daryl reported to an erratic and demanding vice-president. In reaction to this unsettling environment, he had gradually developed a reputation for being defensive, rigid, brittle, and insecure. Being recently divorced as well, he was considered to be especially fragile.

The thought of asking so brittle a person to change long-established work patterns made everyone very nervous. What if he refused, or became angry, or couldn't cope, or simply fell apart?

At length, the hospital's Human Resources director suggested a solution. He would offer the services of a coach to help Daryl deal with the changes in his life. With the approval of the committee, he met with Daryl and told him the news. As predicted, Daryl reacted strongly, by turns angry and resistant. By the end of the meeting, however, he had agreed to meet the coach and to experiment with this new form of relationship.

Coaching turned out to be unlike anything he had ever experienced before in the workplace. When he was angry, the coach didn't panic, she simply listened and empathized. When he was tearful, she handed him a tissue and encouraged him to feel his emotions. When he expressed anxiety that the hospital wanted to dump him, she acknowledged his fears. And as he calmed, she asked if he had any idea how he could make his position more secure.

So began a fruitful partnership. At first, Daryl leaned heavily on his coach for emotional support, while he applied his capable brain to strategies for dealing with his new situation. But soon the coach was helping him to think through ways of dealing with his difficult boss: communicating more fully, taking the initiative to propose new projects, and documenting decisions via e-mail.

His mood lightened. With chuckles, Daryl and his coach referred to his new skills as "upward supervision".

As they began to analyze his experiments in relating to his boss, Daryl was able to fine-tune his responses and saw satisfying results. Within a couple of months the VP had backed off a little, allowing Daryl to ease into his new role. With none of the expected angst, Daryl gradually let go of his supervisory responsibilities in favour of a couple of difficult research projects well-suited to his strengths.

While the executive committee had been correct in thinking that Daryl was rigid, they had not recognized that his reactions were situational and therefore temporary. By changing the situation—by importing an empathic coach—they provided the opportunity for him to swim with the current rather than against it.

Memo from Daryl to his coach:
I'm verrrrrry grateful for all your help and support. When I think I'm about to go mad, I remember that you are here for me. Thanks.
Daryl.

Memo from the VP to the coach:
At the last meeting of the executive committee, we were unanimous in expressing our appreciation. Without coaching, we don't believe we could have turned this situation around.

Needless to say, Daryl continues to succeed with his work, and the vice-president's office has developed an unexpected confidence in—of all things—his flexibility.

A Leadership Coaching Model for the Workplace

To the casual observer, the coaching of Daryl might appear unplanned and spontaneous —a penetrating question here, a tissue offered there, a chuckle of recognition, an impromptu sketch on a scratchpad, and a suggestion for new behaviour.

There is no question that the best coaches are friendly, casual, and responsive to the moment. Probe beneath that easygoing exterior, however, and you will find that they are working deliberately, consciously, from a carefully crafted and time-tested model.

What happens when the coach does not have a model? You have watched it happen on television. The interviewer suddenly asks a question that does not make any sense. It comes out of left field, leaving the person being interviewed mildly annoyed and making the interviewer look stupid. Any empathy the pair may have developed up to this point has been destroyed.

The most important skill in broadcast interviewing is the ability to listen attentively and pick up on cues that your interviewee is certain to offer. As you respond to these cues, the interview flows along natural lines, becoming gradually deeper.

Here is why an interview sometimes goes badly. Inadequately prepared, lacking a sense of direction, the interviewer is too busy searching his mind for the next clever question when he really should be listening. With an empty smile on his face, he is too distracted to take up the multiple cues and suggestions the interviewee is offering, and ends up asking questions that have no relevance at all.

Finding an Adequate Coaching Model

Until recently, the lack of an adequate model for leadership coaching in the workplace was a source of frustration for coaches wishing to improve their work. Training programs tried to cater to students with a variety of interests. Some were focused on coaching for artistic creativity, for spirituality, for personal fulfilment, or for business needs. The available models were often so generalized they teased all but satisfied none.

Our model for leadership coaching in the workplace is described throughout this book. It includes the basic structure of coaching, guidelines, examples, handouts, and hints—all designed to assist workplace coaches in doing their best work.

A Proven Model Provides Invisible Guidance

Coaching is much like interviewing. The benefit of basing your work on a proven model or structure is that it reduces the likelihood of becoming lost. If you examine those professions where the stakes are very high—life and death hanging in the balance—you will find that practitioners work religiously from a model. The aircraft pilot has a checklist of gauges and controls to test before takeoff. The surgeon follows a rigid routine of sterilization. Even the cop shaking down a suspect follows safety guidelines.

Because the coaching model you will meet here provides much of the guidance you need from minute to minute, you will not have to squander energy wondering what question to ask next or how you will cope with the unexpected.

Once you know a coaching model well, you will scarcely have to think about it. It will operate like the autopilot of an aircraft, transporting you and your coachee from the start of the trip to the finish. It will leave you free to focus your attention fully on the conversation and to truly hear what the coachee has to say.

How the Deep Learning Process Complements the Basic Coaching Model

One of the key factors differentiating our model is that it is permeated by a specific process—the Deep Learning Process. How does a process differ from a model? In the case of coaching, the process is dynamic, evoking a subtle series of changes that evolve from the soul and psychology of personal development. The model, by contrast, is the set of structures that contain and support this process of change.

Despite the impact of leadership coaching on organizational life to date, we think it has shown merely a hint of its potential power. Many, perhaps a majority, of the coaches now practising are using only part of their potential. They are often effective, but could be significantly more so if they were to incorporate a learning process like this into their work.

We named it the Deep Learning Process because it enables coach and coachee to move below the surface and visible aspects of a situation, and to work at a more powerful, foundational level by anchoring the changes that the coachee makes, continually producing results beyond the early moments of insight and well into the long term.

We will describe the characteristics of the Deep Learning Process more fully in Chapter Four. For a glimpse at some of its features, let's meet Julian, a senior manager who was supported in confronting serious workplace problems by specific aspects of the Deep Learning Process.

A compassionate coach provided safety in a frank relationship, where Julian's fundamental aspiration to grow was harnessed and focused. Together, the coach and Julian explored significant aspects of his past, as well as his present-day circumstances. The coach attended to his emotional responses and resistance while moving toward practical solutions and seamlessly confronting the possibility of future slippage with practical planning. These elements of the coaching were integrated to form a whole of great strength, providing change that was profound yet sustainable.

JULIAN'S BIGGEST CHALLENGE

Julian gave full credit for his success as VP of Marketing to his pose as a rugged individualist. He needed no one—at least, not until he ran into the biggest challenge of his career.

Increasingly, offshore competition was accompanied by falling prices that began to hammer his organization, an electronics manufacturer. Through caffeine-fuelled days and nights, working largely on his own, Julian developed a fail-safe turnaround strategy.

At length, like any savvy executive, he decided to consult about his plans with his direct reports, some of whom were both clever and knowledgeable. But their response, as he recalls, was no help at all. He felt that they had added nothing new, and that they had only told him exactly what they thought he wanted to hear. It wasn't long before he stopped feeling flattered and began to worry. He knew that he needed direct and honest feedback.

As it turned out, his marketing strategies were a little south of brilliant, and his president let him know that in uncomplimentary terms. The experience was jarring, but it led Julian to realize that, as a leader, he needed to figure out what was wrong with his staff, preferably before the next crisis hit. Having heard about coaching from colleagues, he hired a coach to whom he gave the mandate of explaining why his people were not willing to be honest with him.

UNEXPECTED DISCOVERIES

Julian presumed that the coach would pose a few questions and then tell him the answer. So he was surprised when the coach proposed instead a thorough assessment of the situation. With some trepidation Julian agreed and authorized the coach to survey his staff and compile the results.

What Julian discovered was that the source of the problem was not those who reported to him, but himself. Over the years he had developed an image of unforgiving authority, giving his staff the impression that he knew all the answers, even when he really wanted their help. Every encounter seemed to his staff members like a test that they were in serious danger of failing. Thoroughly intimidated and terrified of Julian's sarcastic style, they sensibly provided carefully sanitized feedback. As one of them put it to the coach, "No sense rocking the boat."

Now, the coach did not look forward to conveying this information to Julian. By this time, she, too, had experienced some of Julian's abrupt, stinging comments. Feeling vulnerable herself, she knew just how tempting it would be to play it safe and provide only the most acceptable part of the feedback.

She also experienced a contradictory impulse. She found it tempting to use her own authority as a coach to bully Julian, meeting harsh words with harsher words. After all, someone had to inform this man that he was dangerously arrogant and ought to clean up his act.

But with restraint and kindness, the coach fed Julian the results of the study a little at a time, which helped him to feel safe enough to digest it. Carefully, after confirming what the staff had said, the coach added her own experiences of his habit of making blistering remarks. That is when Julian realized that an external coach can ask the unspeakable question and propose the unspeakable truth.

Initially, Julian was extremely resistant to this information. After all, he wanted his staff fixed, not himself. So the coach took time to help him to examine the business benefits, the career implications, and the personal satisfaction that could result from a process of self-development.

DISCOVERING ORIGINS OF BEHAVIOUR

Next, the coach asked a series of very probing questions, delivered gently. They were designed to help Julian discover how he had become so caustic and what he could do about it. The origins, as they emerged, had to do with a stern uncle who took responsibility for guiding Julian as a child, providing him with summer jobs and making decisions about his education. Harsh and belligerent, the uncle had permitted no contradictions and had accepted no complaints.

It was a dramatic experience for Julian, seeing the present-day parallels between himself and his uncle. The coach helped him to recognize further that he had followed in the uncle's footsteps as a result of the distinct series of personal decisions he had made throughout his life. If Julian had made such decisions in the past, the coach suggested, he could make new decisions about the future. The question was, did he want to change his patterns?

Around this point in the coaching, Julian became noticeably depressed. He seemed quiet and withdrawn during the sessions, so the coach encouraged him to talk about his feelings. Julian replied that he wasn't sure that he could make the necessary changes. He wondered out loud whether to "try to change myself into someone I'm not."

It was a painful period of reflection, but Julian did admit to the coach that he had never really liked his rough-tough workplace persona and wanted to grow out of it. Gradually, he made a decision to experiment with different behaviours that could reveal his less defensive, more collaborative self to his staff.

RESPONSE AND CONTINGENCIES

Of course, they didn't cheer, and they didn't salute, but very cautiously the staff members did begin to respond. From time to time, they gave him the benefit of their frank wisdom, asking questions of their own and gradually becoming partners with their leader.

So the exercise was a success, but Julian was profoundly puzzled when his coach began to explore the likelihood of a relapse. What if the company hit rough times? asked the coach. What if Julian's boss increased the pressure? What if an employee took advantage of Julian's collaborative approach? What if his personal life took a nosedive?

Again it took time, but Julian saw the point. Everyone backslides on new commitments to some extent, but with a contingency plan, he could save himself from losing the ground he had gained. Julian entered another phase, developing more mutually supportive relationships among the managers in the company. He asked a couple of trusted direct reports to let him know if they thought he was straying from his new path. And he asked the coach if she could check in every few months when their work together was at an end.

Old habits die hard, and the company suffered a dangerous slump, so Julian needed his contingency plan more than he had imagined. But over the years that followed, this self-styled rugged individualist gradually became a true team player, and his marketing initiatives showed the power of collaboration.

Leadership Coaching Takes a Variety of Forms

It would be pleasant to paint a single picture of a coaching engagement, for instance, Julian's story, and suggest that it is typical. The reality is that leadership coaching takes as many forms as there are specific needs and people involved. Its shape and direction is limited only by the needs and imagination of the parties involved.

There is, however, one feature that does not seem to vary from case to case. Leadership coaching is usually offered to the most valued employees exhibiting at least some of these qualities:

- Potential for growth
- Creativity in their approach to work
- Proven results
- A position at the nexus of important relationships
- Leadership, senior rank, or influence
- Irreplaceable skill sets and strategic intelligence

Above all, coaching is offered to people who, having been at the centre of critical developments, carry the organization's corporate memory. In a knowledge economy, such intellectual capital is recognized to be more valuable than machinery, bricks, or mortar. It is information that is too complex to be encapsulated in manuals or memos. It includes, for instance, wisdom that the organization accrued as it developed, such as who works most productively with whom, and which alliances have the greatest effect or symbolic value.

When, for any number of reasons, a person carrying a part of the corporate memory runs into problems and becomes less productive, coaching can help this person accelerate back up to speed. Because leadership coaching acknowledges the value of intellectual capital, it sends a message about loyalty and promise to others. Further, it enables the organization to avoid the disruption, financial expense, and knowledge loss that could result from jettisoning faltering leaders.

Factors Influencing the Coaching Process

The location of the coaching sessions can be as varied as the reasons for initiating the leadership coaching process. The frequency and location of meetings for coaching may take the form of a few informal discussions on the production line or a series of scheduled appointments in an executive office or boardroom. At these meetings, the coach may take the role of a teacher conveying workplace skills; or she may guide the coachee in discovering how to learn, help him to plan a course of action, provide feedback, encouragement, and insight. A coaching relationship may be a covert one, known only to one or two key persons. Or the coach may openly shadow the coachee, by attending meetings, listening in on phone conversations, and gathering other real-time observations to inform the coaching process and to enrich the learning of the coachee.

Similarly, many factors may contribute to the initiation of leadership coaching. Moved by the need to develop new abilities, the coaching relationship could be requested by a highly motivated person, while other times the need for coaching may be suggested by superiors, or even required as a condition of continued employment. Sometimes coaching may be required to help a person manage a benign change in assignment or address a dangerous pattern of dysfunctional interpersonal behaviour.

SIX FACTORS SHAPING THE COACHING PROCESS

1. The culture of the organization
2. The task at hand
3. The nature of the crisis
4. The community
5. The environment
6. Above all, the people involved

Other forms of coaching include those situations where an executive or CEO may coach an up-and-coming manager, teaching the skills needed for promotion. Or, having found that life is truly lonely at the top, the CEO may hire a coach for herself—a confidential, senior-level professional with whom to try out ideas and hone leadership skills. On the floor level, a shop foreman may coach an employee in the use of a new piece of equipment or software. Or he may find his own coach in order to improve his communication or leadership skills.

THE SLEUTH WHO COULDN'T LEARN

Gerry had been supervisor of shipping and receiving for several years. He was known around the plant as "Super Sleuth," because within seconds of a request he could point a forklift at any item in the shipping department. You name it, he or his staff could find it.

One day, seemingly without warning, the firm's ancient, paper-based tracking system was replaced by computer software that permitted anyone in the plant to follow the movement of goods moment by moment. The company's strategy was to enjoy the benefit of carrying less inventory while providing just-in-time service.

But poor Gerry experienced none of the benefits. In fact, it was not long before he had a new nickname, used strictly behind his back. They called him "The Dinosaur." Try as he might, he just couldn't make friends with the computer that had replaced half his staff.

In desperation, Gerry resorted to the ancient adage "When in doubt, read the manual." But it didn't help. The software manual was like a foreign language. It began to be whispered about that Gerry had the dubious distinction of generating more "fatal error" and "file not found" messages on his computer screen than the rest of the employees combined.

His boss was a kindly character, and he sent Gerry off on a week-long software course. "Cost me almost five grand, with travel and expenses," he explained to an associate, while Gerry was at the course. "Of course, it's worth every cent!"

But when Gerry returned, the boss' hopes were dashed. Gerry had worked hard on the course, even spent extra time in the learning lab. Because he was so nervous around the computers, he just didn't get it. Even the few skills he thought he had learned would not translate to the actual computer at his desk, or the goods on his shelves, or the places they were supposed to be delivered to.

"I'm wondering if we'll have to let Gerry go," remarked the boss to his friend. "I sure hope not. Let me see. I wonder if there's someone who could kind of coach him along. What about that guy Marty who runs shipping over at the other plant? He's got the same software and I haven't heard about any problems."

So the neighbouring shipper began to visit Gerry and guide him through the software. They started simply at first. When Gerry made a mistake, Marty reassured him that he'd master the system, then demonstrated how to put it right. The next time, he would let Gerry make the changes himself. When Gerry got upset, Marty stayed calm. Sometimes he took a short walk to let Gerry cool off. Gradually they moved from basics to the more complicated issues.

Marty was exactly like the majority of people who coach. He had absolutely no formal training or certificate in software, inventory control systems, teaching, or coaching. What he did have was warmth, patience, experience, and a willingness to share. And they just happen to be qualities that distinguish a good coach from someone who just shows up.

Gerry required a few weeks of coaching before he was using the software reliably. More than once, he made panicky phone calls to his coach for emergency guidance. But gradually, reliably, he caught on.

"Couldn't believe my eyes," remarked the boss to his friend. "I guess some people don't learn so much from reading the manuals or taking the courses. You put someone beside old Gerry to show him the ropes and he's the 'Super Sleuth' all over again!"

Where Do Coaches Come From?

Coaches currently responding to the need for coaching have emerged from many disparate backgrounds. Some, like Gerry's stock-keeper friend, became coaches without formal training simply because they were thrust into the role and turned out to be good at it. Some decided to add coaching to their existing skills because they like to help other folks develop. It is interesting that the majority of coaching engagements are conducted by people who are not professionals, have no training or preparation for coaching, and, in fact, might not even identify what they are doing by that term. Yet their accrued wisdom has taught us much about the process and skills of coaching.

Today, coaching is practised successfully by a wide variety of people, including those who have dedicated themselves to coaching as a full-time profession and a host of others responsible for assisting an individual's development. These people include CEOs, executives, managers, and shop-floor supervisors, Human Resources (HR) professionals, Organization Development (OD) consultants, as well as Succession Planners and professional trainers. In addition, sales executives, and external organizational, out-placement, and career counselling consultants may all include coaching as part of their skills.

An Accidental Journey into Coaching

Perhaps the most fortunate people are those who established coaching practices on a pre-existing foundation, having begun their professional lives as psychotherapists—as we have. In that role, our fundamental task was to help healthy human beings find solutions to their problems and make crucial changes in their lives. If that description sounds a lot like coaching, it is no coincidence.

We became coaches quite by accident. Many of our early therapy clients were senior managers, and having concluded work with them on personal issues, we would often hear, "Now, there's also a problem at the office I'd like some help with." So we would begin to coach the manager, not even knowing at first that "coaching" was the name for what we were doing. (The term emerged into the public consciousness much later.) It was immediately evident that this was something different: more solution-focused than standard therapy, more immediate, and aimed at meeting specific organizational, educational, governmental, or business needs.

The big surprise was the extent of the welcome we received from organizations that had until then no comparable source for support. As we learned to understand the language and the context of their work responsibilities, our confidence grew. We were being educated by the best of teachers—our own coachees—about the unique demands and pressures of organizational life.

Because they responded with such appreciation for the skills we brought to this new profession from our clinical experience, we decided to dedicate ourselves entirely to coaching.

As the need for in-depth coaching grew, we decided to examine the special skills that former therapist coaches had imported into this field. We also catalogued the additional capabilities we needed in order to coach most effectively in the workplace. The results of that study provided the foundation for the development of the Deep Learning Process.

The same techniques that support former clinicians in becoming effective workplace coaches are turning out to be valuable—with appropriate adjustments—for non-professionals with day-to-day workplace responsibilities that include coaching. Whether the coaches we train are newcomers or highly experienced, no matter the variety of their backgrounds, we are seeing that adding the Deep Learning skill set enables coaches to respond more profoundly to the needs of their clients.

To coach from a more knowledgeable perspective, you may wish to begin by learning more about the history of coaching and how it is practised today. Who typically benefits from coaching? How can you spot the need for coaching? You will also want to understand the unique aspects of coaching that make it work so well. These are the themes of the next chapter.

Dark Days Demand Illumination

With enormous changes and challenges rocking the leaders within our organizations, the evolving profession of leadership coaching in the workplace must respond with precision and clarity about how it will provide support. Visit the executive suite, where people who might seem to be positioned at the very cynosure of power and reward are worrying privately about their alienated families, their looming insecurity, and their uncertainty about whether the next decision might turn out to be an utter dud. With the increase in the possibility of failure, the average period of successful occupancy of the CEO's office is becoming shorter and shorter.

Look into another corner of organizational life, where our brilliant high technology magicians, software programmers, and technical artists reside. Although they represent the elite pioneers of today's work world, they declare themselves to be bored and resentful. They have discovered that it is still a jungle in here: employers continue to eat their young. As for their own jobs, they have discovered that the corporate motto is "Burn 'em out and trade 'em in."

Or talk with managers who have survived rampant re-engineering and the advent of the postmodern, flattened hierarchy. They find themselves supervising near-strangers who sometimes number in the scores. They don't expect to be writing insightful performance appraisals any time soon. Many feel profoundly unprepared for the new tasks they face day-to-day.

Meanwhile, talented rising stars orbit toward unprecedented opportunities for promotion over the next few years, as we anticipate the largest mass retirement of senior executives in modern business and government history. But the successors to those exalted positions are quaking, knowing that they are simply not ready. Few have garnered sufficient experience to step into the shoes of the retirees, and none of their seniors has the time or energy to mentor them.

Dark days we might think.

Coaching Answers Age-Old Dilemmas

Human ingenuity never ceases to search for solutions. Through coaching, our ancestors passed on the contents of tribal memory from one generation to the next, and the wisdom conveyed in this way enabled the human race to survive while adapting to radical climate change, ice invasions, vicious predators, and devastating disease.

Imagine a smoky cave where the chief of a prehistoric tribe is facing a life-and-death decision. Should he lead his people to a new location where the vegetation is richer but the neighbours less friendly? He consults a shaman for advice, and the issues these bearded, skin-clad leaders discuss are not so different from those a CEO and coach face today as they ponder new directions for a corporation whose customer base is rapidly changing, or that educators confront as they meet the challenge presented by the upsurge in on-line learning.

Meanwhile, out in the forest, the hunters of the younger generation are stalking their prey in real-time training under the tutelage of wise old veterans, learning life skills vital to their survival: how to avoid poisonous plants, how to make spears, shelters, and watercraft, and how to capture food. The process is much like that experienced by new recruits to the production line as they learn from experienced supervisors. This is coaching at its most fundamental and pragmatic.

Coaching in Myth and History

Now fast-forward a few million years to an early legend of written history, depicting the famous episode in ancient India when General Arjun stands at the onset of the battle of Mahabharata. Searching for wisdom, he turns for coaching to the god Krishna, who dictates to him the *Bhagavad Gita*, which will become a sacred text of Hinduism.

Shift to Western literature. In Homer's *Odyssey*, the coach's name is—literally—Mentor. He guides the development of Telemachus, son of Odysseus. But in one of the unexpected twists of the story, he is not exactly the nobleman he seems. The coach is actually Athene, the goddess of wisdom, in disguise. Would that we coaches might all be as wise as our pagan patron saint!

Though Mentor is mythology, Socrates is not. In the fifth century BCE, you might have watched the philosopher practising coaching in Athens. Posing his famous Socratic questions to his protégées as they walked in the Agora, he elicited the wisdom that they possessed but had not recognized. And a century later in the same country, the philosopher Aristotle was coaching the callow youth who would become Alexander the Great, the conquering king who imposed Greek culture throughout the ancient world.

Coaches of the Twentieth Century

If coaching is a practice as old as humanity, it is also as fresh as modern times. A few mythical coaches of the century just past even became part of the cultural fabric. Back in the 1940s, the millionaire playboy Bruce Wayne coached a young fellow named Dick Grayson in the skill of fighting crime by terrorizing criminals. They patrolled Gotham City for decades to come under the feared names of Batman and Robin.

In real life, coaches have had a powerful impact on the realm of recreation. The champions of competitive athletics, of acting, and of music have all turned to coaching to help them exceed ordinary levels of performance.

It was a football coach who first made the long pass between success in sports and success in business. Vince Lombardi, the legendary coach of the Green Bay Packers football team, was early in popularizing in 1971 the truth that "leaders are not born. Leaders are made ... and they are made by effort and hard work."

That dictum had little immediate impact on business—the ultimate competitive arena of the past century—because people were generally slow to make that connection. Our corporate leaders rarely acknowledged their debt to the coaches who helped to make them successful. In fact, they encouraged the prevailing but misleading picture of a CEO or president as the lone gunslinger arriving in town, cleaning up the problems, and—just before the credits—riding out of town alone.

That Confusing Term "Coach"

When we think of the term "coach," we may think first of the person who directs an athletic team or player. But the similarities of that sort of coach to a workplace coach are rough at best. Depending on the sport, the coach may develop battle plans, assign plays to an entire team, teach playing skills, offer encouragement, act as a chaperone, or berate and cajole both players and game officials. A few of these roles directly contradict our understanding of the workplace coach.

In 1974 Tim Gallwey's surprise bestseller, *The Inner Game of Tennis*, challenged the harsh, critical habits into which athletic coaches had sunk. Not only did Gallwey establish the importance of a non-judgmental style of coaching, he also urged tennis players to halt the self-criticism that interfered with their game.

The tradition of musical coaching offers a more congenial comparison to workplace coaching in certain respects. This coach works one-on-one with an aspiring musician or singer to help develop abilities and career. The coach's stance is generally senior but respectful. But as in sports, musical coaches often practise with neither standards of accreditation nor guides to appropriate behaviour, and some continue to rely heavily on bullying.

ANOTHER KIND OF COACH

The term "coach" first appeared in the seventeenth century, meaning a horse-drawn vehicle. Two hundred years later it showed up as university slang in Britain, referring to a person who helped students cram for exams or improve athletic skills.

Like a vehicle, the coach carried students from a point of inadequacy to a destination of accomplishment. Today the academic reference has been dropped, but the sporting notion prevails.

Clearly we need to develop our own standards, definitions, and terminology, and do so in a way that will suit an international arena. Although leadership coaching for the workplace began in North America, its influence is rapidly embracing the globe.

Recently one of the authors had the privilege of teaching what may have been the first formal class in workplace coaching to take place in Turkey and found that, despite a business ethos with a more Asian aspect, they faced challenges similar to those coaches face in North America. They had to begin by developing a trusting relationship and demonstrating empathy with the coachee and the workplace context. They had to learn how to work from a helpful basic model and how to include the use of 360-degree feedback (see Chapter 7) to deepen the impact of coaching.

Aside from the basics of the coaching workshops, I was fascinated to discover that when something is new to a country—such as leadership coaching for the workplace—there may be no consensus on how to refer to it. To add to the problem in Turkey, their word koc (which sounds just like our word "coach") refers to a ram. The professionals attending the seminar suggested that this image was less than helpful, being one of butting horns more than the meeting of minds. And to describe the coach of a soccer team, Turks use the imported French term *entraineur*. Thus, with the global spread of workplace coaching, it remains to be seen how each culture will ultimately refer to it.

A Response to Challenging Times

Each recent change in the business environment has increased the demands on leaders, spurring increased appreciation and need for leadership coaching. In recent years massive changes have occurred: the ascent of the knowledge industries, the technology revolution that is rapidly eclipsing the old certainties of conventional manufacturing, and the explosion of biotechnology. In addition, Internet-based businesses, businesses focused on effective waste management systems, and those based on methods of curbing global warming have found their places in the business world. Profound repercussions on every type of organization and business have also resulted from the increase in national and global mergers and competition, and the digital transformation of the monetary system. Mass cultural invasions spawned by worldwide travel, trade, and communications are blurring some cultural traditions, while increasing lifespans are generating growing demands on medicine and health research. Along with advances in computer technology have come the concerns of computer viruses and the problems of copyright and security.

The imminent mass retirement of our most experienced senior executives is spurring a growing and concerned demand for the rising stars of business to gain wisdom equivalent to years of experience in only a handful of months. Yet there is also pressure on older leaders either to leave the field or to reinvent themselves at warp speed for these increasingly rapid changes. As well, we are seeing the emergence of genius entrepreneurs, strong in technical skills, weak in management subtlety, who sometimes endanger the well-being of employees. In turn, a better-educated, more confident class of employee is becoming increasingly vociferous in its growing awareness of its rights and the power of its collective voice. Many of the members of this newly influential workplace community also have the distinction of being under thirty-five years old.

Each of these new and often conflicting realities is like a newly emerged butterfly drying itself in the Caribbean sun, the flutter of whose wings—according to James Gleick's

Chaos Theory—may spawn typhoons in the Pacific. Coaching has arisen out of our need for more sophisticated methods of personal development to help our leaders make these connections and to guide organizations through the subsequent sun and storm.

A SUPERVISOR BECOMES A COACH

The global demand for quality imposes pressure on employees at all levels. In an electronic manufacturing company, a supervisor made several frustrating attempts to induce an assembly line employee to reduce assembly errors.

For instance, the supervisor reminded the employee that her productivity bonus would only apply to fault-free production. You might think that would be sufficient, but although her production improved slightly, the supervisor had to remain constantly vigilant.

At that time the supervisor was provided with training in coaching, and his mind began to open to new leadership possibilities. After talking with other coaches, he decided to introduce the employee to the wider significance of faulty assembly.

First, he asked the assembler to meet with the inspectors whose time was squandered every time a faulty part showed up. He introduced her to the repair technicians, who had to spend more time fixing the fault than the employee did producing the item. He showed her letters from the angry purchasers of faulty items that had slipped past the inspectors.

He even asked the finance department to summarize in black and white how much each mistake was costing the organization, and the impact on wages and profits. Thanks to imaginative coaching by her supervisor, the employee not only "got it," but began to influence others to care about the importance of careful assembly.

Responding to the Revolution

"Be careful how you treat the kid with the green hair." That astonishing piece of advice from a recent recruiting manual suggests the real-time challenges that result from the larger changes we have documented.

Once upon a time (it seems like only last week), we imagined that we could gauge whether young people had a future in business by scrutinizing how they looked and dressed. Now the pace of change itself is accelerating. The nerd with the pens in her pocket might be from the mailroom or the Information Technology Department. The fellow with the nose ring and verdant spikes may be a squeegee kid looking for a washroom or the genius programmer from down the hall who holds the key to your next profitable quarter. No one with an eye for the future would arbitrarily hustle such a person out of the building.

The example is superficial, but it hints at the massive paradigm shifts that managers face. The world of work has become so complex that in isolation no one can expect to master all the requisite skills and information. The days of the manager who knows everything he or she needs to know are truly finished. The only way a manager can function in such circumstances is to develop supportive relationships as guides onto the fast track of personal evolution. It may require a coach to quietly suggest, "Wait a second— think twice. Plan in a businesslike manner how to assess the people who work here."

I am thinking now about a conversation I had during my work in Turkey:

"Most of our businesses are family businesses, run by old-style patriarchs. These people are authoritarian, hold all the information to their chests, and don't prepare the younger generation to take over when they retire. Our greatest need is to develop a new generation of professional managers. But who will help them develop the skills?"

The person who told me these truths was standing on Turkish soil, but managers around the globe—including many in North America, could echo her words.

Emergence of the Professional Manager

Managers at every level are experiencing the need for a mindset that can find answers to puzzling questions while enveloping many variables and contradictions. How to retain clarity of vision while encompassing the logic of chaos and the novelty of technology? How to remain capable of embracing and guiding massive changes yet remain cautious enough to look carefully around the corner and, how in the same breath, be audacious enough to step into the unknown? How to help people resolve their problems in innovative ways while encouraging them to grow in self-knowledge, to learn continuously, and to transcend their perceived limitations of themselves? And overall, how to encourage others—and oneself—to continually think globally and act locally?

The greatest single cause of failure in the workplace, whether at the executive level or the shop floor, is not a lack of skill, such as the inability to operate a machine, read a balance sheet, or write a strategic plan. Rather, it is the lack of an adequate mindset and a lack of self-understanding. When people begin to recognize their own confusing behaviour patterns and understand how others see them, their leaps into greater effectiveness are often dazzling.

Coaching Offers a Path to Productivity

It was not long ago that successful managers could scrape by on one part science, one part instinct, and one part make-it-up-as-you-go-along. Today, as the pressure they experience builds, the stakes are too high for that approach.

With the fat already cut from the bone, expenses slashed and processes automated, businesses face the ultimate and most difficult frontier—requiring those with managerial responsibilities to become even more productive. Instead, what we are actually seeing are the long-term costs of the preoccupation with cutbacks: lagging productivity, physical and emotional breakdowns, lacklustre marketing, and even industrial sabotage.

The quest for commercial advantage is shifting. "In the face of fierce international competition," said Keith Sinclair of Milltronics in an interview, "the people side of organizations has become well accepted as a key competitive advantage, or a competitive disadvantage, depending on how it is handled." The value of coaching in such times is to encourage people to work not harder but smarter.

Clearly though, there is a missing piece to this puzzle. "Coaching? Frankly, I've never heard of it," mused the HR director for a car maker recently. "We've never used anything like that in our business." Asked how his company supports managers who run up against personal challenges, he replied, "Generally, we send them out for a course. Although there is no guarantee that what they learn will transfer back here."

If coaching had its origins in the cave, it has begun to take a valued place in the towers. "The recipe for success," advises Jim Gibson, a wise marketing specialist with Sierra Systems Consultants, "is to recognize that changes in leadership requirements will happen and happen fast. What better recipe can there be for the use of external resources like coaches? Successful high technology firms that I know about are ones that have early in the game invested in the external pair of hands well before the need arises. It is not an option if they are to succeed."

Businesses have done everything imaginable in the past couple of decades to increase competitiveness and profitability. They have downsized and just-in-timed, TQM-ed (Total Quality Management) and right-sized, and become leaner and meaner. What they have rarely accomplished until now is mounting successful projects toward improving the quality of leadership. As *Inc.* magazine proclaimed, "Smart managers have already removed the defects from their business. Now they're using big-league business coaches to do the same for themselves."

THE UNRECOGNIZED WISDOM OF THE COACHEE

The director of finance told her coach, "I'm having trouble getting Monique to stay with the job till it's finished."

"Have you ever had this problem before?" asked the coach.

"Well, something like it, a couple of years ago with Larry."

"And what do you do that time?"

The coachee thought about it for a minute. "Well, I talked with him about how it was affecting the rest of the team when he didn't finish. I also had him talk with another worker and ask for some feedback."

"What happened?"

"His completion rate shot up like a rocket."

"Then it sounds to me," remarked the coach, "that you have a pretty good idea of how to deal with this situation. But before we go any further, let's look for a moment at how Monique and Larry are different, so you can fine-tune your approach...."

Who Uses Coaching?

Coaching has turned out to be especially valuable for four identifiable managerial groups: senior leaders, people identified for succession, managers in trouble, and employees who need new skills.

1. SENIOR LEADERS

This first group consists of CEOs and other executives. They will confirm that the old cliché is more accurate than ever today: It is truly lonely at the top. Confronting massive shifts in technology, shortened business cycles, fierce global competition, and the challenge of new markets, those who carry executive responsibilities experience extreme pressure and isolation. Facing make-or-break organizational and personal challenges, they are looking for all the help they can get.

Most senior executives in office today have the disadvantage of not being graduates of the operating environment. Instead of coming up through the ranks, many have achieved their positions because of their expertise in financial, legal, or other non-operational disciplines. This is part of the reason that some feel profoundly isolated.

Many, too, have identified the need to talk with a wise outsider about their ideas, their objectives, and the challenges they face. They say it sometimes feels downright dangerous to share questions and sensitive information with people inside the organization. They mistrust the feedback they receive, as well, knowing that people who report to them may frequently offer politically motivated responses in an attempt to secure their own positions, or in an attempt to win favour by saying what they imagine senior leaders want to hear.

This is where the gifts of an unbiased coach shine: asking the right questions and providing honest, objective feedback. The coach provides the leader with a forum for thinking out loud. As leadership guru Warren Bennis once reflected, "I wasn't a born leader....You learn about leadership basically through reflecting on experience."

Leaders usually know when their organization needs to take an innovative and creative stance, but they often feel stymied by the resistance out there. They want to make changes in their own management style that will show swift, positive, and lasting results. They need unbiased feedback about their creative plans and strategies.

A leadership coach has a lot to offer here because he doesn't try to fit his message to the leader's assumptions. He can provide objective insight, direction, and support. This confidential relationship enables the leader to feel free and sure as she plans strategy, designs activities, and deals with complex interpersonal situations.

And like the three groups listed below, it is these coachees who set the style for the coaching, based on what works best for them. Do they get the best value from face-to-face interviews, telephone conferencing, or e-mail? How often do they want to meet? What location works best: their office, the coach's office, or neutral ground? As far as possible, the effective coach will meet them how and when they wish.

2. PEOPLE IDENTIFIED FOR SUCCESSION

The second group who benefit from coaching are seasoned managers and rising stars. These are people who have done well. They have achieved all they can with all the brilliance at their command. Now they need to do something utterly different and make a life-defying leap into the unknown.

As we brace ourselves for the mass retirement of senior executives, coaching is providing a way to develop those talented mid-level people who have not had the opportunity to develop mature skills simply because they have not been around as long as the retiring generation.

Rather than sending promising managers away to take the standard workshops, succession planners have discovered the value of referring them for customized coaching. They find that it assists in the transfer of vital skills into the operating environment, encouraging retention and re-use. And when it comes to the development of strategic skills, coaching offers the crucial supports: individual attention and frequent feedback.

3. MANAGERS IN TROUBLE

The third group who benefit from coaching are managers who are experiencing workplace or personal difficulties. Organizations that are trying to run lean and fast to remain competitive sometimes discover that they are losing momentum because of problems that certain managers may have with productivity, flexibility, self-understanding, relationship issues, or people skills. The behaviour of some of these managers is, in the words of IBM executive Bill Etherington, "like lighting your hair on fire and putting it out with a hammer."

Yet these managers in trouble are often the most talented people in the organization, possessors of remarkable abilities, the repositories of invaluable knowledge, and keepers of the corporate memory. Because they are such valued contributors, the organization will not lightly discard them. The bill to replace them could easily run to six figures.

Officers of the organization may already have offered these individuals a variety of suggestions and interventions to induce them to face their issues and change their approach. But when they prove unable to break through to the next level of effectiveness on their own, it is time either to strike up the last dance of the dinosaurs or to start coaching.

4. EMPLOYEES WHO NEED NEW SKILLS

The fourth group of staff who benefit from coaching are employees who need to discover and master new workplace skills. For this group, depending on the focus, the most effective coach is often an insider who has been through the same learning curve and understands what the organization values. In a majority of cases, this will be the direct supervisor of the coachee.

Coaching this group can take many forms. One may be individualized skill training to increase effectiveness. Here, important aspects of the coaching may include strategic planning, decision-making, conflict management, communication, and equipment operating procedures. Or a more productive management style may be needed, which would include, perhaps, managing change, developing a highly functioning team, as well as balancing work and personal life. At other times, the resolution of value conflicts may include clarifying values and attitudes, managing diversity, understanding dual relationships in the workplace, and building a values-based culture for the organization.

Robert Haas, chairman and CEO of Levi Strauss & Company, has minimized the old division between "hard" skills and "soft" skills, "What we've learned," he says, "is that the soft stuff and the hard stuff are increasingly intertwined.... Indeed, values drive the business."

COACHING A HARSH CEO

Senior managers with rough tongues not only demoralize their employees but also erode their businesses. Frequently they remain unaware of the damage until it is too late to do anything but pick up the pieces. Cynthia, a talented, difficult CEO of a mid-size firm, experienced a very close call.

A couple of years ago, Cynthia was astounded to read an employee survey that depicted her as distant, unpleasant, and unkind. The use of anonymous questionnaires allowed staff to reveal that her style was costing the business money.

Because she was always a committed learner, Cynthia decided to analyze critical incidents with the help of a coach and to test more effective ways of communicating. "I would not have guessed that the way I talk to my employees would cut into our profitability," she told her coach. "I've always prided myself on a no-nonsense approach. I am very direct and they know where they stand. I don't waste their time or mine by saying they are doing a good job if they aren't."

With Cynthia's blessing, the coach spoke in confidence with a number of employees. After a harsh encounter with Cynthia, they said, they might spend several hours spinning their wheels, trying to recover their self-esteem. Some managers admitted they avoided decision-making, playing it safe to minimize the risk of being criticized. Not surprisingly, productivity and profit were on the decline, while griping around the water cooler was on the increase. There were even, the coach discovered, subtle instances of sabotage.

A MORE POSITIVE APPROACH

"The whole thing leaves me confused," Cynthia told her coach. "I've taken courses in communication, so I certainly wasn't prepared for this."

Together she and the coach designed three initiatives fine-tuned to her situation.

First, Cynthia began to balance her critiques with affirming comments. She then made a point of expressing her respect for genuine accomplishments. She discovered that a leader who shows appreciation for employees' good qualities will earn the necessary credibility to request changes in behaviour. It is human nature to respond to praise with redoubled efforts.

Second, she took a more positive approach to criticisms that were necessary. "Here's exactly what I'd like you to do, and here's why it will work." This turned out to be more effective than her usual approach, "This is all wrong. How many times do I have to explain it to you!"

And third, she experimented with revealing herself. Everyone on staff knew Cynthia was human, so it helped when she acknowledged that fact. She discovered that there was nothing unprofessional about letting them know that she was proud of her nephew, or that she had been embarrassed when she forgot a customer's name.

Still, Cynthia felt awkward as she began to practise these changes. So she made sure that whenever she miscalculated or faltered in her resolve, the coach was there to encourage her. As she saw improvements in the atmosphere at her firm, she grew more confident. Gradually, managers began to confide in her, and staff became more motivated.

UNDERSTANDING THE ROOTS OF THE PROBLEM

Then she began to worry that she would not be able to sustain the changes. What would happen when her coach was no longer working with her, or when the pressure built to the boiling point? That's when her coach asked her if she understood what led her to treat employees the way he did.

Cynthia thought about it for a moment. "Maybe it's how I grew up. My parents never praised us as kids, and if we messed up, they were pretty harsh. In fact, I can remember hiding in my closet after one confrontation with my dad."

That conversation was pivotal. As Cynthia realized that she had learned her harsh approach at a finite time and space in her life, she recognized that she could unlearn it, too. Her confidence took a leap. Yet one puzzle still remained. Why were her subordinates so frightened when she thought of them as her equals? One morning on the way to work, she listened on her car radio as a leading politician was questioned about his reputation for exploding at his staff.

Keenly aware of the similarities with her own situation, she listened with fascination. The politician brushed off the interviewer's questions with the comment that such outbursts are quickly forgotten. He didn't say by whom, of course. Prodded by the interviewer, he related the story of a subordinate whom he had chewed out and who petulantly threatened to resign. A few days later, he said with just a hint of pride, this same employee blew up at him, but he, the politician, did not threaten resignation.

Cynthia discussed the interview with her coach. "When a subordinate explodes," she said, "the politician seemed to experience it the same as I do. It's like a mosquito bite—annoying but minor. So when I get angry, why do my employees behave as if it's thermonuclear?"

The coach helped Cynthia to understand the imbalance of power that exists between herself and her employees. Even when they're at their most confident, she remains the person with power to hire and fire, to reprimand or reward.

MAINTAINING PROGRESS

Even on days when she doesn't feel very powerful, Cynthia continues to remind herself that, for employees, the workplace is never a level playing field. That's why only an aware leader can make it safe for employees to take the kind of risks that lead to business success.

Of course, people don't change their style overnight. Under stress, Cynthia sometimes reverts to acerbic behaviour with her staff. But because she is aware of her impact, she also knows when it is time to make amends. Gradually she has become more encouraging, and her people continue to respond. In particular, she has learned to reward her managers verbally for their fresh thinking. As a result, she is seeing a lot less activity around the water cooler and a lot more at the shipping ramp.

Is Workplace Coaching a Fad?

The reason that so many seemingly brilliant insights about organizations have faded into fads during the past two decades is that they are not congruent with the human personalities they are supposed to support. They may be intriguing mental constructs, but they do not represent the way people really work.

When an organizational discipline like coaching bursts onto the scene, it gets attention because it is exciting, powerful, and we need it. The mystery of how coaching actually works remains largely unexplained. The truth beyond the hype is that coaching is both simple and complex. And why does it work? Because it incorporates the most effective processes through which we human beings learn, develop, and change. In addition, each coaching intervention is customized for the recipient, solution-focused, time-limited, productivity-oriented, and designed to maximize effectiveness by enhancing strengths that leaders already possess.

Furthermore, the roots of coaching lie in the most basic, primitive requirements for human development: the importance of relationships for learning, the value of personal feedback, the power of encouragement, and the stimulus of well-placed challenges.

Most importantly, the strength and longevity of leadership coaching in the workplace arises from the fundamental qualities of the coachee: curiosity, ambition, flexibility, and experimentation. That is why coaching is so good at unlocking creativity, relaxing the anxiety that often hobbles workplace efficiency, and building loyalty—a commodity without price in these uncommitted times.

Coaching Is Like Product Development

Coaching is no magic carpet. It requires dedication and hard work from the coachee. Those who receive the most benefit are those who have chosen their coach carefully and then invested a considerable amount of courage in the process. Because coaches tend to be ruthlessly oriented to results, they are not for the meek, warns Claire Tristram in the magazine *Fast Company*. "They're for people who value unambiguous feedback. ... Executive coaching isn't therapy. It's product development, with you as the product."

In the magazine *Report on Business*, observer Tracy Johnson offers her take on the coach: "Part work shrink, part nag, part new-age feel-good hand-holder, part confidant." She called coaching "the latest competitive edge ... the meeting of traditional business and psychology."

How Does Coaching Work?

From childhood on, we learn to look to others for encouragement and instruction. To develop not alone but in community is to experience a lively alternative source of energy. Coaching is so powerful because, stripped down to the essentials, it is a relationship and a form of community that provides a great deal of individual attention.

Individuals learn best in relationship with another human being who is committed to that person's growth. How did we learn to use a fork, to dance, make love, play baseball? By spending time with someone else who had already learned those skills, or was at least engaged in the process of learning. Generally it was a person with a quality of caring who helped us to learn.

Coaching is powered by communication, sheltered through confidentiality, lubricated by trust, and smoothed by positive regard. The coach listens attentively, hearing what the coachee needs. The coach then responds, offering what is required while acting as a sounding board and providing guidance with frank feedback. The value of these transactions, repeated over a period of growth, is immense.

Evolutionary magic

Although the circumstances of our lives evolve at a dazzling rate, we human beings evolve gradually. It has required seven million years to differentiate us from our ancestors in the cave. That is why it has required evolutionary magic to build civilizations, to improve our physical health, to travel across and beyond our planet, and to learn how to love the diversity of humankind.

We have developed this magic through the sharing of understanding and history, and through connecting old thoughts in new ways. Coaching provides a means of combining the accumulated wisdom of a mentor with the untapped wisdom of the coachee. For the coachee, this eliminates the expenditure of creative energy on reinventing the wheel.

People with broad experience in leadership development often become the most effective coaches. When coaching incorporates in-depth processes, it enables people to make profound personal and professional changes. Data evolves into information leading to knowledge that turns into wisdom. People develop into better managers, leaders, and team members not just because they learn improved skills, but also because they are becoming better people.

Coaching is Customized to Individual Needs

It may be that "mass customization" is the hottest trend in merchandising, but it has always been essential that coaches customize their involvement to the coachee's individual needs. An effective coach will allow the individual's requirements to establish the agenda for the relationship, rather than relying on off-the-shelf solutions.

Good coaching fine-tunes not only the subject matter but also the style of learning to suit the coachee, showing respect for the individual's preferred methods of learning and helping to harness his or her power.

These days, it seems that we rarely take the time to reflect on the consequences of our actions. The next crisis is always crying for attention, so we plunge into an attempt to resolve it without attending to what we might learn from events of the recent past. But in relationship-based learning, we permit the coachee to stop us in our tracks. His curiosity about our experiments helps us to focus on the educational opportunities implicit in our own behaviour.

Rather than studying theoretical or textbook examples, the coach helps the coachee to review actual workplace experiences in order to shape their work together. Through a commitment to privacy and confidentiality, as well as a positive encouraging stance, the coach develops a safe zone that encourages the best creative and strategic thinking.

Then, as a team, they plan a strategy to match the specific needs of a particular workplace. Within hours, the executive or manager can test the design in action and bring the results back to the coach for immediate fine-tuning.

To See Ourselves and to Value One Another

The poet Robbie Burns offered a succinct diagnosis of the need for coaching, two centuries ago:

> *Oh wad some power the giftie gie us*
> *To see oursels as others see us!*
> *It wad frae monie a blunder free us,*
> *An' foolish notion.*

To make lasting changes, we need to address what is not obvious to us—those unseen factors inhibiting us from taking creative risks and persevering with difficult tasks.

The kindest, most courageous act in the corporate environment occurs when one person says firmly to another, "You need to change this. It is not an option. You must." The second kindest act is to say, "I know someone who can support you in making that change." Coaching works in part because it reveals how much we value one another.

Unquestionably leadership coaching is gaining such momentum because it feeds the bottom line. But that is only a partial explanation. The crucial other part of the equation is that it enables us to contribute to a leap in the evolution of a valued fellow human being.

What Coaching Is Not

From a certain perspective, the process of coaching may appear to be like a number of other forums in which people develop: training, mentoring, psychotherapy, and simple friendship. But it is important that we understand how these forums for learning are alike yet different. Otherwise, we become confused about what we are trying to accomplish and may inadvertently hurt the very people we are trying to assist.

Coaching has significant differences from training, mentoring, psychotherapy, and friendship. What is confusing is that it also shares some of the territory occupied by each of those relationships and derives some of its power from the similarities. In both friendship and coaching, for instance, the positive regard one has for the other is the basis for building trust and good self-esteem.

It is difficult to precisely define the boundary where coaching ends and training, mentoring, psychotherapy, or friendship begins. It is best to differentiate between them by recognizing that their centres are in different locations. For instance, training generally centres on the group, while coaching generally focuses on the individual. Mentoring is usually undertaken to help prepare an individual to follow in one's own footsteps; coaching is designed to develop enhanced performance.

1. COACHING IS NOT TRAINING

Coaching is clearly differentiated from training, although it may include a certain amount of personalized training. Adult students in classrooms and seminars usually complain about three issues: content, speed, and personal attention.

Instead of addressing the specific challenges they face in the workplace, training requires them to settle for learning whatever everyone else is learning. Although the world of work is shifting rapidly and radically, they are forced to slow their development to the pace of the slowest. And although they face issues of great urgency, subtlety, and complexity, they must compete for the individual attention of the instructor. Small wonder that people sometimes return from courses carrying little more than high hopes and good intentions.

Because coaching is a one-on-one relationship, it is more readily customized. It is also less constrained by time and provides an ongoing process with opportunities to experiment and to refine new attitudes and behaviours. Further, it is a highly confidential process that encourages the coachee to take risks and to be more open about uncertainties than could typically occur in a training course.

COACHING IS EFFECTIVE FOR THOSE WHO LEARN BEST

- in a person-to-person situation;
- at their own speed;
- when they have help identifying and addressing the areas where they're having difficulties;
- when the learning is in-depth, confronting unseen blocks and barriers that could otherwise subvert their best efforts.

2. COACHING IS NOT PSYCHOTHERAPY

Similarly, coaching is not psychotherapy, although like therapy, it may assist the coachee in bringing hidden or submerged ideas and feelings to a conscious level of awareness. Like therapy, coaching emphasizes positive change.

In practice, psychotherapy is often addressed to the "inner child" and so is rooted in the traumas of the past and examines how current problems derive from the family-of-origin.

Coaching appeals more to the adult within, concentrating on the present and the future, is resolutely solution-focused and optimistic, and more concerned with developing strengths than examining weakness. The emphasis in coaching is that we are not determined by our past, but we are accountable for our present behaviour. And where psychotherapy frequently restricts itself to the personal life of the client, leadership coaching looks at various aspects of the coachee's life with particular emphasis on the workplace.

3. COACHING IS NOT MENTORING

Coaching also differs subtly from mentoring, although practitioners use many of the same skills. The mentor is usually a senior manager who undertakes to guide a less experienced person with potential for development. That relationship is often built on the good chemistry between them. The mentor enjoys receiving admiration and regards the mentored person as a protégé. Coaching is based less on inherent chemistry between people and more on the maturity and wisdom of the coach in managing relationships.

In mentoring, the emphasis is often on how to prepare for promotion. Coaching may focus on succession or on the requisite skills for doing the job right now. Either role requires expertise and friendship, but the coach tends to be more of a professional, where the mentor is more of a friend.

4. FRIENDSHIP

Coaching is not friendship, although it is a very friendly relationship offering a high level of support. An important quality of a friendship is the acceptance of each other's frailties, often without comment. But leaders, managers, and administrators generally need more than friendship. They need someone who will tell the truth about what they see—the mistakes they make, the perception gaps that keep them from optimum performance, and the areas where they could improve their leadership abilities.

In coaching, the focus is on identifying frailties (with kindness and compassion) and developing greater specific competencies.

A good coach offers many of the generous qualities of a friend. The distinction is that the coach is scrupulously careful in his practice to leave the coachee with no confusion about his role. It is the inherent professionalism of the coach that creates a safe set of boundaries around the relationship.

Matching the Coachee's Needs to the Forms of Coaching

Coaching takes a variety of forms. There's coaching for

1. Basic skills
2. Support

3. Problem-solving
4. Strategic planning skills
5. Independent learning
6. Self-discovery

1. COACHING FOR BASIC SKILLS

At its simplest level, coaching is valuable when it conveys information and skills. For instance, a foreman explains to an employee how to use a certain piece of equipment on the production line, watches while the employee tries it out, suggests a few changes, then keeps a watchful eye until both are sure that the employee has mastered the necessary skills.

There are plenty of jobs that cannot be performed until the employee has been carefully instructed. No one wants an employee to use a metal-stamping machine or the payroll software without supervision. That is why this form of coaching has no detractors. It is quick and effective. It leaves the employee with no doubt about how to proceed safely and efficiently.

But the impact of basic skills coaching is limited. It does not ensure that the employee will develop the habit of building on what she or he already knows. It may not convey the positive regard that motivates people to find extraordinary solutions to ordinary problems. And it does not address the unseen blocks that sometimes hold back even the brightest and most highly motivated people from further development.

2. COACHING FOR SUPPORT

Supportive coaching, which operates at the next level of sophistication, is marked by a strong positive regard for the coachee. An expressed belief in his abilities helps motivate her self-development and allows growth in productivity.

For example, a good supportive coach may say: "I have a lot of a faith in your ability to make these changes. You are more capable than you think. I know you'll be great!" Supportive coaching sets just the right tone for the coachee's development.

There is a risk. No matter how enthusiastic the cheerleader may be, when a player fails to score, the cheering can sound hollow. At first, the coachee may be merely puzzled that the coach thinks so highly of her, but she may gradually learn to discount what she recognizes as meaningless cheers. Cheering for the coachee on the basis of enthusiasm rather than demonstrated skills may lead to some small successes, but quickly loses its credibility.

The workplace is often a very critical environment. "You didn't do this correctly" is heard much more frequently than "I know you'll be great!" That is why a supervisor or other coach who provides support and expresses legitimate faith in the employee is likely to see morale jump and productivity follow close behind.

3. COACHING FOR PROBLEM-SOLVING

Many professional coaches are excellent problem-solvers. They take a tried-and-true analytical approach to the problems faced by their coachees by asking coachees (1) what their goals are, (2) where they're starting from, (3) how big the gap is and what they need to learn in order to get where they want to go, (4) how they can learn this, and (5) how they will put these new concepts into action. Problem-solving coaching is limited in that it offers few alternatives when unexpected difficulties arise. Like a map showing the relation between places but ignoring the topography, it fails to address the deeper questions of motivation and blocks. What looks like a half-hour hike on a flat map may actually require two days of hard climbing up and down mountains.

The major criticism levelled at professional coaches to date is that their work is sometimes shallow, providing enthusiastic but simplistic solutions to complex problems and offering little in the way of substantial, long-term impact.

Yet problem-solving coaching is valuable because whenever the problem is amenable to direct solutions, coaching provides them. And because it is a shared activity, it reduces the coachee's sense of isolation and provides encouragement.

SOMETIMES JUST SHOWING UP IS ENOUGH

Every few days the IT director of our business asks us to coach him around a problem.

Often he will stop abruptly in the middle of his description of the issue to say, "Of course, that's the answer. Thanks for talking with me."

Sometimes our role is "lazy coaching." We don't hear the whole problem. We don't even propose a solution. Our presence alone is enough to change how he looks at the issues.

We help just by being there in a trust-based relationship.

4. COACHING FOR STRATEGIC PLANNING SKILLS

This form of coaching enables people who have previously operated with a limited tactical vision to transform themselves into leaders who possess panoramic insight. Sometimes the sole factor holding them back from the use of strategy is a lack of familiarity with strategic planning skills. The coach responds by teaching the skills and monitoring the practice.

Strategic planning may be particularly difficult for those whose early lives made it risky or useless to look into the future. If they grew up in extreme poverty or were at constant risk for physical or emotional violence, they may have learned to keep such a close eye on the present that the future may become obscured. Such people often develop into fine tacticians, but lack the ability to develop long-term strategy, and the coach attempting to teach strategic skills is likely to frustrate both the coachee and himself. The coach's work here is to enable the individual to discover why she has trouble seeing the woods for the trees and then, armed with that knowledge, to begin to shift paradigms. This is a task requiring considerable patience and determination.

As the coachee evolves an inner perspective of greater personal security, this is usually accompanied by a greater freedom to see the big picture. Then she is equipped to develop plans for the future, as no mere lesson in strategy planning could have accomplished.

5. COACHING FOR INDEPENDENT LEARNING

Enabling a workforce of independent learners makes them more efficient and productive —like removing a superfluous layer of management. Self-directed learners require less hand-holding, freeing supervisors to become managers, and managers to become strategists.

This form of coaching guides the coachee to discover what he already knows and how to build on that knowledge by seeking further learning.

Independent learning skills are generally discouraged by the control-and-command approach to management. Bosses are assumed to be those in the know, and employees reporting to them are assumed to be less knowledgeable. As a result, all information must pass through the leadership ranks in order to be considered valid and be acted upon.

For independent learning to flourish, the coach may need to become involved with those who influence organizational culture, coaching the individual in a way that encourages independent learning, while helping the organization to develop a culture affirming individual learning. This will increase efficiency by freeing the coachee from relying exclusively on the resources of the boss or even of the coach.

This form of coaching can be more costly than other forms, because it may initially require additional time and energy from both coach and coachee. Also, for reasons of self-esteem or organizational culture, the coachee may be reluctant to enter this unfamiliar territory. So the coach may have to "sell" the project, consulting with the coachee about his expectations and providing the rationale for continuous learning.

6. COACHING FOR SELF-DISCOVERY

Coaching for self-discovery is grounded in the use of interpersonal skills and effective assessment. More than any other form, it requires the coach to be highly responsive to the person in front of him, rather than importing his own expectations to the coaching situation. The coach's task is to encourage the coachee to articulate and trust her own wisdom.

The key issue is whether the coach is really listening—active listening and feedback skills are absolutely essential—and knows how to respond to the cues that are coming back, often unconsciously, from the coachee.

In coaching for self-discovery, sustainable results are achieved because the coachee is viewed not as an isolated object but as a person within an organizational context where her influence on her environment and its influence on her are carefully weighed in planning for action. Further, inner conflicts, not just skill deficits, are addressed.

> To become a coach is not like becoming a driver: take lessons, practise, pass your test. It requires competence, experience, adherence to standards, and above all, aptitude.
>
> The next chapter describes the person of the workplace coach and highlights the seven core competencies of this challenging role.

The Challenging Role of the Workplace Coach

Let's look at the coach through two different lenses: the *standards* that challenge us to develop the best practices and the *competencies* that encompass the necessary personal skills. From these developing standards and competencies, our growing professionalism emerges with principles that become so much a part of our thinking that they guide us almost automatically. This chapter raises the bar, setting standards for coaches that are fair but unquestionably challenging. It also describes some ineffective coaches in the hope of helping those who should probably not coach to assess themselves with honesty.

Of course, no book can assess whether you in particular have the qualities required to be an effective coach. You bring your own peculiar mix of talents to the work. For instance, you may fall short of the bar in formal training, yet you may soar above it when it comes to personal development and ethics, with the result that you could be an exemplary coach. Or not.

In the absence of meaningful agreed-upon standards, the best person to decide whether you have what it takes to be a coach is you. This chapter will support you by pointing to the most important questions to ask yourself and others, and gives you a chance to reflect rigorously on whether you have the qualities to be an effective leadership coach in the workplace.

But first, let us take a broad view of coaching and the person of the coach. To be a coach is a privilege. The people we coach reveal their hopes and fears, confess their vulnerabilities, and share personal information. They listen with rapt attention and respect to whatever we have to say and, in many cases, open to us the very doors of their souls. To live up to the standards of this demanding role, the workplace coach must be a special human being.

First, a coach must be a lover of humanity, passionate about the potential for growth in each person, and a believer in the infinite capacity of individuals to transcend limitations and achieve heights that might otherwise seem impossible.

It is no exaggeration to say that a coach needs the keen eyes, ears, and balance of the surgeon, the insight of the philosopher, and the skills of the therapist—not to mention the love of a parent! The coach must also be extraordinarily alert, fully responsive to the person being coached, and always conscious of the danger of importing personal expectations into the coaching situation.

Coaching is rewarding work, but it is extremely complex. The best coaches combine personal maturity, self-awareness, people skills, a keenly developed ethical sense, technical skills, workplace skills, and professional training. A reliable marker of good preparation is that the coach has herself been coached. A professional charged with helping others to grow has an ongoing responsibility to be involved in a continuing process of self-development and be at the growing edge of personal learning.

You might think that developing your abilities as a coach for the workplace is valuable only if you are planning to make this work your full-time career, or that becoming a superb coach will have little impact on your job as an executive, manager, or consultant. But nothing could be further from the truth. If you have already succeeded in your career to date on the basis of superb technical skills and can add to them the personal qualities described in this chapter, you will be unbeatable.

To be an effective coach, it is not sufficient to have natural talent, although it helps. It is not enough that people like to confide in you. It is not enough to have taken a course. And it is not enough that from time to time your job may put you in a position to coach others.

What we are discovering, as leadership coaching in the workplace develops toward maturity, is that becoming a coach requires much effort and sustained hard work. To hang out a shingle that says "Coach for hire" is simply to engage in marketing. To become a dedicated and professional coach will stir you to your depths. You can count on it.

You may be a full-time external coach or consultant. You may be an executive within an organization and find yourself coaching others without necessarily calling it coaching. You may be a manager whose major responsibility is to convey knowledge and attitudes to the people who report to you. Whoever you are, these pages are intended to challenge, to guide, and to encourage you.

Toward Professionalism and Standards

We have spoken of "professional" and "coach" in the same breath, but at this point in its development, coaching cannot be described as a profession by any strict definition. Unlike medicine, law, or psychotherapy, the practice of coaching is still too young to have developed generally accepted standards of education, training, practice, discipline, effective regulatory bodies, or even an agreement as to the nature of the profession.

As a result, there are few protections available to the various constituencies affected by coaching. These constituencies include individuals and their organizations, co-workers, friends and family, and society as a whole. Our work as coaches also has an impact on other coaches, whose reputations may rise or fall depending on how we practise coaching.

A variety of people are engaged in workplace coaching. At one end of the spectrum are supervisors. They are called upon every day to coach those who report to them regarding basic workplace tasks. In the middle are people who, on an irregular basis, provide coaching to individuals who do not report directly to them. At the other end of the spectrum is a growing number of people who have devoted themselves to being full-time coaches, some of whom describe themselves as professionals.

In time, coaching may become a profession in the formal sense of the term. But for the present we suggest that all of us who practise it—from the line supervisor to the HR manager, from the consultant who occasionally coaches his clients to the full-time dedicated coach—should regard ourselves as being "on the road toward professionalism." It is in that sense that the term "professional" is used in this book. Because all of us are still in the process of learning and growing, a professional quality of behaviour and practice must be our goal. We cannot be complacent about the perfection of our skills.

Therefore, our place on the road to professionalism is based not on official role descriptions or titles, but on whether we bring minimum standards to our work. Such standards would have to include a well-developed ethical response and a commitment to confidentiality. We will need to see ourselves as accountable to fellow members of the profession and to our public as we apply a body of appropriate skills to our work. We must learn to recognize our own limits and be prepared to hand off responsibilities to more appropriate professionals whenever indicated.

As with all committed professionals, there must be a dedication to personal, as well as career, growth.

Discovering Standards of Coaching Excellence

To clarify the qualities of an ideal coach, on the basis of your own experience, think about a time when someone helped you to learn a skill. It may have been a parent, piano teacher, physical education instructor, driving instructor, classroom teacher, older sibling, workplace supervisor, doctor, nurse, or therapist. You could choose anyone, but likely it will be a person who, for at least a few minutes of your lifetime, could be described as your coach.

Which aspects of their personality and practice made that person effective in helping you? It may be helpful to pause now to write them down. Hundreds of people have responded to this exercise, and they have commonly identified qualities that included "patience while caring for me as a individual" and "believing in my capacity to grow and change." Others have noted that the coach either "possessed a good knowledge of the subject matter" or "was willing to learn alongside me." Frequently they noted that the coach was "always raising the bar and pushing me gently to exceed previous limitations." Many considered it important that the coach "noticed my hidden capabilities and encouraged me to believe in myself."

Now make another list including the ways that coaches have interfered with your progress, discouraged you from learning, and left traces of misery in your memories. Failures most commonly identified by those we surveyed included coaching that exhibited a "bullying approach," "the coach who saw me as a product rather than a person," and "becoming discouraged when I stumbled." Also listed was "Being inconsistent or unavailable," together with "taking advantage of our relationship to satisfy selfish needs: usually sex or ego."

As you discover by attending to your memories, you already know a great deal about what makes effective or ineffective coaches.

Not everyone should skydive. There are people who should not aspire to become brain surgeons. Others are not suited to basketball. A few will not make good parents. And some should not coach. At this stage in the development of coaching as a field of practice, many people are hopping onto the bandwagon, and for a variety of reasons: greater income potential, having others look up to them, good experiences in helping clients problem-solve, or pressure from their organizations.

The problem is that many self-proclaimed coaches possess only minimal training and an uncertain amount of inherent skill, and may lack a depth of self-knowledge. Because the field has no meaningful accreditation or legislative guidance, talented and skillful coaches hang out their shingles every day next to those of the truly terrible.

As we consider the value of developing standards for leadership coaching in the workplace, let us look at the negative side of coaching and some case examples.

Dangerous Coaches

A grim history looms behind the concerns expressed here. For years now, the media have been littered with stories about professionals who have abused clients and patients. These dangerous individuals slipped through the safety nets of a dozen or more professions better regulated than coaching. For every case that actually hit the news, be sure that a dozen were not brought to public attention.

What drives those professing to serve others to display destructive behaviour? It may be that they were ill prepared for a professional relationship of intimacy. Or it may be that they have a tendency toward self-indulgence or even a naivety about the complexity of a helping relationship.

Workplace coaches face additional risks because they work within the magnetic field generated by the power and demands of organizations. Since many organizations have priorities that are shaped by production, profitability, or systems, they tend to be relatively insensitive to the worth and frailty of individual human beings. It requires great wisdom to find the balance between one's responsibilities to the employer and to the person being coached.

The vulnerability of our clients requires that we constantly grow in our professionalism. Our responsibility is not only to continuously monitor our own work, but also to engage others to help us to see the subtleties that we might otherwise miss.

KNOWING ALL THE RIGHT ANSWERS

To heighten the skills of coaching students, we often ask them to undertake practice exercises in coaching. In the early stages, we sometimes find it painful to watch as they attempt to figure out the right answers for the person they are coaching. You can almost see the doors in their brains opening and slamming as they mentally try out and reject various bits of helpful advice. Only later do the students begin to realize that the coach who thinks she knows the answers has the lowest probability of success. The know-it-all tends to drive the coachee to blind obedience or to a rejection of the process.

The most dangerous of these coaches are those who shoot from the hip with solutions that sound plausible but lack depth. If you watch the coachee's face closely in such situations, you will see some puzzling over the advice given, appreciative and respectful of the effort and expertise of the coach, but not entirely certain that one-size-fits-all is the right solution.

Human beings are terrifically complex. Anyone who claims to know the correct answers for someone else is either omniscient (as in divine) or deluded. The best coaches are those who know clearly just how much they do not know.

Admittedly it is sometimes evident that the emperor has no clothes. At such times, the coach has a distinct responsibility to help the coachee discover the truth. And there are plenty of times in a coaching relationship when the conscientious coach is required to persistently but gently challenge a coachee to see the truth that is invisible to him.

But for some self-appointed coaches, usually those without the benefit of rigorous training, pointing out the mistakes of others can provide them with a subtle and seductive high, which gives them a bent feeling of personal fulfilment. The coach who believes that she knows all the answers for the coachee (or the client) is demonstrably dangerous. But it is equally true that the aspiring coach who does not know any of the answers is likely to be impotent.

JANE'S REVENGE

As a small child, Jane often fantasized about how she would wreak her revenge on older children who routinely intimidated her in the schoolyard. But as she grew up, those events gradually receded from conscious memory into her unconscious mind.

In her thirties, Jane showed a talent for coaching; she attended a few workshops and developed her skills by taking on coaching assignments. One of these was with a senior executive who had a tendency to push others around. In fact, at the beginning of the coaching relationship, the man demonstrated this trait, testing Jane to see how far she could be pushed.

As Jane recognized later, that behaviour evoked the same response she had experienced with the bullies of years ago. Instead of working with her coachee from a perspective of detachment and objectivity, she began to show subtle changes.

Now Jane was much too smart, too self-protective, to become openly aggressive with her coachee. She never said out loud what she was thinking—that the executive was an insensitive creep.

But Jane got the message across in infinitely subtle ways. She took pleasure in reporting criticisms from the executive's peers. She showed little empathy for the impossible task of leading a large organization. Watching Jane closely, you would notice a tiny sparkle of glee when the executive made a serious mistake in communication.

And somehow the executive knew it, though not consciously or directly. He began to feel vaguely unsafe with Jane and began to close up, yet he never knew why. His tentative trust came unravelled, and soon he was cancelling coaching appointments.

Jane had an unspoken feeling, as she and the executive parted for the last time, that this relationship could have been richer and more effective than it had turned out to be. But unrecognized factors had defeated the relationship. Jane had paid back the bullying executive with her own bullying, in a fashion so subtle that the executive could never identify what had happened.

The irony of the story is that once the executive had satisfied himself that Jane was no pushover, he stopped trying to push her around. Jane had been handed an ideal coaching opportunity, but she blew it. She never did provide first-person feedback to this powerful manager about what it was like to be pushed around by him.

In fact, Jane did not recognize her mistake until much later, when she sought out a supervisor for her coaching practice and told the story. For the first time, she began to recognize that her unconscious responses sometimes leaked unknowingly into her behaviour, polluting and spoiling her work. By learning to pay attention to those responses, she began to manage them and avoided bullying her clients.

THE COACH WHO DID NOT SPEAK THE LANGUAGE

Jeanine was an excellent psychotherapist with a quiet, steady practice who decided to take up the challenge of corporate coaching.

Unfortunately she knew next to nothing about the day-to-day pressures people face in the organizational world. She did not speak the language of business, and what little she had to say about coaching was focused exclusively on the need for personal development with no reference to business or to organizational needs.

As you can imagine, although Jeanine made the rounds and scored a few interviews, she rarely received a coaching referral. The moment she opened her mouth, the sponsors recognized that she was an outsider, someone from a different planet.

While the prospective coach who doesn't understand business needs is unlikely to get the work, there is another way of not knowing the answers. Self-designated coaches who have not undertaken sufficient personal exploration are equally unlikely to fulfil their coaching responsibilities.

THE CHEERLEADER WHOSE TEAM LOST

As a member of a midsize consulting firm, Nicole had been successful in organizational development for more than a decade. She was bright, gregarious, and a quick study. More often than not, the solutions she offered her clients were successfully implemented.

Because Nicole was likable, people sometimes told her their secrets or cried on her shoulder. Watching the coaching movement develop, Nicole began to describe what she did as "coaching." Never one to miss an opportunity, she obtained permission to set up a coaching unit within her firm, and given her corporate credibility, the unit soon attracted work.

Nicole was a good cheerleader with plenty of ideas for her coachees to try out. But the outcomes were not always as satisfying as expected.

Coached only rarely during her career, Nicole had never explored her own professional or personal life at any depth, and she was incapable of leading clients through their own personal explorations. And though she was good at designing business models for her new unit, she was not effective in supervising the coaching needed by her people.

Gradually her corporate clients began to doubt that coaching was as effective as advertised in providing solutions for their needs. Nicole had unwittingly contributed to a small backlash against her new profession.

Dangerous Psychological Traps for Unwary Coaches

Even though they may not be actively dangerous, unwary coaches may still pose risks both to their coachees and to themselves. As you develop your own standards and core competencies, especially in self-management and the study of the patterns of the mind, you will also need to develop a working understanding of four psychological traps—projection, transference, counter-transference, and porous boundaries—which are recognizable pitfalls in the relationship between the coach and the coachee, and an area thoroughly researched by psychotherapists during the past century.

1. PROJECTION

Projection is a very powerful force, because it occurs without the individual being aware of it happening at the time. Here is how it works. Think of yourself as a film projector with the other person as the screen. Watching him, you may think that he appears angry, and because you think so, you assume that this is true. But if you were to enlist the help of a colleague or coaching supervisor to help you to examine the situation, it might turn out that the fury you imagine seeing in his face is actually the projected image of your own anger.

A key skill for a coach is to learn how to find out whether a coachee is truly feeling what he appears to be feeling. Until we develop that ability, we risk treating our own disease in the other person. The simplest way to discover the truth is often just by asking.

Projection may occur in the opposite direction, as well. For instance, the coachee who is feeling despondent about his lack of progress may project his feeling of hopelessness on to the coach. The alert coach will notice the assumptions that the coachee is making and investigate whether projection is at work. It is possible to do so effectively only if you have confronted your own tendency to project.

2. TRANSFERENCE

When a coachee attributes to the coach qualities that actually belong to some other important person in his life, this phenomenon is called transference. Because this happens without conscious awareness, the coachee will behave as if it were the most obvious truth.

A common example is that the coachee may transfer onto the coach the judgmental stance that once was taken by his parents. Even though the coach is not critical of the coachee, this assumption can be so powerful that it can stall the coachee's progress.

The coachee may also transfer onto you such flattering qualities as vast wisdom and overwhelming attractiveness. As pleasing as it is to be regarded in this way, dangers lurk for the coach who takes this seriously. In your special role, you will need to be alert to clues that the coachee is transferring an attribute to you, and to develop the skill of addressing this in a graceful, non-judgmental manner.

3. COUNTER-TRANSFERENCE

Psychotherapists recognized that it was also possible for them to unconsciously transfer certain attributes to their clients. To distinguish their responsibility for this phenomenon, they named it counter-transference.

Here is an example. Without being aware of it, a coach may transfer to the coachee qualities of her own child who, let us say, is a very meek individual. As a result, the coach may make the incorrect assumption that the coachee is behaving submissively in the workplace. Too certain of this proposed problem, the coach may frustrate the coachee and miss the actual difficulties in his work life.

A good cure for counter-transference is to ask—preferably in the presence of a colleague—"Who is this coachee to me?" By recognizing that counter-transference could be happening, the coach should seek further supervision. It is easy to fix, but if you do not, it can sabotage your work.

4. POROUS BOUNDARIES

It may seem obvious I am me and you are you, and that there is a boundary between us. But for proof that professionals sometimes ignore or forget this distinction, we need only recall the notorious cases in which they have used clients for sexual gratification, have borrowed money, have asked for favours, or in other ways have failed to establish healthy boundaries. Good fences make good neighbours, and to know where the fence must stand will make it unlikely that you will take advantage of the vulnerability of your coachee to satisfy your own needs.

Further, a lively awareness of boundaries will alert you to cases where the coachee wants you to identify inappropriately with him. For instance, when your boundaries are firm, you can empathize with a coachee who feels angry with the boss without getting dragged into a fruitless argument with his supervisor. Healthy boundaries also assist coaches who may hear crushing amounts of detail about other people's burdens to let go of that load and to sleep at night.

As you can see, there exists a hefty body of knowledge for the coach to possess. Although she resists taking an expert stance in the sense of prescribing solutions for others, her expert knowledge of human behaviour is absolutely essential to smooth the coachee's path to development.

PLACING A VALUE ON KNOWLEDGE

David Hallam Bentley, grandfather of one of the authors, was living in Hampshire, England, and was involved in the twentieth-century development of the motorcar. Around 1930 when he was working in his garage, a visibly distraught man pulled up with his sputtering auto. He complained that he had been to three garages and no one could fix it. Bentley agreed to take a look, pushed the vehicle into the garage, and firmly closed the door in the face of the owner.

Minutes later Bentley emerged with the car engine running perfectly and announced that the repair cost ten shillings—a considerable sum in those days.

The customer began to fume. "Ten bob for only ten minutes work!" he exploded. "That's far too much!"

Bentley took a deep breath and replied with the assurance of a man who understands the value of what he knows. "The ten shillings, sir, are not for my time. They're for my knowledge."

Bentley got his payment. Members of the family, passing the story down through generations, reinforced the value of keeping their body of knowledge up-to-date.

Seven Core Competencies of the Effective Coach

Competencies are the well-honed skills and abilities that we regularly display in our work. They seem almost automatic—at the least, they are becoming so. The fact that we have developed them helps to make us competent in our work. A "core" competency is one that has been identified as central or essential to a profession, or is regarded as the basis for the success of a particular enterprise.

In the past century it was easy, even stylish, to identify failure, inability, disability, or a deficit. It was an era marked by an obsession with those factors that make people incompetent. We now recognize that human beings whose value is calculated based on their deficits quickly learn to regard themselves as flawed. As a result, they show less eagerness to change and less capacity to grow.

We now increasingly recognize the importance of focusing on competence. When a coach inquires in an appreciative tone about the coachee's ability and success, rather than highlighting disability and failure, she conveys in a convincing fashion that the coachee must be capable of further success. The value of such an approach will be no surprise to anyone who has raised a child or learned a new skill. Yet this approach has been slow to manifest itself in workplace culture. Identifying ourselves with a proven and productive learning style, we can list seven core competencies for effective coaching:

1. Coaching orientation
2. Coaching skills
3. Teaching ability
4. Values in action
5. Personal qualities of the coach
6. Interpersonal skills
7. Business or organizational understanding

Each competency comprises a host of challenging ideas, and probably no coach will exhibit each competency in all its aspects. These competencies are not intended to eliminate anyone from the game, but rather, to set a standard to which we can aspire. If you feel that you are less effective in certain areas, it means that you are just as human as other coaches. Regard this as a challenge rather than a dead end, for if you have read this far, you probably possess determination enough to get help in developing your abilities.

At the end of this chapter, you will find a checklist of behavioural descriptions based on the seven core competencies. You can use this list as quick self-assessment.

1. Coaching Orientation

A good starting point when we examine the crucial competencies of coaching is to note the importance of developing a theoretical orientation. Theory is valuable because it provides a sound structure to guide your personal development and skills development. We will examine several considerations here: a practical coaching model, the importance of self-management, understanding how the mind works, and the value of clinical experience.

A PRACTICAL COACHING MODEL

A coaching model is a complex description of the design, the tools, the procedures, and the philosophical perspective that makes it possible to pursue this profession.

The best way to familiarize yourself with a coaching model is to take an extensive course in coaching—more than a year in length to allow you the necessary time to grow—measuring your practice against a particular model. Additional benefits of taking a course include exposure to others who are eager to think out loud about the practice of this profession.

How can you know whether a particular program offers the best model? This question is not that important, because you will soon find yourself refining whatever model you are first presented with, attuning it to your own experience and your real-life clientele. In the end, your model will be well designed precisely because you have developed new knowledge and made it your own.

THE IMPORTANCE OF SELF-MANAGEMENT

Part of your orientation to coaching will be awareness of whatever personal "baggage" you might be bringing into your coaching sessions. Examples include your needs and expectations, acute problems in your personal life, and aspects of personal style, such as moving slowly or quickly. The coach's awareness and self-management around issues such as these cannot be over-emphasized.

For example, what impact do your expectations have on the outcome of coaching? Perhaps you feel a strong desire for the coachee to follow a certain direction or to move at a faster speed. The unhappy result is that he will feel pushed and you will feel frustrated. But once you become aware of your expectations and begin to manage them, both you and the coachee will relax and get on with less stress. Is this a tall order? Perhaps, but it constitutes another of many arguments for having an experienced coach with whom you can talk regularly about self-management in your work with coachees.

UNDERSTANDING HOW THE MIND WORKS

Gaining an understanding of how the human mind operates is a question of unending importance to all people, and the innovations in theory about the mind are continuous. There will never be a last word, only a latest word. While this may disappoint those who treasure absolutes, it will delight those who value the opportunity to expand their information and to examine life from many perspectives. As a coach, the mind is your workplace, so enjoy the privilege and responsibility of remaining abreast of knowledge in this area.

Your coaching model will include a tentative understanding of how the human mind functions. You will want to become better acquainted with psychology and psychotherapy—and especially with the closest cousin to workplace coaching: solution-focused therapy. You will want to learn all you can about human motivation and relationships, as well as individual and group behaviours. (See Resources.)

THE VALUE OF CLINICAL EXPERIENCE

Controversy rages among coaches as to which background best qualifies a coach. Understandably those whose training was outside the therapeutic realm—in finance, or strategic planning, or marketing, for instance—will argue that they are ideally suited to convey "hard" business skills.

Coaches with a background in human growth and development will assert that a psychological or clinical foundation is crucial. They say that when successful leaders become stalled, it is a sign that they have hit a psychological wall. These leaders are smart, action-oriented people, they say, otherwise, they would not be successful. If all they required was to understand what went wrong, they would fix it in a flash.

The coach who understands the workings of an individual's mind and the impact of relationships is likely to have the most profound impact on morale, productivity, and loyalty in the workplace. She can look beyond external behaviour to the conflicts—whether external or unconscious—impeding a person's growth. She can also reach with confidence for selected tools to assess the current state of a coachee. (See Chapters Six and Seven.)

The intention here is not to insist on a lengthy psychological exploration, but to provide information enabling the coach and coachee team to move toward solutions respecting human reality. Because the sophisticated coach understands the deeper drives of individuals in the workplace, she can chart strategies to deal with complex work relationships, and she is less likely to rely on simplistic, off-the-shelf solutions. Also, she is comfortable making appropriate referrals in cases where it would help to have another professional take part of the load. Whenever the personal issues are deep or subtle, the clinically trained or psychologically developed coach does indeed have much to offer.

For a variety of coaches in the workplace who may lack such a background, the Deep Learning Process provides valuable insight and support (see Chapter Four). Such coaches include those whose professional development focused on quantifiable, rather than descriptive, factors, for instance, in accountancy and information technology. Many HR professionals, who have specialized in systems like payroll and benefits, want to understand better how others think and feel. Still other HR professionals, whose work focuses on human interactions, may need a more comprehensive framework to guide their development. Executives who have taken on coaching roles already recognize that people are their greatest source of productivity, but now find that they are challenged to improve their mentoring skills. Industrial psychologists, attuned to testing and interpretation, may now be called upon to help employees enhance their effectiveness. The list also includes professional coaches whose original careers were in business and wish to develop greater psychological sophistication.

2. Coaching Skills

Coaching is essentially an extended conversation leading to positive change. Its strength is in addressing the entire person of the coachee: the intellect, the emotion, the history, and the relationships.

One of the crucial skills required for the coaching dialogue is the ability to ask insightful questions that others routinely shy away from. While you may feel awkward doing this at first, you can hone your ability so that you deepen the conversation. As a result, you will become more sensitive to the coachee.

One caution: although it is important to have a good set of coaching tools and techniques ready in our back pockets, it is equally important not to be dazzled by our skills.

Otherwise we are likely to be distracted by planning our next great manoeuvre while our clients are speaking to us.

As we gain experience, we find ourselves relying on techniques less (because they have been integrated into an instinctive way of working) and simply "being" with our coachees more. That allows us to attend deeply to them in the moment and to show more genuine care. Sensing the sincerity of our attention encourages them to commit themselves to the growth process.

ACTIVE LISTENING SKILLS

To make the coaching conversation powerful, the coach must possess a high level of skill as an active listener. Fortunately there is more to this than the comedian's stereotype.

Coachee: I'm really tired today.
Coach: I hear you saying that you are really tired today.
Coachee: That's right. I sure am.
Coach: So you sure are?
Coachee: Yep.
Coach: I really hear you. You're saying yep.
Coachee: (Snores gently.)

The active listener is unobtrusively busy. She maintains eye contact and body language that reassures the coachee of his importance. Looking out the window or retreating behind the desk are behaviours guaranteed to keep the coachee feeling distant and lacking in involvement.

Active listeners pay attention to thoughts expressed by the coachee and respond in a way that shows they are listening. For instance, the coach thinks to herself, "My coachee looks like a pet that has been beaten." She is about to say this when the coachee mutters, "I feel like a worn-out tire." The coach jettisons her own formulation at once to inquire, "What's it like to be a worn-out tire?"

The challenge in every session is not just to hear the literal words of the coachee, but also to listen to the deeper messages he is communicating, deliberately or unconsciously, and to reflect those back. In this way, you will affirm the value of the coachee and encourage him to trust his best instincts.

Coachee: I'm really tired today.
Coach: What impact does feeling so tired have on your work?

DEVELOPING EMPATHY AND A CARING ATTITUDE

"Where am I in this relationship?" is a question we must ask ourselves as coaches. It is through their relationship with us that coachees begin to make the changes they want to make. Because the relationship continues over a period of time, it has a profound impact on our coachees, carrying both power and risk. So it is important that we do not lose our awareness of how they are responding to us as people—not just as question-askers.

Empathy is the ability to feel alongside the person we are with. Some people developed this skill so long ago they don't remember doing so; they are naturals. For others, it takes time and commitment to clear away the buzz of our own concerns so that we can respond in a caring and intuitive way to the feelings, thoughts, and attitudes of others.

THE PRIMACY OF FEELINGS

People who are being coached experience various feelings during each session, and those feelings must be addressed for the coaching to be effective. To do so, the coach must be comfortable with the expression of emotion, not just at the office, but in all parts of his life. Emotions have many functions in a coaching session. At any given moment they might serve as a barrier, a source of energy, a clue about unspoken aspects of the coachee, or a gift to the relationship.

Feelings As Barriers: Focusing on emotion may seem contradictory to the ultimate aim of coaching, which is to help people move out of their doldrums and inspire action. This action orientation sometimes deludes coaches into reducing the importance of emotion in their work, and it may also explain why some see little permanent improvement in their coachees. The emotional barricades against which they collide are invisible, implacable. For people to make changes and to move effectively into action, their feelings must be acknowledged.

Why? Because such emotions as anger, despair, and fear often pose a potent barrier to positive action. Let us imagine that the coachee is frightened about the impact of some change he is about to embark on. The fear may cause him to delay, to fudge, or even to set up circumstances so the experiment will fail. And all of this will happen quite unconsciously. He will not be aware of it nor be able to acknowledge it without help.

That explains why it is so important to address the fear, to normalize it, to ask some questions about it. A good question is, "What is the worst thing that might happen when you change in this way?" The coach might help the coachee to explore first the worst and then the best scenarios out loud. With such emotions exposed and examined, one of those little miracles of coaching takes place. Disruptive feelings move further into the background and allow the individual to proceed with the planned behaviour for change with less distraction.

Feelings As a Source of Energy: The coachee's feelings are sometimes not a barrier, but a driving force for change. For example, he may feel sad when he thinks of the wasted time in his current, ineffective ways of doing his job. When the coach notices those feelings and asks about them, he can help the coachee shift his passion and energy into the change process.

Feelings As a Clue about Unspoken Aspects of the Coachee: When the coach senses that the coachee is experiencing an emotion, she may discover that it can tell her even more about the individual. Signs like fidgeting or abrupt movements may convey anxiety about life at work or at home. A withdrawn, low-energy mood may convey depression. A bright, upbeat approach may signal the right time to experiment with new directions.

But do not assume anything. Patient inquiry about how the coachee is feeling or thinking is essential before the coach can begin to respond with accuracy to the emotion.

Feelings As a Gift to Relationship: The coachee's gift is to show his feelings, inviting the possibility of an empathic response. The painful risk he faces is of not being heard accurately. The coach's reciprocal gift of acknowledgment acts as a catalyst for one of the most enduring aspects of the coaching relationship: the building of trust. To acknowledge a coachee's feelings is to say, "I see you as you are, and I accept you as you are."

While a sensitive willingness to work with your client's feelings is a basic requirement for effective coaching, it is best not to charge blindly into this area. With many individuals, you will need to be gentle and patient, holding back a little, allowing them to get used to the idea of talking about emotions.

THE TOUGH, CONSTRUCTIVE COACH

The coach shows the courage to confront as needed, after carefully charting whether the coachee is at a point on his learning curve where he can get maximum value from frank feedback. Understanding how fragile people are, despite the tough exterior in which many garb themselves, she maintains—even in confrontation—a gentleness that encourages the coachee's sense of self-esteem.

CONTRARY COACHING

The audience watched in dismay at a recent conference on corporate coaching as two male presenters stumbled into a competition about who was, in their word, the most "contrary." To the embarrassment of the viewers, they began to promote a tough guy coaching style.

Both tried to stake a claim of shoot-from-the-hip, brutal honesty. "Someone's got to tell the coachee the bad news," proclaimed one.

"Someone has to level with the organization," said the other.

Their discussion looked more like a schoolboys' pissing contest than a serious evaluation of coaching styles.

Tell it like it is, they advertised. No more Mr. Nice Guy.

As well, they suggested, no more empathy. No more caring. No more understanding of how frightening it can be to set out on the uncertain road of change.

DIFFICULT GENTLE TRUTH

A coach was struggling to find a helpful way to confront a coachee. The coachee showed subtle signs of choosing not to grow, preferring to stay stuck in painful circumstances. At length, the coach approached this difficult issue with a question.

"Are you willing," she asked in a kindly voice, "to live with less pain in your life?"

Reflecting afterwards, the coach said, "The highest value I was holding at that moment was to be gentle in how I spoke a hard truth."

The coachee was able to acknowledge for the first time the possibility that he was so used to discomfort that it felt normal. And he began to envision the possibility of changes that could improve his life.

While the effective coach provides frank objective feedback, it is always offered in a thoughtful, constructive manner. In doing so, she differentiates herself from those whose approach to feedback is to give it "right between the eyes."

Many of the problems brought to coaches result from the coachee's inadequate understanding of the workplace, the family, and society. In such cases, the coach who has developed a high competency in coaching skills will sometimes earn her pay by helping the coachee slow down his thinking, so that he can take into account the needs of the organization or reformulate his responses to important people in his life.

3. Teaching Ability

The coach may never write on a flip chart or set an exam, but there is no question that she is a teacher. She guides the coachee to discover new capacities within himself and new things about the world. To be effective requires, along with the requisite educational skills, that she possess a profound belief in the capacity of the coachee to learn and change.

As a professional educator, the coach learns to recognize and appreciate a variety of learning styles, so that she can adapt her methods to the people involved. And in the face of the inevitable obstacles, the coach maintains a sense of composure. Rather than pushing ahead impatiently, she allows individuals to set their own best pace for development. As a result of this perspective, she can calmly select among a variety of options to help coachees to surmount their problems.

TECHNIQUES FOR SMART LEARNING

A common stumbling block appears when one tries to fix a huge insoluble problem all at once. The wise coach helps the client break down complex tasks into manageable pieces. The coachee may fear at first that doing a bit at a time will delay the process, but will be pleased when it manages to speed it up. Often by the time they reach the third step, steps four, five, and six have already resolved themselves.

A key concept in change is to learn through action and reflection. This process helps the coachee to experience partial successes without crippling discouragement. When each success can be analyzed to see what made it work, and each apparent failure analyzed to find the changes that will convert it into success, the coachee will see the world of work in a much clearer light.

4. Values in Action

Although there is confusing talk these days about value clarification and value conflicts, there is actually nothing particularly complicated about values. Everyone holds them. Our values are, to put it simply, whatever we value. As coaches, we confront and clarify our values so that we are consciously aware of their impact when we work with our coachees.

The problem is that values frequently compete with each other. The coach who wants to resolve everyone's problems, for instance, holds a value. But at the same time she may also value allowing people the experience of resolving their own issues. The challenge she faces is to choose which will be her preferred value in a given situation and to put it into action.

A value held by most professional coaches is respect for the inherent wisdom of the coachee. The coach shows this value in action, for instance, when she reveals her belief that the coachee already possesses at least the beginnings of the answers he seeks.

An important value is an appreciation of the diversity of human beings and their experience. All of us have strengths and weaknesses. All of us diverge from the norm in certain ways, and in other ways we all resemble the norm. There is not a single way of being that is superior, but only an infinite chain of human possibilities. Coaches rejoice in the widely differing qualities of the people they work with.

COACHING IN TWO LANGUAGES

I pulled up a chair for the coachee and asked what he would like to talk about. I could not understand a single word of his reply. Then I slipped a receiver over my ear, and from a booth at the back of the conference room, a translator converted his words into English and mine into Turkish.

I had been invited to his country to introduce executive coaching and 360-degree feedback (see Chapter Seven) to an enthusiastic audience. As executives and human resources leaders, they represented the banking, manufacturing, and retail sectors of Istanbul.

The volunteer "coachee" was a human resources manager for a multinational beverage company. He described his feeling of isolation in trying to respond to a real-life workplace problem.

As usual, I had no prepackaged solutions to offer. I had to trust the magic of coaching—not to be clever myself, but to assist the coachee in discovering his own wisdom. Still, I felt like I was floundering. Listening to my own words repeated in another language is no way to relax. But as I released my anxiety, I noticed that he had hinted at a solution. He might turn out to be less isolated than he had thought.

I asked whether there were allies who might support him. With visible relief, he identified a particular executive who had endorsed other initiatives. He said he would seek his help, and I asked when. He replied in Turkish without hesitation, "Tomorrow morning."

I was reminded again that, no matter what the language, when the coach ceases to be attached to finding a solution, the coachee will reliably develop his own.

5. Personal Qualities of the Coach

The personal nature of the coach is the root of her success. She has developed significant personal maturity as a result of her life experience, and she will add a commitment to continuous learning and the pursuit of personal growth experiences.

The coach puts down strong roots by developing self-understanding—understanding of her own motivations, memories, and behaviours. She uses personal coaching and/or psychotherapy to shine a powerful light on her inner processes. As a committed learner, she approaches her clients with humility and a tolerance for ambiguity. Because she is not motivated by a need to dominate or to win points, she responds to the reward of a job well done. The coach's delight is in seeing others flourish.

CONTINUOUS PERSONAL GROWTH AND LEARNING

Inherent in the definition of the coach is a commitment to growth—as a coach certainly, but also simply as a person. Look at it from the perspective of the coachee. If you wanted to learn to drive, you might be willing to take a classroom lesson about the rules of the road from a teacher who had never driven a car. But if someone who lacked many years of driving experience offered to teach you to actually drive a vehicle, you would walk away.

So it is with coaching. People who have honed their awareness through many years of involvement in the workplace have an inherent advantage as coaches. They cannot help having learned and grown. The best coaches do not rely entirely on the passage of years. They deliberately align every aspect of their lives with the process of continuous growth and learning. In their personal lives and relationships, they are committed to discovering all they can be. In their professional life, they take every opportunity to develop their skills and capabilities.

Such phrases as "the learning organization" and "continuous learning" do not represent an empty fad. We human beings are physically limited creatures who cannot run as fast as the ravaging lion, swim as well as the shark, fly from danger like the sparrow, or even survive infancy on our own like the turtle. But we possess the ability that has kept humanity alive for seven million years, and that is our desire to keep on learning, and learning, and learning. This is the power we demonstrate as coaches when we work with our clients. The resource list at the end of this book will provide plenty of suggestions for your own exercises in continuous education, on-line, in the classroom, and on the page.

To understand yourself, it is necessary to undertake training in how the human psyche works, as well as a journey of self-knowledge in which you are on the receiving end of coaching or psychotherapy. Here's a story from one of the authors.

On my way to becoming a coach twenty-five years ago, I applied for training as a psychotherapist. I was surprised that the interviewer, Dr. Helen Morley, decided at once to reject me.

I had presented myself as smart, successful, and very sure of myself. But Helen had serious doubts about whether I was ready to suspend my certainties and self-defenses long enough to discover what might be going on below the surface, within my psyche.

At length she relented, allowing me into the program. But there were conditions. She challenged me to become more vulnerable, open, and questioning. I was required to work with my own personal psychotherapist; my work was closely supervised; and I was coached by a number of excellent senior practitioners.

Today I am convinced that I would have long ago burned out as a coach had she not insisted that my first priority in training was to know myself.

Self-awareness is partly determined by gender. On average—although with many exceptions—women show more self-awareness than men. Something about the factors that affect women's lives (estrogen, menstruation, pregnancy, and mothering) impels them to reflect and, equally important, to talk with one another about their feelings and experiences, about what it means "to be me." Testosterone and other factors that shape male experience, by contrast, have the useful quality of orienting us to survival and victory in a hostile outside world, but seem to encourage little in the way of self-understanding and reflection. For that reason, males in general have a greater need to develop in the disciplines of self-knowledge.

THE ADVANTAGE OF PSYCHOTHERAPY

An absolute prerequisite for being a leadership coach in the workplace is to have been coached yourself. To increase your likelihood of success, consider entering personal psychotherapy. Look at it like this. If you knew that you were going to take a job slinging one-hundred-pound sacks of grain, you might build up to it through weight training. If you developed your muscles to the point where you could lift one hundred pounds, you would be confident that you could manage the new job.

But what if you could lift 120 pounds? Then you would know that you could not only manage the routine, but also have extra resources for times when the floor was slippery, or a bag broke, or you had to work an extra hour at the end of a long day.

That is what psychotherapy is like. It helps you to understand a little more about yourself than you may need for routine coaching. You will begin to see below the surface of your mind, your relationships, and your culture. By extension, you will understand your coachees better.

The therapies that offer the best payback for coaches are generally solution-focused, behaviour-oriented, and relationship-focused. Be aware that with some exceptions, traditional psychiatry, psychoanalysis, and psychotherapy tend to be oriented more to the past than the future. You can find the best therapist for your needs through research: call therapist associations, ask your friends for information about their therapists, and question therapists about their orientation. Use these buzz words: "solution-focused," "behaviour-oriented," and "relationship-focused," and note how people respond.

YOUR OWN COACHING

Coaching, by its very nature, is a collaborative exercise. It relies on an ability to work intensively with one or more human beings. The coach must be or must become a collaborative person. To put that in more specific terms, the coach who has not been coached is playing at being a coach.

There are several benefits to this collaborative exercise. They include the fact that the senior coach "models" the process of coaching for her—live and in person. Observing another coach close-up allows her to discover which behaviours support her own learning, and which ones hold it back. This is a generous source of information, helping her discover what it is like to sit in the coachee's chair and vastly increasing her dexterity as a coach. An added benefit is that it demonstrates her integrity; her coachees see that she practises what she preaches.

This is not to say that the coach must be in the coachee role at every moment of her career. But if she has not been involved in significant and extensive coaching relationships in which she is the coachee, she will be flying in the dark.

YOUR OWN SUPERVISION

A student in one of our coaching classes, uncertain about whether she should be sharing information about her coachees, asked, "Should I have someone I can talk with about my cases?" The reply was a resounding yes. To do her best work, a coach should be constantly "in supervision." Being coached and being supervised enables us to renew our reserves, making us more flexible and resilient. Without these reserves, there is a significant danger of running dry, like a car with an empty fuel tank.

Supervision is a relationship with an experienced fellow coach to whom the coach voluntarily yields a certain amount of authority. We take to the supervisor the difficult issues facing us in certain coaching relationships. We may ask the supervisor how she has handled similar situations. We listen, we explore our practice, and we learn. The relationship gives us a forum where we can recognize our limitations and see beyond our usual borders. None of us is so clever that we can resolve all issues by ourselves. None of us owns so accurate a mirror that we truly see ourselves as our clients do. Of course, the coach reveals only information actually required, with high respect for confidentiality. And the supervisor has a commitment to keep all information confidential.

Supervision can take a number of forms. It may be a mentoring relationship involving a more experienced and a less experienced coach. It may be a complementary relationship in which two coaches of roughly equal experience provide each other with feedback—no holds barred—about their work. Or it may be in the form of a coaching support group, bringing coaches together on a regular basis to discuss the challenges in their work.

It is sometimes an advantage to exchange money in this transaction, although it is not obligatory. In many professions, practitioners have found that to pay for supervision by a more senior practitioner helps to cement their commitment to work hard on the development of skills, understanding, and ethics.

AUTHENTICITY AND CREDIBILITY

The coach often has access to private, confidential, and vulnerable places in people's lives. But when the unprepared coach starts to experiment on innocent people, the result can be catastrophic.

A minister of religion described himself in almost every sermon as "a psychologist and sociologist." From this expert perspective, he dissected many interesting social phenomena.

On investigation, however, it turned out that the reverend gentleman had taken exactly one undergraduate course in psychology and one in sociology. Knowing that, it was a bizarre experience for us to listen to him misrepresenting himself.

The biggest problem was not truth in advertising, although he did develop serious credibility problems with the more knowledgeable members of his congregation. The danger lay in the fact that he himself did not recognize his limitations. As a result of pretending to skills he did not possess, he put himself in a position where he could do significant damage.

In the intimate and powerful arena of his counselling office, he offered parishioners his good intentions, but none of the appropriate discipline. Erratic and opinionated, he sometimes diagnosed their personalities inaccurately or pressed them to follow a course that could have disastrous outcomes.

Like the majority of coaches, you may have no formal training at all. Perhaps you are a line supervisor who coaches employees every day in the course of your job. And what keeps you out of trouble is your ethical commitment to coach only in areas appropriate to your level of skill.

You do not try to diagnose the unconscious conflicts of your reports. You do not interfere in their personal lives. But when you help them to improve their effectiveness in the workplace, you are, like many other fine supervisor-coaches, extremely effective. Your coaching is effective because it is business-driven. It produces results. It is rewarding for the employee. And the reason is that it covers ground that is appropriate for both your job specifications and your skills.

FEEDBACK ABOUT YOUR COACHING SKILLS

An excellent way to discover how others see you is to use a feedback instrument like the one provided at the end of this chapter. Unlike a casual conversation, an instrument has the advantage of allowing you to formulate your questions in a thoughtful manner and cover ground that might not otherwise be surveyed. If you are not already familiar with the use of 360-degree or multi-source feedback, there is an additional benefit to using a questionnaire with a variety of responders. You will experience a foretaste of the value it can offer for your coachees. (See Advanced Assessment, Chapter Seven.)

One additional suggestion: Plan to do this in partnership with your own coach, supervisor, or other person who can offer you guidance, balance, and support. And remember, you are going to see some critical comments—they may sting at the moment, but they are gold, for they point the way toward making you a better coach.

6. Interpersonal Skills

Coaches are "people persons." They show a genuine liking for others and develop good relationships with people of all varieties. Their openness to relationship is not limited by race, colour, national origin, gender, sexual orientation, physical appearance, or disability. Their communication skills enable them to get their message across clearly and to hear what others want them to know.

The very nature of their profession means that coaches are engaged in a lifetime study of human behaviour, so nothing they hear is likely to surprise them. They are primed to understand both the individual's "shtick" and what makes him or her "tick." Carl Rogers, the great pioneer of the human potential movement, said it earliest and best when he prescribed "unconditional positive regard" for the person being counselled as the precondition for their development. He was reacting to the pose of cold superiority that he saw insecure professionals adopting to feel more comfortable. He recognized that this pose was costly, for it reduced the coachees' sense of power and restricted their confidence in their own potential.

By contrast, the professional who sees the coachee as her peer is showing respect for his capabilities. The coach's high regard for the coachee helps ensure success. A caution: to think so highly of this person is not the same as to develop a personal friendship. It does not minimize the helpful boundary between coach and coachee, and it imposes no obligation or burden on the coachee.

A GENEROUS RELATIONSHIP WITH THE COACHEE

The coach who is personally secure will have no need for self-aggrandizement. She can reveal herself to the coachee with honesty and humility. She reveals herself to be a fellow traveller along the challenging road of life, a person who has made some mistakes, scored some victories, and gained some wisdom. Because she is open about mistakes, her wisdom is all the more convincing.

This is a stance of generosity. The coach sees the pattern of his life from the perspective of abundance, rather than deprivation. She knows that she is drawing from a well that is full and that replenishes itself. So she never needs to hoard her goods and her goodwill.

MODELLING FOR THE COACHEE

The coach recognizes that, as a person in a position of power or authority—whether she likes it or not—she stands as a model to others. This can be a problem, but it has the benefit of forcing the coach to make certain that she lives with integrity. Coaching is a life of self-awareness. The coach keeps on checking herself to be sure that she is modelling the same behaviours, skills and attitudes that she encourages for her client.

Coaches often encourage their coachees to take good care of themselves and not sacrifice their well-being to their work. Speaking to others about self-care serves as a reminder to look more closely at our own lives, to measure how we are balancing the demands of personal and business life, relaxation and effort, relationships and solitude.

7. Business or Organizational Understanding

Reading these pages, you might believe that psychological sophistication is the main requirement for success as a coach. While it is certainly central, it is not enough. In our early days of workplace coaching, we recognized our most urgent learning curve was to increase our understanding of organizations, their patterns, and their needs.

The coach cannot hope to be effective if she functions like a therapist whose client happens to have a job. Not only must she understand the organization, she must empathize with those who carry responsibilities within it. The task of providing leadership in organizations today is more complex and onerous than ever before in human history.

For that reason, the ideal candidate to provide leadership coaching in the workplace might be a trained psychotherapist who has spent the past ten years working as a senior manager in a business. But since there are not many of those to be found, all of us, whatever our origins, must focus on broadening our perspective and filling the blanks in our experience to date.

ACCUMULATING ORGANIZATIONAL EXPERIENCE

The organizational experience of effective coaches allows them to check their own ideas against known realities. When a beginning coach desires to work in a corporate setting, she will have to use every means possible to develop an in-depth understanding of corporate life. For those who lack business experience, a period of paid or volunteer work in a company with the purpose of gaining broad knowledge can be helpful. Make a habit of reading magazines, journals, corporate reports, the business section of newspapers, and the Internet, on trends in the organizational and business world. Pay attention to everything that will help you to pick up the language of the work world and, more importantly, the thought-forms and theories that infuse the words.

Probably the best sources of information about business are people who have senior positions in organizations. They are often generous in describing the complex dimensions and needs of their systems. They can also elucidate the enormous changes being forced on their organizations by the changing context of global business, relentless competition, and the pressure to balance budgets and ensure profits.

A LEADERSHIP TEAM CONFRONTS THE EARTHQUAKE

The president of a software-development firm asked a coach to work with him and the three other owners of the company. He explained that, despite the fact that they were co-owners and friends, they had never worked as a team and were in disarray. It turned out that they had previously reported to a charismatic leader, recently departed under unhappy circumstances. Now they had to discover for themselves how to lead.

Because in the past they communicated with the CEO in a vertical fashion, they had developed little skill or experience in communicating with one another on a horizontal level. Even months after his departure, they persisted in sending one another information—and challenges—not directly, but through the new president.

The four owners had many strengths working for them, including genuine goodwill. But each had unique needs that required the skills of a coach. For one owner, it was discovering the nature of leadership through experimentation and reflection. For another, it was rebuilding commitment to the firm, and yet another needed to learn how to work as a team member around issues of mutual need, such as communication about product development and marketing. The fourth owner simply needed to build confidence as an executive.

The executives met with the coach for almost a year, individually and as a team. Their task was not only to build up individual and team skills, but also to improve the functioning of the company so that they could market it to a new owner. Within a year, they had sold it successfully.

This situation imposed a wide range of demands on the coach. She had to have the flexibility to meet each leader around a different task, depending on need, and the confidence to track and to guide four very different people at a time when their organization was shifting radically under their feet. She had to be comfortable providing leadership to a group with terrible communication practices, helping them to be explicit about their unspoken assumptions, politics, and patterns. Success in this assignment required the coach to have an understanding of how people behave in teams, a capacity to help individuals balance personal needs and corporate demands, and the ability to think along several tracks at one time. As well, she needed to dedicate time to reflecting about the individuals within the larger picture.

A Systems Perspective

The coach's first tool in comprehending organizations is the study of systems in general to guide her interventions. For our purposes, a system is any set of interrelated elements, such as an organizational structure, or any grouping of people that has an impact on the coachee and on which the coachee has an impact. Systems can spur workers on to greater productivity, tie their hands, divert them to respond to other needs, and even affect their emotional condition. Examples of systems include the family, the friendship circle, societies and associations, and the workplace. Even within the workplace there are many active systems, and each may have its own culture. People who work physically close to each other or work interdependently form a system, as do those who report to a common supervisor, those who belong to the same bargaining unit, and those who eat lunch together in the cafeteria.

It is important for the coachee to understand the various systems in which she functions, and the specific cultural norms of each. The coach helps him to discern the differences between the acknowledged official culture of the organization and the unspoken but powerful unofficial cultures, enabling him to understand the competing sets of needs within the organization and how to balance his efforts for individual change against their force. The coach also helps him to see the dichotomy of how his systems may gently encourage him to change, at the same time as they attempt to maintain their own stability by subtly restraining him.

Attending to the Context

Extensive past experience with organizational systems helps a coach to assess whether plans that the coachee may propose for making change are realistic.

Coachee: So I'll just go in there and tell them I am upset with how they have treated me.
Coach: I understand why you would like to do that. But I wonder how they are likely to react.
Coachee: I don't know. I guess they would think it was pretty weird. Personal feelings aren't exactly the biggest topic of conversation at the office.
Coach: Are you saying this might not help?
Coachee: I suppose. I could end up feeling even worse.
Coach: So maybe we could look for another way you could get more respect from your peers.

Marketing to the Organization

The practice of coaching is impractical without a ready supply of customers. The coach must therefore know how to communicate to the organization the ways in which she will add value. It is not enough to say that he will help a particular employee feel better. The coach must present a case for how coaching will benefit the organization, whether through increased productivity or profit, improved morale, reduced disruption of production, steadier direction of the enterprise, or other gains of a tactical or strategic nature. To do so requires a certain amount of empathy with the aims and methods of the organization.

Further, from the outset, the coach makes certain that the contracting process with the organization is not only clear and covers all relevant bases, but also that any conflict between the organization's need for information and the coachee's need for privacy is balanced and maintained. (For more on the Contracting Phase of Coaching, see Chapter Five.)

In the marketing process, the rare coach who sees the organization as an enemy and himself as a covert infiltrating agent is likely to be found out and shunned. While there is nothing unusual about having a love/hate relationship with big organizations—most people do—you are likely to have a positive impact as a coach only if you are prepared to give the benefit of the doubt and to hold the organizational sponsors of coaching to their highest aspirations. It is respectful and useful to clarify precisely where your values complement those of the organization and at what points they may diverge.

Making Your Commitment to Continuous Learning

In this chapter, we have presented a wide range of standards and competencies, and depicted many of the cautions and skills that will enhance the performance of a workplace coach. Our intention has been to pose a meaningful challenge to ourselves, as well as to the reader.

You should not expect to fulfill every demand that is implied on these pages, but you are likely, at this point, to have begun thinking about making some changes. You may find it helpful to pause here and make a few notes to remind yourself of these development directions. If you would like further guidance, complete the survey that concludes this chapter.

Check Your Skills Against a Competency-Based Questionnaire

Developed for two purposes, the following survey will help coaches to assess themselves and will assist those who engage coaches in deciding whether a particular candidate may be effective. The questionnaire covers each of the seven core competencies, using descriptions of observable behaviour. Not intended to be comprehensive, the survey was designed to be a manageable length and to cover most of the skills and competencies required for good coaching. Take a few minutes to check how well you fit this profile. You are likely to uncover areas where you would benefit by further development, and in other areas be encouraged about the strengths you bring to the work.

You are welcome to copy the questionnaire if you wish to respond without marking up the book. Or you may want to adapt it to better reflect your own values and practice.

INTERPRETING THE RESULTS

Like all surveys, this one has built-in prejudices, specifically those of the authors as described throughout this book. For instance, it includes some items that may not be important to you if you are providing a basic, skills-oriented level of coaching. Once you have filled out this questionnaire, you should be clear about what you hold in your hand. It is a very limited document—your own take on your own abilities.

A better way to assess your abilities is to try to see them as others do. You can develop a more panoramic view of yourself by making copies of the survey and soliciting feedback from your coachees, sponsors of coaching, fellow coaches, and others who know your work. For the sake of maintaining their anonymity, ask someone else to average their scores. At the end, you will find that you have a rich picture of your strengths and the areas on which you need to work.

This is not a test—it has nothing to do with passing or failing. It is not designed to tell you whether you should or should not coach. It will, however, reveal the areas where your skills are fine, and those where they need improvement. Where you see the need for further development, we recommend that you undertake some of the excellent training that is now becoming available. For more specific information, you could join a coaching association or check out Resources at the end of the book.

FIGURE 3.1 **COMPETENCY SURVEY FOR WORKPLACE COACHING**

Person being assessed: _____

Instructions to responder: Using a scale of 1 to 10, please indicate in the boxes below whether you strongly disagree, disagree, agree, or strongly agree, that the person named shows each of the behaviours described. If you do not have enough information to respond to an item, write the letter "N" in the box and that entry will be ignored in the averaging of scores. The scale below indicates how to express numerically the degree of your disagreement or agreement.

Strongly Disagree		Disagree			Agree			Strongly Agree	
1	2	3	4	5	6	7	8	9	10

(continued)

FIGURE 3.1 CONTINUED

COACHING ORIENTATION

- [ ] Operates from a well-designed coaching model
- [ ] Operates from an effective working theory about how the human mind functions, including motivations, relationships, and individual and group behaviours
- [ ] Looks beyond outward behaviour to the conflicts, whether external or unconscious, that may impede a person's growth
- [ ] Possesses excellent assessment abilities
- [ ] Has access to appropriate assessment instruments
- [ ] Operates in a solution-oriented mode
- [ ] Avoids off-the-shelf solutions for complex problems

COACHING SKILLS

- [ ] Shows good ability to ask insightful questions
- [ ] Is effective at helping coachee see new possibilities
- [ ] Possesses high level of skill as an active listener, reflecting and mirroring what the coachee presents
- [ ] Demonstrates empathy and a caring attitude as a skilled witness to growth
- [ ] Has courage to confront as needed, along with gentleness that maintains the coachee's self-esteem
- [ ] Provides frank, objective feedback in a constructive, nonjudgmental manner
- [ ] Skillful at inspiring coachee to move from contemplation and insight into positive change/action
- [ ] Draws on previous experience with organizational systems to help assess whether coachee's plans for change are realistic
- [ ] Possesses ability to elicit wisdom from others in a wide network
- [ ] Knows when and how to make referrals to other resources
- [ ] Possesses good boundaries, including the skill of not carrying other people's burdens
- [ ] Maintains a professional relationship with coachee, including clearly defined boundaries

TEACHING ABILITY

- [ ] Believes in the desire and capacity of the coachee to learn and develop
- [ ] Possesses sufficient patience to surmount coaching obstacles
- [ ] Assesses the difficulties the coachee may face in learning new skills
- [ ] Encourages learning methods based on action and reflection
- [ ] Understands, adapts to, and gently challenges the coachee's personal learning style
- [ ] Has ability to break down complex tasks into manageable pieces

(continued)

FIGURE 3.1 **CONTINUED**

VALUES IN ACTION

☐ Has confronted and clarified her or his own values and ethics
☐ Assists the organization in balancing its need for information with the coachee's need for confidentiality
☐ Protects the organization's business secrets
☐ Shows integrity by presenting self and skills in a frank, open, and professional manner

PERSONAL QUALITIES

☐ Has developed significant personal maturity through life experience
☐ Shows commitment to continuous personal growth and learning
☐ Has developed strong self-understanding, through personal coaching and psycho-therapy, for example
☐ Is present, authentic, and credible in relationship with the coachee
☐ Is passionate about helping others grow
☐ Has the confidence to seek feedback from coachees, sponsors of coaching, and other stakeholders

INTERPERSONAL SKILLS

☐ Has a genuine liking for people, relates well with people
☐ Shows unconditional positive regard for the coachee
☐ Practises personal generosity and humility
☐ Models the behaviours, communication skills, and attitudes recommended to the coachee
☐ Models self-care and life balance

ORGANIZATIONAL UNDERSTANDING

☐ Has a breadth of experience in organizational and leadership development
☐ Understands the complex dimensions and needs of business organizations
☐ Knows how to communicate to the organization the ways in which she or he can add value
☐ Expends effort to understand the culture of a particular organization
☐ Works effectively within both the official and unofficial cultures of an organization
☐ Assists coachees in balancing their efforts for individual change with the corporate culture
☐ Holds a systems-oriented perspective

(Adapted with permission from *PanoramicFeedback.Com*)

Having looked closely at yourself as a coach, you are ready to discover in the chapter that follows a description of your most vital tool set, the Deep Learning Process.

A Look at the Basic Coaching Model

There is a basic, reliable structure that stands behind the Deep Learning Process. It is, in fact, the model on which everyone who coaches, instinctively relies. For our purpose, it will provide an excellent starting point for the understanding of Deep Learning.

This basic coaching model begins with the decision that coaching will be helful or necessary—a decision made by the organization and its representatives or by the individual. In response, the coachee withdraws briefly from workplace responsibilities to engage in a coaching session. There, the coach helps her to clarify what she wishes to accomplish, and together they plan a personalized and viable strategy. The coachee then re-enters the workplace and experiments with the new behaviour.

Even in its least sophisticated forms, coaching accomplishes great results through the use of a simple set of tools:

1. Personalizing the learning: "No more cookie-cutter solutions."
2. Applying intelligence to a problem: "Two minds are better than one."
3. Adding enthusiastic support: "Go get 'em! You can do it."
4. Standing back to watch the fireworks: "You were great!"

Such tools underpin all the varieties of coaching, and if the coach is attempting simpler tasks that pose a minimal threat or challenge to the client, these tools can be very effective by themselves. Examples of less complex outcomes are the learning of a new technical skill and the learning of how to plan productive meetings.

There is a problem, however. The basic model limits our vision of the extent to which people can learn and change. It does not meet the needs of individuals requiring performance development at a deeper level. And while it encourages a strong sense of motivation in the immediate moment, it may fail to deliver persistent results once the coach is off the scene.

Suppose that you are working with a manager who needs to learn to run meetings more effectively. Using a basic coaching process, it is possible to coach her to improve her skills, and likely there will be positive results. But there is no way of predicting whether the improvement in skills will last. With the basic coaching model, much depends on the person's state of readiness for coaching and the encouragement already available within the workplace.

This basic coaching model, although useful as far as it goes, is limited in its ability to respond adequately to complex and ambiguous realities. It ignores much of the complex structure of the human mind. As a result, it may fail in two major respects: it does little to ensure deep change and little to support sustainability.

A Process for Deep Learning

The Deep Learning Process provides additional value as it guides us into the fascinating territory of the human development process, enabling the coach to confidently approach situations that others might avoid as intractable. Understanding and working with the process helps to unleash the potential of highly valued and accomplished leaders who have somehow stalled. It also provides reason to hope for those whom most others have declared hopeless.

The Deep Learning Process is effective because it addresses not simply the aspect of the mind that we define as rational, but the mind in all its fullness. It attends to emotions and instinctive responses, to memories, beliefs, assumptions, values, and principles. It helps us to connect equally with the conscious mind and the deep and powerful flow of the unconscious mind that sometimes sweeps us through our lives without our ever noticing it.

The Deep Learning Process is universally applicable, encompassing not just techniques of human development (what to do, when, and how) but equally the subtle motivations of personality (why we cling to archaic behaviour, why we change). It enables the leadership coach to respond, with respect and effectiveness, to the complexity of human nature. Rather than simply resolving external problems located in the workplace, it helps people to change their lives.

Central to the process is the conviction that human beings in their natural condition have an insatiable urge to grow and to learn, that they are intensely curious about what they can accomplish, and that they have more power to develop than many believe.

For some people traumatic life events may have hidden or frustrated this natural drive. Think, for instance, of the person who was told repeatedly as a child that she or he would never learn, or of the person who is struggling for emotional survival within a poisonous work environment. Without the stimulation offered by outside help, many may never realize that they have an innate capacity to exceed the limitations of personal history and circumstance and keep on learning and developing. Even in lives clouded by cruel circumstances, the ability to grow remains a foundational aspect of our humanity.

Human beings bring much more to any new learning situation than the demands of the job. We each carry intelligence and skills, unique memory-driven behaviours, and a complex of emotions. Frequently these factors tug us in opposing directions, complicating new learning, increasing the possibility of failure and a backward slide into familiar routines. Our natural human condition is a contradictory mix of motivation and apprehension, enthusiasm and complacency, confidence and diffidence, energy and resistance, vision and fear, future-oriented thinking burdened with past memories.

The Deep Learning approach reminds us as coaches to keep our eyes wide open to this complex reality of human nature and behaviour. Because the process provides an in-depth framework for the coach's work, the coachee is guided more deeply into reflection and is supported in exploring underlying hindrances to successful performance. Most importantly, the Deep Learning Process is powerful because coachees learn how to learn, increasing the likelihood of retaining their accomplishments. Gradually the patterns that lead to success in the workplace become habitual, even in cases where coachees did not initially expect to make deep personal changes.

For the coach, the Deep Learning Process reduces the dependence on chance, circumstance, and stereotypical techniques. Applying the characteristics and the principles of the process, the coach guides the coachee to an awareness of how her skills were inadequate, helping her to discover the root causes and deciding how she can practise improved skills. With the goal of sustaining these new skills, together they take the time to consider and predict where she would be most likely to stumble and then deliberately plan what she can do to avoid that.

Learning about learning and learning how to learn offer tremendous benefits for the new coachee. Through this process, she not only gains an awareness of hidden barriers to her learning, she also comes to understand how she learns best, how to manage her learning, and how to reinforce her changes. Most importantly, the coachee discovers that learning is transferable because the basic process applies to any situation or relationship.

Learning in this penetrating way also demonstrates substantial career benefits, helping the person to become not only a better manager or leader but also one with better individual and team relationships. Such personal improvement can result in a better bottom line and better chances for promotion. Because the individual gains in both self-awareness and an understanding of her effect on others, the learning is not here today, gone tomorrow. It will last and continue to affect her work and her relationships throughout her career. Furthermore, the coachee will feel more confident about acquiring new skills and enhancing her knowledge. Her increasing self-awareness and self-understanding will also have a positive effect on her awareness of others and her impact on relationships.

Characteristics of the Deep Learning Process

This process is many things:

1. It is not a goal we reach but a path we follow.
2. It is based on professional and ethical principles.
3. It addresses the problem of learning retention.
4. It builds on an understanding of the human mind.
5. It requires us to assess the individual qualities of the coachee.
6. It means a willingness to engage at the level of personal issues.
7. It means seeing beyond the conscious mind.
8. It is powered by love.
9. It requires the coach's commitment to personal growth.

Let's look at each of these characteristics in more detail.

1. IT IS NOT A GOAL WE REACH BUT A PATH WE FOLLOW

The Deep Learning Process is like a map providing a path toward the goal. The challenge posed for the coach is to actively guide this exploration. The more we consciously practise the characteristics of the Deep Learning Process, the more profoundly it will affect both coach and coachee.

Our task as coaches is to remain engaged in understanding the process and in learning how to use it. Because this philosophical path is not based on conventional qualifications, it can be just as valuable to the supervisor who works at a production line level as it is to the CEO or the professional external coach.

2. IT IS BASED ON PROFESSIONAL AND ETHICAL PRINCIPLES

Deep Learning invites you to become more professional in the way you do your job, whether you are a supervisor, an executive, or an external coach. To be on the road to professionalism is to see your job as an aspect of your own continuous learning, and one that makes a meaningful contribution to the well-being of society.

Becoming more professional has implications for how you see the value of your work: taking care to do your job in a state-of-the-art way, and understanding and respecting the limits of your skills, while maintaining high ethical principles.

3. IT ADDRESSES THE PROBLEM OF LEARNING RETENTION

People do not necessarily learn just because they are presented with a new task, a training course, or a book of instructions. Studies show that even in straightforward how-to courses, people remember and use only a small percentage of the information conveyed to them.

The retention problem becomes far more acute whenever the new skills involve personal changes. When the stakes are high and the issues are subtle or threatening—improving one's management skills is a prime example—people need more than information.

We learn best when we experience personal support and guidance that makes us feel safe—secure enough to experiment and to practise taking risks. When we are frightened and feel unsupported, we usually revert to old behaviours—exactly the wrong thing to do—because we equate their familiarity with our safety. The Deep Learning Process helps us to explore what motivates success and what holds us back.

4. IT BUILDS ON AN UNDERSTANDING OF THE HUMAN MIND

In the past few decades we have all become more aware of the impact of our mental states and processes on our behaviour. Deep Learning is founded on that psychological insight and experience, and is best practised by those who approach coaching from two directions simultaneously: by exploring and engaging their understanding of what makes people tick, and by training their understanding through disciplined study.

The most effective leaders, managers, and coaches are those who are curious to discover as much as they can about how the human psyche works.

5. IT REQUIRES US TO ASSESS THE INDIVIDUAL QUALITIES OF THE COACHEE

It is not sufficient for a coach to understand human nature and psychology in general. Successful change lies in the details. For example, one person facing an enraged ton of live beef in a bullring will wave a brightly coloured cloth at it. Another will run for the fence. A host of invisible qualities determine the difference: personal values, previous experience, family ideals, the inner response to the roar of the crowd, and the mystique of the matador.

Similarly, the individual setting out to make changes through coaching brings much unseen material to the enterprise. Only through a disciplined assessment of these individual qualities can the coach understand the experience of the coachee standing in the "bullring" of her personal and workplace life. A careful exploration of her life experiences will help her to transcend the strictures of her psychological makeup.

6. IT MEANS A WILLINGNESS TO ENGAGE AT THE LEVEL OF PERSONAL ISSUES

Our culture exhibits an enormous fascination with people's personal lives and psychology, as manifested in biography, exposé, and rumour. Yet in the workplace we are often hesitant to acknowledge the influence of personal issues. It is understandable. Our work is more complicated when we have to see people as complex, emotional creatures with long memories and a life outside work. Management would certainly seem tidier if we did not have to attend to such issues as the employee's feelings, home life, or physical health.

The Deep Learning Process provides a set of tools enabling the coach to work with the personal issues of each coachee at a safe level, one appropriate for the individual and suited to the coach's skill.

7. IT MEANS SEEING BEYOND THE CONSCIOUS MIND

Coaching is complicated enough when we acknowledge the emotions and the personal life experienced by the coachee. But there is yet more to consider. The unconscious, unacknowledged aspects of the mind contain powerful forces affecting people's ability to change and develop. If our mind is like an iceberg, the unconscious part is truly the nine-tenths lying invisible below the surface.

As a coach, you can gently probe the coachee to bring blocks and barriers—those unseen assumptions, memories, and values that may have restrained her from developing fully—into the light of day. You will help her to harness the immense powers that buffet all of us at times: memories, courage, fear, peace, strength, rage, recurring thoughts—indeed, the very life force.

8. IT IS POWERED BY LOVE

"Unconditional positive regard." The phrase originated with Carl Rogers and may not sound particularly businesslike, but it is solid and trustworthy as a basis for workplace coaching. It means that only those who have a positive passion for people should engage in coaching. It is our love for those with whom we work that provides much of the energy for our work.

Of course, many people claim to love humanity. So how do you distinguish the effective coach from the self-indulgent meddler? The key evidence of the coach's commitment to this sort of professionalism is that a love for people is yoked to rigorous learning and self-discipline.

9. IT REQUIRES THE COACH'S COMMITMENT TO PERSONAL GROWTH

Coaches are business people, and their business is the business of growth. To be credible and effective in this enterprise, they must continually and fully engage in their own personal development process.

People being coached have an uncanny ability to sniff out those who can tell a good story but do not walk the talk. They may not consciously recognize that the coach is sending out discordant messages, because they are used to receiving such messages frequently in the workplace. Yet, they will respond just as they do at work—only half-committing to the coaching process while holding a great deal of themselves in reserve.

Principles of the Deep Learning Process

Six principles define the operating nature of the Deep Learning Process:

1. Respecting the coachee.
2. Exploring the coachee's wisdom.
3. Helping to move barriers.
4. Encouraging learning.
5. Coaching by rigorous ethical standards.
6. Creating a safe working zone.

UNIVERSAL PRINCIPLES FOR PERSONAL CHANGE

The principles espoused by the Deep Learning Process are not exclusive. They are similar to those of other professions focusing on health and personal change, and many of these principles are also practised in no-frills, basic models of coaching. But when consolidated with the other aspects and characteristics of Deep Learning, they set a challenging standard for the coach's growth in professionalism.

1. Respecting the Coachee

The coach sees coaching not as a technique but as an engagement with human nature, the emotions, and the unconscious mind, viewing his work not as a mechanical task but an organic process. His trade is more an art form than a routine method. Coaching must work that way, because human beings are like that: complex, contradictory, and rich with unexpected wisdom. The coach expects to be fascinated, attracted, amazed, and sometimes shocked.

Coach: Looking at you as we talked, I thought for a moment that something went across your face.
Coachee: Not really. I'm okay.

Coach: Lots of people would find it hard to talk about this situation. What's it like for you?

Coachee: Well, I'm kind of overwhelmed right now, so it's a little difficult.

Coach: I bet it is. So what does that tell you about yourself?

Coachee: I don't know. Either I'm too soft or I'm really into this project.

Coach: Which do you think it is?

Coachee: I don't know. I was always told I'm too soft.

Coach: Do you believe it?

Coachee: Not really. It really does get to me when things go wrong, but that's normal, right? So I think it's that I'm really into the project.

Coach: From my point of view, that seems more like you. I guess it matters a great deal. ...

Here, looking closely into the face of the coachee, the coach detects a change. It is enough to start a conversation that reveals unspoken self-doubt, allowing the coachee to begin to counter it.

The coach understands that no matter how stoically the coachee may present herself on the outside, strong emotion is an aspect of every personality. Not only is the coach undisturbed when powerful feelings arise, but he understands them as the engine that will ultimately propel the coachee into productive change. He understands, too, that the greater part of every human mind is unconscious, that it drives our behaviour without our being aware. That is why we so frequently surprise ourselves. So, to an extent appropriate to his level of skill, he guides the coachee on an inner journey of discovery into the unconscious mind, which holds the potential to reward her with potent new ways of self-understanding.

Given the complex nature of the coachee, the coach must be highly flexible to maximize his effectiveness, responding quickly to each variation in the person.

2. Exploring the Coachee's Wisdom

The most seductive and dangerous notion a coach can entertain is that he must be wise. On the contrary, his job is essentially to facilitate. A mark of his skill is that he knows how much he does not know.

The coachee is a great paradox. Her mind, though sometimes cloaked in mystery, is often a fount of information, memory, interpretation, insight, and wisdom. The task of the coach is to help the coachee discover her wisdom. The key skill used by the coach to accomplish that is the ability to listen actively.

Coachee: ...but you're the expert. You tell me.

Coach: Actually, I'm not the expert here. You're the one who knows how to run this company.

Coachee: Most of the people who work for me are more committed to getting home by 6:30 PM than in propelling us into e-business.

Coach: You sound a little frustrated.

Coachee: You're right. I don't like being the only one with a commitment to the company.

Coach: I don't understand. This company has achieved a lot. You've got great potential. What could be keeping them from giving a little extra for a while?

Coachee: Isn't that what you're supposed to tell me?

Coach: That's one approach. Another is to assume that perhaps you already know the answers
but don't trust what you know.
Coachee: Well, I guess I do know some of the history here. Do you want to hear about it?
Coach: You bet.

Here, the coach politely *refuses to be responsible for the coachee's growth*. He listens attentively, helps her surface her feelings, and names contradictions that might otherwise have lain untouched. As a result, the coachee develops increasing trust in her own wisdom and offers to share it with the coach as her partner in the investigation.

Many people were taught from childhood to mistrust their own insights. One of the great gifts the coach brings to the relationship is his firm belief that the coachee knows best. His task is to help her to hear and to trust her inner wisdom. In this age of cheap certainties, the coach's humble statement, "I don't understand," can be tremendously liberating for the coachee. Paradoxically, it is not by immediately understanding but by curiosity and openness to new insights that the coach demonstrates his wisdom.

3. Helping to Move Barriers

Identifying the changes that the coachee needs to make is the easiest part of the coaching job. And it is not much harder to plan how to accomplish them. The major challenge in coaching, and one too often ignored, is to figure out why people do not change, even when it is clearly in their interests. To attempt to coach without attending to this vital issue is like trying to drive a boat away from the dock without untying the rope. The engine roars, the water boils, and the boat bucks—but the passengers remain where they started.

Why do some people simply accept their lot in life without resistance? Why don't they spontaneously transform themselves as needed? Why does the coachee sometimes hit a brick wall and stop developing? Why do people make dramatic, satisfying changes, then backslide to where they started?

A valuable contribution of the Deep Learning Process is that it goes below the surface of conventional coaching, exploring issues deeper than mere behaviour and probing how the hidden barriers of memory, emotion, and the unconscious get in the way of development. It enables the coach and coachee to untie the restraining ropes and address the deeper causes of success and failure.

Coach: Do you ever wonder why you haven't changed in this respect before?
Coachee: Not really. I guess it's just me.
Coach: How would you say you think about yourself? Are you always the same, or are you a
person who is constantly changing?
Coachee: I think of myself as being steady.
Coach: Sounds like you really value being stable and reliable.
Coachee: Right.
Coach: Is there any downside to that?
Coachee: Well, the people who seem to get ahead are constantly changing. You never know
what pose they'll take next.
Coach: So do you wonder whether changing the way you operate might help you progress?

Coachee: Sometimes.
Coach: But you worry that you might lose something of yourself in the process?

Here, the coach begins a reflective conversation about an important characteristic of the coachee, asking questions that do not require the "correct" answer. He does not let himself get caught in an argument about "poses," but guides the coachee to reveal her inner attitudes, hopes, and fears. By getting these out in the open, he encourages the coachee to address them.

Deep Learning produces sustained results because it addresses inner conflicts, not simply skill deficits. And when the coachee is an active participant in her own assessment process, she learns skills she can use for a lifetime to navigate the waterways of her own mind. Ultimately the coach is expendable, for the coachee will have learned to do this for herself.

4. Encouraging Learning

Coaching is possible only because human beings harbour an insatiable desire to develop new capabilities and enhance even those that are familiar. With the exception of the tragic few whose spirits have been utterly crushed by circumstance, we find it natural to innovate. Those who are strong and fortunate can influence macro-changes in their culture and community. Those whose estate is more humble develop endlessly new and better ways of doing whatever they do to survive.

The genius of coaching is that it allies itself with hopefulness at either end of the scale. Coaches believe that until proven otherwise, they can support anyone in learning. And while they sometimes experience frustration and disappointment, almost without exception they prove correct in their hope.

Coachee: I don't ever want to be the kind of person who fits in with the popular opinions and politics of the office.
Coach: Were you ever close to someone who acted that way?
Coachee: Let's see. When I was a kid, my uncle stayed with us when he was out of work. One day he'd sit at the table talking as though he was super-educated, because he was applying for a job selling encyclopedias. The next day, he'd be talking like a farmer because he was trying to get farm work.
Coach: Even though you were young, you saw through that?
Coachee: I hated it. I felt embarrassed.
Coach: Did it affect what kind of person you wanted to be?
Coachee: Just not like him. I wanted to be consistent, sure, reliable, and always the same.
Coach: And those have turned out to be genuine strengths for you, haven't they?
Coachee: According to my performance appraisals ... (The coachee's voice trails off.)
Coach: But?
Coachee: But I don't get high marks for flexibility.
Coach: Do you ever wish ...?
Coachee: That I could be more of a leader and less of a drone? Sure I do. I have much more to contribute than anybody here guesses, and I'd really like to figure out how to show it.

Here, the coach helps the coachee learn through guided recollection. When the coachee hints at discomfort with the status quo, he tentatively asks questions that allow her to express her urge to develop and be recognized. Because the coach helps the coachee identify a pivotal life experience, she is able to move from longing to expectation. This is the genius of coaching: the quiet confidence of the coach creating an environment in which the coachee can recognize and grasp her own potential.

People are rarely satisfied when they make only surface-level changes. While employees may seem satisfied in learning a new set of methodical procedures or a particular skill from time to time, what many actually yearn for is the opportunity for deeper learning.

The production line worker may long to transform her self-image from a simple worker bee performing rote tasks to a reflective, generative person. The unpleasant executive, who appears to care only about the bottom line, may wish to become a leader who can inspire people. Deep Learning is built on such aspirations, which are at the very foundation of human nature. It satisfies these instinctual desires by encouraging a process of self-reflection, evaluation, and analysis. The coach helps the coachee to examine the different and unrecognized possibilities facing her and encourages her to risk the experiments she longs to make.

5. Coaching by Rigorous Ethical Standards

The role of the coach can be defined in part by the needs of his employer. Because the organization pays the coaching bills and benefits from the value-added results, it can justifiably claim to be the coach's "client." But from the moment the contract with the organization is signed, the coach's immediate commitment shifts to the growth and well-being of the coachee.

The coach has made it clear to the organization that during the course of the coaching his commitment will be to the individual with whom he is working. Without that certainty, the coachee will always be looking over her shoulder, wondering if she is being judged on the basis of information leaked from the coaching session—a preoccupation with feeling unsafe, rather than being able to be honest with herself and the coach.

Coachee: But don't you have a responsibility to tell my boss what's going on in the coaching?
Coach: With your permission, the most I might say is, "We've started," or "It's going well," or "We're struggling with some important issues." But my commitment as a professional is not to provide details. I told him from the beginning that would be the best way for us to work. That it would leave you free to deal with things in your own way.
Coachee: On the other hand, they're paying the bills. Don't they have a right to know?
Coach: Theoretically, sure. But if they were offered a choice between exercising that kind of right and having the coaching succeed, which do you think they'd choose?
Coachee: Success.
Coach: So I explained to them that the best way to succeed is to make our relationship an island that only you and I can visit.
Coachee: And they bought that?
Coach: They did. It's in the contract. Of course, it's up to you how much you tell me, but it's in the organization's best interests to allow this to be a safe and private relationship.

Here, the coach describes explicitly the protections surrounding the coaching relationship, stressing that they are both contractual and common sense. Beginning the session with suspicion, the coachee now ends it with clear information about confidentiality. Based on her question, it is likely that there is something on her mind that she will benefit by talking about in confidence.

The coachee's worrying about safety is never in the best interests of the organization, because it hampers growth. Like so many issues, the ethical way is also the most pragmatic.

The most dangerous people in the field of coaching are those talented, empathetic individuals who have experienced little training or supervision. Because of their natural abilities, they experience a certain amount of success, which is sufficient to obscure the necessity of clarifying the ethical requirements of their chosen vocation.

Ironically, one of the reasons that such coaches present a high risk is that they are initially very effective, sometimes charismatic, and always confident. With such individuals, the coachee is likely to become dependent and suspend her normal protective boundaries. Later on, because the coach's ethics are in a vague and disorganized state, there is always the possibility that he may step over the line and harm the now-vulnerable coachee.

Some ethical issues to be faced by the workplace coach are:

- balancing your responsibility to the organization with your responsibility to the coachee;
- being clear about the limits of confidentiality;
- handling positive and negative emotions you may feel toward the coachee;
- knowing how intimate you should become with a coachee;
- understanding how to treat insider information that you pick up as a coach;
- understanding your responsibilities when a coachee is at risk but does not recognize it.

6. Creating a Safe Working Zone

When coach and coachee are working together, the relationship between them could be described as a kind of sacred space. It is private and intimate. It allows the coachee to drop her protective mask and become utterly open and honest. It allows for vulnerability and the taking of risks.

Coachee: I'm under huge pressure from the VP.
Coach: How is that for you?
Coachee: Not good.
Coach: I'm wondering what kind of "not good" it is. I'd like to know about that so I can support you better.
Coachee: Like how?
Coach: You can tell me whatever you like about it and be sure that I won't say anything to anyone. Maybe talking about it will help you figure this out.
Coachee: Don't worry. It's nothing serious. We can talk about something else.
Coach: Can I pursue this just a little further?
Coachee: I guess.
Coach: Are you at all angry with the VP?

Coachee: How do you mean?

Coach: Well, he's putting a lot of pressure on you. People often feel angry when someone makes demands without negotiating.

Coachee: I don't think there's much room in this organization for anyone to be angry.

Coach: That's probably true. I wouldn't necessarily advise you to express it in the office. But you might find it useful to talk about it here, confidentially, and then we can plan how you might manage your feelings.

Here, the coach moves from the vagueness of "not good" to pursue an educated hunch about emotion that can be discussed only in a secure environment. By differentiating between what it is safe to talk about in the office and in the coaching interview, he assures her that he has a realistic grasp of organizational reality. He also clarifies that the discussion will be for the coachee's benefit and will not endanger her.

It is the coach's responsibility to function as the guard and gatekeeper of the safe space, vigilant against anything that might reduce the coachee's safety. The primary factor in making this zone safe is the coach's ability to demonstrate great respect and care for the coachee.

Coaching Involves Commitments

Several commitments distinguish the practice of coaching: a commitment to work with the coachee, a commitment to frankness in all matters, a commitment to the workplace as a force for potential good, and a commitment to recognize when a situation is beyond the coach's expertise and to suggest a referral. Throughout their professional practice, coaches must retain a firm commitment to the continual renewal of their inner resources.

Coaching Involves a Commitment to the Coachee

A crucial characteristic that marks coaching as a professional calling is the coach's maintaining a commitment to the coachee. The commitment is to keep going until the job is done and to work through any difficulties—including difficulties in the relationship—that may arise.

Coachee: I don't think I'm making any progress here.

Coach: Well, the changes you're trying to accomplish here are really hard. Have you ever thought that even making the attempt is a form of progress?

Coachee: Not really. I guess you don't usually coach people who get stuck like this.

Coach: Actually, everyone I work with gets stuck at some point. I do, too. And then, at another point, they also get wonderfully unstuck. But I'm wondering, what is it like for you to think you're not making progress?

Coachee: I don't like it. I start comparing myself to other people. And I wonder if this is the best use of your time.

Coach: How do you mean?

Coachee: Well, I feel guilty when you're being paid to work with me and I'm not changing.

Coach: I'm sure that's not a nice feeling for you. But it sounds like you're being really tough on yourself. Since we're not in a race with the calendar, why don't we relax our expectations a little and give you more time to come up with some successes?

Coachee: Well, I'd really like to succeed.

Coach: Then let's talk today about what's holding you back. Do you think it has anything to do with excessively high expectations of yourself?

Here, the coachee hints repeatedly at a fear that the coach will soon back out of the relationship, but the coach makes it clear that he is committed for the long term. Because he is self-revealing and provides the coachee with a sense of security, she becomes ready to reflect on her emotional patterns and brutal self-expectations.

Coaching Involves a Commitment to Frankness

The coach also maintains a commitment to frankness. Within the private conversation of the coaching relationship, the coach is never neutral. He has a responsibility to provide direct and honest feedback to the coachee. He can ask what seem like impossible questions and propose truths that insiders would consider unspeakable.

While this relationship with the coach is safe, accepting, and protective, it is in no sense isolated from reality. In fact, it provides the primary testing ground for the coachee's development. The way that she presents herself to the coach reflects how she presents herself to other people in the workplace. The coachee's management of their relationship is often the coach's primary source of information about how she goes about her day-to-day responsibilities.

Interacting with her, the coach sees and hears things, gains impressions, and feels emotional responses. To learn deeply about herself, the coachee needs to understand her impact on the coach. Far from pretending to be neutral and unaffected, the coach helps out by frankly describing what he experiences. Otherwise the coachee may never become aware of her impact on others.

Coach: Would you like some feedback about that?

Coachee: What do you mean, feedback?

Coach: I could tell you how your handling of the situation looked to me.

Coachee: Uh-oh!

Coach: Or I could refrain if you'd prefer. I know it's often difficult to receive feedback. Right?

Coachee: It leaves you feeling exposed.

Coach: Right. That's why I'd like you to get it from me.

Coachee: Why is that?

Coach: I'd like to support you in your development.

Coachee: It always makes me nervous when people hit me with their perceptions. "You're an idiot and I wish you'd go work somewhere else."

Coach: I'd certainly like to avoid "hitting" you with my perceptions. I would just tell you what I saw. Remember, I don't have any reason to want to hurt you.

Coachee: But I don't see how the way you see me has any connection with what happens in the office.

Coach: You can be the judge of that. But let me tell you a little about my experience. I see aspects of the people I am coaching that people in the workplace see as well. But because they don't feel comfortable discussing those things with my coachee, these aspects usually remain under the rug. So one of the special contributions I can offer is a friendly and open approach to feedback. Anyway, it's entirely up to you....

Here, the coach is not neutral. He's got things to say and wants the opportunity to say them, knowing that no one else will. But he makes it clear that his feedback has no hidden political agenda and is solely for the sake of the coachee. Ultimately, he underlines his respect for the coachee by offering a choice.

This question of feedback from the coach is a matter of ongoing confusion among coaches. Some like to see themselves as neutral facilitators, simply encouraging the coachee to find her own wisdom. They would like to believe that they do not import any of their own perceptions into the coaching relationship. There are, however, two problems with this stance. One, perceptions influence the behaviour of even the most skillful professionals. The best we can do is to be aware of them, and to manage their impact on our work. And two, this stance circumvents a basic strength of the coaching relationship. Deep learning is impeded if the coach is not prepared to be frank about what he experiences within the relationship.

But there are a few coaches, like those described in the last chapter, who take unwarranted pleasure in their so-called honesty. Driven by an unmet need to "call it as I see it," they are dangerously unaware that honesty without caring translates into brutality. They cannot comprehend that it is the enduring responsibility of the coach to be kind and frank, gentle and firm—all at the same time.

Coaching Involves a Commitment to the Workplace

To coach effectively in the workplace, it is essential to maintain a belief in the workplace and its leadership as a force for great potential good. Coaching provides a peerless opportunity to nurture the most benevolent forces within the organization and to encourage the most humane instincts of its leaders. Many coaches, however, harbour serious concerns about organizational motives and actions. Some corporations have maximized profits or balanced budgets by thoughtlessly minimizing costs, and the commitment of some leaders and organizations to their employees and the environment has been uneven. But when coaches help leaders to understand themselves, those leaders increase their understanding of their employees, the community, and the environment. With increased appreciation, the benefits may trickle down to scores, even hundreds of people, both inside and outside the organization.

Coaching Involves a Commitment to Recognizing Your Limits

Good coaches develop a keen sense of the level at which they are effective. For instance, when faced with signs of strong emotion—tears, anger, anxiety—a coach with little experience may say, "This is outside my area of expertise. Why don't you come back when you're feeling better?" Although not particularly helpful to the coachee, this is an appropriate response, because at this stage of development, the coach is apparently uneasy with deep feelings. With more time and experience, the same coach will become sufficiently comfortable to offer warm support, rather than simply withdrawing.

Sometimes it is best to make a referral. For instance, even a highly experienced coach, on hearing that the coachee's marriage is on the rocks or that she is suffering from depression, may say, "I'm not equipped to work at this level, but I'd be happy to give you a hand finding help." As well as having resources to recommend, a crucial factor here is the warmth he displays with the offer of support.

Specialized problems respond best to specialized forms of assistance, and the wise coach has learned when and how to make a referral. Whatever the need—medical treatment, credit counselling, treatment for substance abuse, legal advice, anger management, time management, psychotherapy, computer training—the coach who tries to be all things to all people will ultimately disappoint and may, in fact, be dangerous. It is a mark of professionalism in any field to know one's limits.

Coaching Involves a Commitment to the Continual Renewal of Inner Resources

Coaching is very demanding. To avoid burn-out and continue to do his best work, the coach must maintain his intellectual, emotional, and spiritual well-being. That means getting enough relaxation and stimulation, exercise and rest, hobbies and continuing education, solitude and warm intimate relationships.

While self-care is important, a coach can be effective only if he himself has experienced a process of self-exploration. Coaching diverges here from other professions. If we were in trouble with the law, we would not ask if our lawyer had ever been in jail. We wouldn't ask whether a surgeon had suffered the same illness as we do. But, as described earlier, the coach definitely needs to have been on the receiving end of coaching, counselling, or psychotherapy in order to be effective and to understand how the process works from the coachee's perspective.

This also tells us a great deal about whether the coach is walking his talk and is prepared to be vulnerable and humble enough to learn from someone else. Only if the answers were consistently positive would we consider him adequately experienced to be a coach.

In addition, the need for self-renewal requires that a coach engage a supervisor of his work—a mature, experienced coach who can help him to reflect. Even coaches who have a great deal of experience seek frequent input from others about their case management—for example, in the form of peer supervision or consultation.

Coaching Is Based on a Commitment to Building a Relationship

If you were a surgeon dealing with a malignant growth, you would not need a personal relationship with your patient to do good work. You would need to know where to cut and how to heal. But when the task is psychologically subtle—nurturing the growth of a human being—the essential matrix of the work is a relationship. Whether you are a parent, priest, therapist, manager, or coach, the conversations within this relationship will continue and change over time.

Your interpersonal skills are central to the success of this extended conversation. You will need to be as responsive as possible to the person in front of you, monitoring the extent to which you may be importing your own expectations into the coaching situation, expectations that may blind you to what is really happening.

The building of a relationship is not automatic. It requires generous amounts of time, mutual vulnerability, trust and trustworthiness, and a sharing of wisdom. Be a coach only if you are willing to give yourself over to developing this kind of ongoing conversation.

Coach: So I've been wondering if you might be a little angry with me.

Coachee: No, not at all. Why do you think so?

Coach: I'm not certain. I've been noticing that you've arrived late for our sessions a couple of times recently. And you've seemed more distant.

Coachee: No, I was late because of some problems at the office.

Coach: I think it started when I questioned the way you handled the technology problem. In retrospect, I think I wasn't very diplomatic. Wouldn't you agree?

Coachee: Well, it did set me back a bit when you said that.

Coach: If you're like me, it's not easy being challenged.

Coachee: You're right.

Coach: And I was pretty blunt. Right?

Coachee: Yes, you were. I was upset.

Coach: Upset with me?

Coachee: Yes. Not angry but a little upset.

Coach: I'm sorry I hurt you.

Coachee: Thanks. But you were right. I'm actually glad we talked about it because. ...

Here the coach surveys the ongoing relationship to find out why it is less effective. Are the coachee's feelings a barrier to progress? It is generally difficult for coachees to acknowledge when they are angry with their coach, who is a quasi-parental authority figure. But by being gently persistent, he enables the coachee to bring the issue to the surface and move beyond it.

The relationship of coach and coachee is complex. Not only is the relationship the "location" where the coaching takes place, it is also a primary tool of the coaching. This is an immense benefit, for as the coach reflects on his experience within this relationship, he discovers the nature of the person he is coaching.

A coach found himself often confused by the coachee. Sometimes he couldn't understand what she was trying to communicate. Sometimes he was tempted for a moment to tune the person out—that's human nature. Other times, he blamed himself for not being able to understand.

But because he was committed to being frank with the coachee, he talked about it. "Just now, I realized that I wasn't able to figure out what you meant. Has anyone ever suggested to you that you are sometimes difficult to understand?"

Later he asked, "Do you have any idea why people might have said that?"

And later still, "Why don't we look at this issue together to figure out why it happens and what you can do about it?"

Here, he demonstrated his commitment to the relationship by continuing to ask relevant questions, each of which went a little deeper. Similarly, when the coach feels criticized, sweet-talked, or bamboozled, he can use this experience of the relationship to deepen the impact of the coaching. For reasons already discussed, there is much value here; how the coachee manages the relationship with the coach will generally reflect how she manages relationships within the organization.

Workplace Coaching Is about Leadership

A key theme of coaching for the workplace is about being an effective leader. To remain a follower requires little in the way of skill or imagination, but today even the humblest worker is likely to be called from time to time to the role of leadership.

There is, of course, no gene for leadership. Among the countless numbers of leaders, few are instinctively effective. And those who need the most help with this responsibility find little challenge or support within the organization. No one has time to mentor them. Who will offer honest feedback? Who will remind them of simple truths and best practices?

Those for whom leadership is the primary task—CEOs, CFOs, COOs, CAOs, CIOs, CTOs, other executives, directors, and managers—find themselves in a paradoxical bind. If they insist on their authority, they stunt the growth of others. If they require obedience, they invite revolt. If they consult only themselves, they are accused of arrogance. If they consult widely, some will assume that they have no opinions and no authority. The art of facilitative leadership is not only crucial in this age, but also very complicated to perform.

Coach: We've discussed how you handled that situation. So let's talk about leadership.

Coachee: Leadership in what sense?

Coach: It looks to me like you've changed your communication style for the better. Do you think so?

Coachee: I sure do.

Coach: I'm wondering if the next frontier might be for us to talk about your relationships in terms of the leadership you're displaying.

Coachee: Isn't that implied in everything we're doing?

Coach: It is. But I'm thinking that it might be useful for you if we began to be more explicit.

Coachee: How would that work?

Coach: Let's take an example. Recently you've been practising being less critical of people. What's the impact on how they regard you as their leader?

Coachee: I'm hoping they see me as demonstrating how their relationships should go, too.

Coach: So you're hoping that your behaviour will improve the atmosphere throughout the department?

Coachee: Right.

Coach: The way you behave is a form of leadership?

Coachee: That's it.

Coach: So let's think some more about you as a leader. Do you deliberately decide to take a leadership role at certain times when it's necessary? Or do you feel that it is just you—constantly a leader—all the time?

Coachee: I guess it's more something I decide to do at times. I wouldn't say I've ever been a natural leader.

Coach: So maybe this is a good time to see if we can unearth more of your natural leadership ability....

Here, the coach moves leadership out from the wallpaper of the discussion to the centre of the room, helping the coachee uncover her uncertainty about her role and suggesting that she will find further benefit in reflection and experimentation.

The coaching process itself is the practice of leadership in action, as coach and coachee in turn lead each other. Coaching is not only a tool for change—it is the laboratory.

Workplace Coaching and the Organization's Needs

Although the roots of coaching are established in ground that is essentially person-centred, the coach never forgets that he has been engaged by the organization and that his task includes satisfying the organization's needs. While the coach works closely with an individual, his contract is with the organization, which means that leadership coaching in the workplace is a remarkably complex activity. The coach must make choices in the midst of a constantly shifting conflict of interests, providing care for the coachee while satisfying the needs of her employer. The effective coach keeps several balls in the air at the same time.

1. THE ORGANIZATION'S NEED

The first "ball" is the organization's need, which is usually why the coach was engaged in the first place. The organization may require

- Better performance from the coachee
- Better leadership from a particular manager
- Improved productivity or profit
- Moving people smoothly through a change process

Usually the organization is providing the time for coaching, and if an external coach has been hired, it is also paying the bills. The organization has a right to expect positive business results.

2. PLAYING DETECTIVE

The second ball in the air is that the coach must sometimes operate like a detective. He may uncover information unanticipated—or even initially unwelcome—by the organization. The coach may discover, for example, that the organization is operating inefficiently in certain respects, or that its policies or culture are lowering the productivity of personnel. Finding the best way to communicate such information to the appropriate level in the organization and having it heard is a coach's additional responsibility to the organization.

3.THE COACHEE'S STRESSES

The third ball is the needs of the person being coached. That person will in most cases be committed to the same results as the organization, but will usually have additional concerns. Unknown to management, the coachee may be coping with stresses ranging from illness or substance abuse to family problems or cultural difficulties. These stressors may reduce productivity and flexibility. They need to be addressed in order to provide the business benefits for which the coach was engaged, but must at the same time be handled in a confidential way.

4. CONFLICTING NEEDS

To put another ball in the air, the desires of the coachee may in some ways be in opposition to those of the organization. She may, for instance, want to feel secure when the very nature of the business is shifting radically, increasing everyone's insecurity. Or she may be thinking of leaving the company. It is indeed a complex performance to do good work, to respect these differences, to care for a vulnerable coachee, and to continue to serve the greater good of the organization.

5. IMPACT ON OTHERS

The fifth ball represents other people in the workplace. The coach knows that any changes the coachee may make—or not make—can have a considerable impact on other parties. The clerk who continues to misfile documents despite coaching, for instance, will continue to be ostracized and will reduce the productivity of others around her. A manager who decides to spend less time around the water cooler may become more efficient in providing vital services to her boss, but will be less available to catch the valuable buzz in the workplace. And people who once relied on her to provide a listening ear may—on finding her less available—become hurt or angry. This may in turn affect their productivity. The effective coach maintains a watchful eye on such environmental factors.

6. THE AGILE JUGGLER

Finally other balls may be in the air, depending on the situation, for example, the community, the environment, and office politics. The coach must maintain a clear head and a decisive understanding of his loyalties in the midst of these varied demands. Only the most agile professional can juggle all these issues, maintaining a concern for each of the constituencies encountered without losing sight of the business needs of the engagement.

Workplace Coaching and the Impact of Systems

The coachee is a member of many different sets of relationships, each with a different stake in her behaviour. These "systems" include the people in her local work area, the organization as a whole, the family, intimate relationships, the community, and others. The differing needs of the various systems may pull her in contradictory directions.

Organizational hierarchies often complicate relationships. They may force people to associate who are not appropriate partners, and they may establish a vast gulf between those who would otherwise accomplish a great deal of productive work together. Similarly, organizational processes sometimes reduce the effectiveness of relationships. For example, rank-oriented decision-making may discourage those who are not senior but have good ideas, while consensus-based processes may frustrate those who want to move quickly and get on with a task.

Furthermore, when a coachee is involved in a change process, her relationship with other systems complicates her progress. She cannot alter her behaviour in one area without the effects—which may or may not be appreciated—leaking to other areas. The coach will need great breadth of vision to anticipate such outcomes and to guide the coachee in preparing for them.

Coachee: I'm really pleased. I can see that I've become more assertive than I used to be. I'm not being aggressive toward other people, but I am making it clear that I need to get my job done properly.

Coach: How are people responding?

Coachee: It's interesting. They seem to like it. And I'm getting a lot more cooperation.

Coach: So is there a downside?

Coachee: I don't think so.

Coach: Does this have any impact outside the workplace?

Coachee: Let me think. To tell the truth, I'm wondering if it's affecting my personal life.

Coach: Do you have an example?

Coachee: I seem to have been tougher with my parents recently.

Coach: Change isn't always limited to one place. So how do your folks take that?

Coachee: They seem a little hurt, maybe a little bewildered.

Coach: Any idea why they are reacting differently from your co-workers?

Coachee: Well, we're closer.

Coach: Yes, and the other factor might be that your family is very used to you being a certain way. Even if it's not the best, they kind of count on you never changing. So that might help explain it.

Coachee: I feel kind of sorry for them. I wonder what I should do.

Coach: Have you tried talking with them about the changes you're making in your life and how much happier you are these days?

Here, the coach helps the coachee to recognize that because some barriers to her changing may also be located in the systems of which she is a member, they can impose an almost imperceptible drag on her progress. Yet, the coach suggests, systems are often amenable to change once the issues are raised out loud.

Perhaps the most potent but unspoken truth about people within systems is that they often prefer members of their group to remain more or less the same—even when they appear to be demanding transformation. Systems sometimes promote stability regardless of cost.

So the coach has a responsibility to understand how an organization (a system) may respond to change in unexpected ways. Only then can he can help protect the coachee from becoming a victim of her own success.

Deep Learning and Self-Knowledge

The Deep Learning Process is effective because it begins not with planning the actions required for new behaviours, but with discovering the barriers that have blocked the coachee from taking those actions successfully in the past.

Those barriers typically include unrecognized assumptions that keep people from learning, or rigid defences that they unknowingly carry to protect themselves. Only when these blocks have been made explicit and addressed is it possible for profound and sustainable change to occur.

At each phase of coaching from contracting through to the moment of completion, the coach requires the ability to confront such blocks. This ability is the foundation that can make the work resilient, thorough, and comprehensive.

The most common cause of failure of leaders in the workplace, and indeed throughout history, has been not a lack of intelligence or skill, but a lack of self-understanding. "Know thyself" was inscribed for good reasons at the mouth of the Delphic Oracle in ancient Greece. When the eighteenth-century poet Alexander Pope echoed those ancient words in *An Essay on Man*, he added his own famous dictum, "The proper study of mankind is man." Pope's view was that humans are often a riddle to themselves; the great promise of Deep Learning is that it helps coachees to deepen their self-awareness and self-understanding. They may begin to resolve their riddles through a relationship with their coach, but they often continue on their own, making significant progress in their personal relationships. The process of coaching can help the coachee to see the other person with increased reverence, and in the words of Martin Buber, not just as a "you" but as "thou."

SELF-AWARENESS CHANGES HOW WE SEE OTHERS

- With self-awareness comes a deeper understanding of others.
- Through the understanding of others comes impact awareness (an understanding of the ways we act on one another).
- Through the exercise of this understanding, skills in management accelerate.
- As the results reinforce the learning, the coachee begins to see the workplace and indeed the world differently, with a competitive stance yielding to one of collaboration.

From Stagnation to Change

The results of deep coaching are remarkable. People who were fooling themselves have had the opportunity to get honest with themselves. They see themselves as others see them. Those who were round pegs forced into square holes have moved to new positions. Those who operated like loose cannons, leaving havoc in their path, have learned to be steady and sure. Those who were subtly abusive of employees have learned to cherish them. And those who were only marginally effective have developed greater skill.

For the organization, this means that its people are now developing in ways required to maintain success over the long term. Because the changes are lasting and deep, they markedly improve the conditions of the workplace, rewarding the organization with greater productivity and potential for profit.

The chapters that follow will detail the four phases of the coaching process embedded in the Deep Learning Process: Contracting, Assessment, Development and Integration, and the Completion Phase. Also included is a special chapter on Enriched Assessment.

PART 2

The Phases of the Leadership Coaching Engagement

Clear Contracting Deflects Confusion and Conflict

Contracting is the front door of the coaching engagement. People sometimes associate the process of contracting with protracted negotiation and dusty obligations, the nasty but necessary process of trading off one's interests against those of others.

In coaching, however, the development of a contract goes beyond the negotiation of terms. It is an opportunity to undertake stimulating detective work. Effective contracting is a precursor to coaching at its earliest phase, and serves as a basis for deep learning, because it makes explicit the important information about the coachee, the environment, and the meaning of deeply held concepts. Contracting that lacks such precision can go seriously adrift.

A teenager tells her father she wants to visit her girlfriend for the evening. It is a school night, so her loving Dad agrees with a stipulation, "If you want to go out, you have to be home early." And just to make sure the terms are clear, he checks with his daughter, "Is that understood?"

The cheerful teen replies, "Sure, Dad, early. See you 'round!"

This contract incorporates a number of simple and foolproof features. First of all, the terms are straightforward: the teen is allowed to go out on this school night, providing she returns early. Second, there was a formal acceptance of the contract: "Sure, Dad, early." Finally all the words in the contract are in simple English, none of them longer than three syllables.

So what happens that evening? Dad consults his internal clock and decides that "early" should mean about 10 PM, but because he is a very flexible person, he will be happy if his daughter is home by 11.

Meanwhile, the teen consults her inner clock, and because she is a responsible young person, she also checks for good measure with her best friend. It is crystal clear to both of them that the term "early" means anytime before 2 AM.

Needless to say, at 1:55 AM, an angry exchange ensues between a worried father who has been waiting up for hours and an astonished teenager who cannot believe that her parent could be so totally unreasonable.

The source of the conflict? Sloppy contracting between two decent, caring people. Specifically, a failure to examine exactly what each party meant by the term "early."

Had they recognized the need to find a common meaning for that apparently simple word, there would have been no argument, and everyone would have enjoyed a good night's sleep. By comparison, when a contract for coaching is clear and unambiguous, the groundwork is set for a relationship that is productive and encouraging, free from unwarranted tension.

CONTRACTING PHASE

The process that begins with the gathering of relevant information and leads to a clear agreement between sponsor, coachee, and coach about the expectations and objectives for coaching that will guide them throughout the process.

The Key Participants

Assuming the most common scenario in which an organization contracts with a coach to provide coaching for a staff member, the typical coaching engagement includes a cast of people, each with her or his own agenda. Clarifying their roles increases the effectiveness of the process.

THE ORGANIZATION
The employer of everyone listed below, the organization is the ultimate beneficiary of the coachee's increased productivity or other improvements, and in return it pays the bills.

THE SPONSOR
Usually a representative of the organization, the sponsor is the person who arranges for and contracts with the coach. Most frequently this will be an executive, the coachee's supervisor, or a member of the Human Resources (HR) or Organization Development (OD) department.

THE SUPERVISOR
The coachee reports directly to the supervisor. Ideally, the supervisor is either the sponsor of the coaching or works in close collaboration with the sponsor.

THE COACHEE
The coachee is the person employed by the organization whose need for development has been identified, and who receives the coaching.

THE COACH
The coach could be a staff member of the organization or an outsider who is selected and hired to guide and inspire the coaching process.

So Who Is the Client?

It is natural for the executives of the organization to think of themselves as the coach's client. After all, they may make the policies that enable people to be trained and to function as coaches within organizational ranks. They may also authorize the selection and hiring of outsiders to perform coaching. Further, they bear the responsibility for developing the organization's employees through coaching and other means, and they must balance those benefits against the corresponding financial costs. (If this were a standard consulting arrangement, the organization would be regarded as the ultimate client.)

Still, a case can be made for another party to be viewed as the client. The sponsor of the coaching intervention is the organization's representative on the scene. She authorizes and monitors the coaching process. (If she were to arrange for the services of a consultant, she would be regarded as the immediate client.)

But from still another viewpoint, the supervisor might appear to be the client. After all, he oversees the coachee and has direct responsibility for whether he is effective in his work.

While each of these parties must be recognized for contributing to the success of the coaching enterprise, none of them can ultimately be regarded as the client.

The Client Is the Coachee

To say that the coachee is the client is not to slight the management of the organization. It is simply a recognition of the difference between coaching and consulting, and the immutable reality of human nature.

In the coaching relationship, the coachee allows himself to become highly vulnerable. He permits another human being to see him in unguarded moments and in absolute honesty. He thinks, "If I cannot count on this coach to be fully with me, then I cannot fully collaborate with the process. If coaching is to engage my undivided energy, the coach must regard me as the client."

If the coachee does not feel that he, directly, is the client of the coach, that the coach has his interests primarily at heart, he will not develop trust in her. Without this key quality of the coaching relationship, the coaching will not mature.

Whether the coach is an internal employee of the organization or a hired external, this understanding will lie at the heart of all effective contracting with the organization. It is the coach's professional responsibility to develop boundaries that protect the relationship with her client, the coachee. To do so will ensure that the necessary conditions are in place for the organization to receive full value for its investment.

The Contracting Parties

But it is also true that the coach establishes contracts with as many as three interested parties:

1. The organization through the sponsor of the coaching. Here the nature of the contracting depends on whether the coach is an internal or external person. If external, the contract is usually on paper.

2. The supervisor of the person to be coached. This contract may be spoken aloud but is often implicit.
3. The coachee. The contract is usually expressed in words, with great care to be complete. There is some movement today, for the sake of clarity, toward the use of written contracts with the coachee, as well as the organization.

Reporting and Confidentiality

Confidentiality sets the safety standard for coaching. Everything the coachee tells the coach is strictly private and confidential, with the possibility of two common sense exceptions. If the client authorizes the coach to reveal information to the organization, the coach will do so, with the stipulation that the coachee must first review it. In the rare event that the coach discovers that a coachee is likely to do serious harm, the coach has a responsibility to alert the proper authorities.

REASONS NOT TO PROVIDE REPORTS TO THE ORGANIZATION

The organizational sponsor or supervisor may ask a coach to provide reports, either during the process or at its end. There are several reasons for the coach to discourage this:

- The coach's hunches about how the coachee behaves at work are less valuable than the direct observations of members of the organization, which are readily available without resorting to a report.
- The coachee may develop trust more slowly, fearing that the coach may be reporting any uncertainty, confusion, or weakness, and may therefore make less progress.
- The coach may find that her contract with the client is less direct, less personal, when the sponsor is an ongoing third party to the engagement.

Reporting to the Organization

Some organizations will not provide coaching for their members unless they are promised a report or reports. In such cases—providing that the coachee is aware and agreeable—for the coach to accede to such a request would assure the coachee of the valuable experience of being coached. The coach should then set the parameters ahead of time, on paper if possible, so that there are no surprises. It is best to report back only information to which the coachee has specifically agreed. With this assurance, most coachees will feel they can confront and resolve personal issues without running any risk of humiliation or great loss of privacy.

The most crucial provision is that any report must be read and approved by the coachee before delivery to the sponsor.

Usually the report can be written in a way that provides additional value for both the coachee and the organization. For instance, it may highlight factors in the corporate environment that need to change for the benefit of the coachee and of others. And, given that the majority of coachees respond enthusiastically to coaching, a report may also provide the coachee with encouragement by describing the commitment and energy that he has devoted to the growth process. Furthermore, the report may actually enhance the coachee's organizational file, providing a positive conclusion to a series of notations about problems.

Conversational Reporting

Less formally, it is common for the coach to have one or more brief telephone conversations with the sponsor during the process. For reasons of accountability, the sponsor often wants to know how the coaching is proceeding or if the coachee is getting some value from it. Providing the coachee knows about the sponsor's wish, there should be no problem in providing the requested information in a circumspect manner.

An informal conversation constitutes a report. Therefore, it is the coach's responsibility to provide the information that the sponsor wants, without revealing any confidential details. Keeping a record of the conversation is a good idea, in case there is a dispute at some future point. Furthermore, it is important to qualify the remarks. Rather than pretending to report unquestionable facts, the coach should be clear that his opinions are based on observation, belief, and expectation.

To build trust, the coach should tell the coachee about the conversation and relate, accurately, what was said. That way there are no surprises and no secrets. When the coach holds no secrets, the coachee is, of course, encouraged to be frank and open, too, which makes the coaching more productive.

Following are brief examples from conversations that respond to the needs of the sponsor without infringing of the privacy of the coachee.

"We have had several sessions already, and he has never missed an appointment. I believe he is making good progress in understanding what needs to change. As far as I can see at this point, he is committed to make progress and I am very hopeful.

"I would encourage you to have a talk directly with him and find out about the coaching in his own words."

"I am not certain how well this is going to work out. We haven't had as many sessions as I hoped, and I am not certain whether he is committed to this process. This may indicate that we are not going to get anywhere, or it may just be a difficult start.

"I think it would be useful if you were to talk directly with him and get his impressions."

For the Sponsor: Selecting a Coach

Most of this book is addressed to coaches, but as we look at the outset of the coaching engagement, it is valuable to address two additional groups. The first are individuals within the organization who are responsible for sponsoring coaching engagements. The second are coachees who, for the sake of their own development, select and pay a coach privately without involving the organization. Below, we aim to help both groups understand the contracting process from the perspective of their interests and concerns. Readers who are coaches will find that this discussion will help them to anticipate the challenges they face in contracting and to understand the forces at work behind the scenes.

Those who select coaches need to know that the few current standards of accreditation are largely untested, so it is difficult to objectively determine which coaches are effective. You will need to do some investigative work to ascertain the qualifications and the ability of coaching candidates. Often the best way to begin the investigation is through your network of contacts. Ask trusted sources about coaches who come highly recommended. Then, with great care, interview the candidates. Be aware that few responsible coaches will guarantee outcomes. Although the skill of the coach has a significant influence, the outcome is largely determined by the organization and by the individual being coached.

An In-House or External Coach?

To decide whether to look for a coach in-house or externally, you must ask yourself

- Are there in-house staff members who have the necessary qualities, training, skills, and qualifications for this particular coaching job?
- Is the time required for coaching available in-house? Does the coachee need coaching regularly or in quantity?
- When you balance the direct costs to hire an outsider against indirect costs of staff time, how do the numbers look?
- What kind of coach does the situation merit—a qualified professional or savvy inside mentor?
- Does coaching in this situation require an insider's knowledge of organizational procedures or other in-house information?
- Are confidentiality or professional secrets an issue?

FIGURE 5.1 **OUTLINE FOR INTERVIEWING A POTENTIAL COACH**

1. Get to know the coach by asking pertinent questions, such as
   - What makes a good leader?
   - How do you see your role with leaders?
   - What training do you have as a coach?
   - What experience do you have as a coach?
   - With whom can I speak about your coaching work?
   - What is your history in the world of work?
   - What is your personal experience of professional growth?

2. Trust your instincts. Ask yourself
   - How am I reacting to this person?
   - Is this someone who seems really present in this moment?
   - Would I like to be coached by this person?
   - Is this someone I would trust with information that I do not usually share?

3. Clarify the boundaries of the intervention. If you decide to engage the coach, discuss
   - Length of contract
   - Location of coaching

(continued)

FIGURE 5.1 **CONTINUED**

- Fees for coaching
- Who will be involved in the intervention
- The issue of confidentiality and its limits
- How to ensure a reliable ongoing evaluation process
- What tangible results can we expect from coaching?

Keep the Contracting Moving

Once you have settled on an effective coach for the client, the following three steps will enable you to maintain the momentum.

1. *Get approval from all those affected.*

   If you are the sponsor hiring a coach on behalf of an organization, the contracting will proceed best if you consult thoroughly.

   - *Be certain that you have the support of the potential coachee's supervisor.*
     Occasionally, sponsors will try to sidestep the supervisor either for the sake of confidentiality or because they fear the supervisor will interfere. The supervisor who has been explicitly involved is more likely to support the coachee, to provide flexibility to enable maximum learning, and to supplement the coaching with personal mentoring.

   - *Take time to explore all aspects of the referral with the coachee.*
     The coachee will want to know whether the coaching is mandated, meaning that it is a requirement of his job, or whether it is a suggested option. He needs to know what objectives the organization has in finding him a coach, and what will be expected of him. He will benefit from seeing the contract on paper, knowing everything that has been agreed with the coach. Even the money? Yes. The coachee who knows how much the organization is investing in him is more likely to respond with enthusiasm.

   - *Leave space for the potential coachee to express concerns.*
     Common worries are whether his job is at risk, whether the coach will really be able to help him develop, and whether it really will be confidential. Have your answers ready.

2. *Make the contract*

   Words on paper represent an attempt to outline our commitments in a succinct and clear fashion, assisting us to satisfy each other's expectations. But the coaching contract is more than words on paper. Its power involves such intangibles as attitude, communication, believability, and character. These are qualities too complex to be squeezed through a laser printer.

   If you are choosing an external coach, you will certainly need a written contract. Even if you choose to involve a coach who is internal to the organization, a simple document can be helpful in clarifying expectations.

   The external coach may suggest that you use her standard contract. The benefit is that it reflects extensive experience in this particular kind of contracting. The down-side is that it may be excessively protective of the coach's interests. Still, it is likely to be a more valuable starting point than the consulting contract your organization gen-erally uses. That contract is usually not appropriate for the more intense, personal relationship of coaching.

* Ask the coach to draw up a contract based on your discussion.
* Read through it carefully and negotiate any adjustments necessary.
* Sign the contract only when it entirely meets with your satisfaction, and you are confident that it will satisfy other parties.

You will find more guidance about the written contract below.

3. *Let go.*
   If you are the sponsor, you are about to fade from the scene. You will remain avail-able in the background as a potential resource for the coach and coachee, but you will not be actively managing the situation. You can ask to be notified when the coaching actually begins. When the contracting reaches an end, you may meet with coach and coachee separately to formally conclude the contract and clarify what kind of reports you expect, if any. You may also discuss with coach and coachee the best way of intro-ducing them to each other. Be prepared to facilitate the introduction, providing sup-port and continuity by introducing them personally. Now you must back off and allow coach and coachee to set up their next time and place to meet and get the coaching process under way

Making Difficult Referrals to Coaching

If you are the sponsor of coaching, it is useful to know two or three coaches well enough so that you can respond quickly whenever the need for coaching arises. There are three kinds of referrals, differentiated by whether it is the individual or the organization requesting the coaching, and, if the latter, whether the coaching is posed as a suggestion or a demand.

1. THE COACHEE'S REQUEST
The least difficult situation is one where the potential coachee asks to be provided with a coach. The process of referring in this case is usually straightforward, with minimum tension and anxiety.

2. THE ORGANIZATION'S SUGGESTION
The tension level is higher when you or the supervisor recommends coaching because of your perception that the individual needs to make changes.

3. THE ORGANIZATION'S REQUIREMENT
The highest level of tension, along with the possibility of resistance and anger, comes when coaching is mandated (that is, demanded as a condition of employment) by the organization, with either you or the supervisor in the role of its spokesperson.

In the second two cases, the likelihood of a successful outcome increases when you handle the referral in a graceful but clearly structured fashion. First, inform the individual's supervisor, if he is unaware of your intentions. In advance, secure his agreement that change is essential and coaching is appropriate. Second, prepare on paper ahead of time the case for coaching and the recommended strategy, and ask a trusted colleague to comment on them from the point of view of thoroughness and fairness. Finally, convene a meeting with the individual concerned. Depending on the situation that precipitated the need for coaching, this meeting may include you, the supervisor, and a representative from Human Resources, as well as the potential coachee. Having these people present displays the organization's commitment to provide the opportunity for change. In cases of dispute, they can also provide witness to what happened during the process.

Making a Non-Mandated Referral for Coaching

- Ask the potential coachee to meet with you.
- Express your concerns and listen carefully for signs of stress or distress.
- Suggest that he or she would probably benefit from having a coach.
- Explain the process of coaching, emphasizing that it is confidential.
- Be empathic.
- Reflect back whatever you hear in response.
- Stress that coaching is being arranged not as a punishment or because you think he is weak, but because he is highly valued in the organization.
- Ask for a commitment.

Making a Mandated Referral for Coaching

- Call a meeting between the supervisor, the potential coachee, and yourself. If disciplinary issues are involved, and if you are not a member of the Human Resources department, include a representative from HR.
- State the problem as you see it clearly and concisely, providing a written description of the problem and a rationale for coaching.
- Allow the potential coachee to respond.
- Reply in a reflective and empathic manner.
- State clearly the decision of your organization to provide a coach.
- Explain the process of coaching, emphasizing that it is confidential.
- Stress that coaching is being arranged not as a punishment but as a potential solution to the potential coachee's current difficulties.
- Reassure the individual that he is highly valued in the organization.
- Explain the next steps.
- Take extensive notes during and immediately after the meeting.

Making the Case for Coaching

It is preferable for all parties that the coaching process be voluntary wherever possible, and it usually is. However, mandated coaching can be very successful, provided that the coach has developed the specialized skills described in this book. She will be able to encourage trust, by making genuine personal contact with the coachee, demonstrating respect, and showing empathy.

It is never easy to tell an individual that he needs help in doing his job. You know from the beginning that what you have to say will not be easy to hear. So you will see it as normal when you run up against a certain amount of resistance. It is important not to let yourself become discouraged or stalled by an apparent lack of motivation, and certainly not to take it personally. Here are additional guidelines for the referral conversation.

Address time and productivity issues. Ask the individual to explain any concerns. Listen carefully so that you understand the precise areas: resistance, anxieties, confidentiality concerns, and time pressure. Then you can respond to them directly. Make sure you do not inadvertently minimize the individual by minimizing her concerns, and be sure that the expectations of coaching are both reasonable and challenging.

Threaten or promise? Make it clear whether you are suggesting coaching (a) because of your observation that the person could improve his work style, or (b) because his future with the organization depends on making constructive changes. There is nothing wrong with either option, but it is crucial to be clear.

Affirm his strengths. Let the individual know your suggestion is a compliment to his abilities. He is a highly valued contributor to the organization—that is why coaching is being offered.

Facilitate, don't delegate. Provide support and continuity by offering to introduce the individual personally to a coach. Do not expect him to act on his own. If he had felt confident, he would have done this already.

Respond to blame and denial. If the coachee is reluctant to commit to the process or blames others for the problems that have been identified, it is valuable to take as much time as required to explore this reaction. The most reliable approach is to listen empathically, to take the concerns of the individual seriously, and to allow for some venting of emotion—all without becoming intimidated or confrontational yourself.

What amazing power there is in making personal contact, demonstrating respect, and showing a little empathy! In most cases, the result is that the potential coachee will sense that he is being treated with respect and become willing to experiment with coaching.

As we've said, when coaching is mandated, there is an additional hurdle to surmount. Most people resist doing things that are forced on them—even if, like yucky medicine, they know it will be good for them in the long run. That is human nature. But again, the most effective strategy is to smooth the way by listening intently, showing that you understand the person's reluctance.

The trick is to combine gentleness of spirit with firmness of intent. You will have to inform the employee in an unambiguous way that coaching is a condition of continued employment. For that reason, you may suggest, why not give it a good try? Why not make it work for you? It is no favour to the individual to provide a vague description of the problem and the need for change.

When sponsors look back at situations where they had difficulty making a referral, they usually trace their problems to not having delivered the message in a manner that was both caring and firm. So be clear, and make sure you do not lack backup. In fact, do not even consider presenting mandated coaching unless you have it on the highest authority.

The Delicate Dance of Referring Leaders

Mandated or not, it is often difficult to convince executives and other senior individuals that they will benefit from coaching. A lack of trust and collaborative skills characterizes the senior ranks in many organizations, and leaders tend to be proud and therefore nervous about appearing weak. Needing help of any kind is seen as weakness. As a result, they tend to avoid what they may regard as a one-size-fits-all program and may even prefer to stay away from sources of support associated with the HR department, concerned that these may not be private and confidential. Some leaders may view coaching as a form of training or an extension of the Employee Assistance Program, and therefore inappropriate for them. Unlikely to confide in co-workers, who might make a referral to coaching, the leader's need may not be obvious and there may be few opportunities to recommend coaching.

A pre-emptive strategy is to make the availability of coaching widely known through a variety of media addressing senior people. Once executives begin to speak openly about their positive experiences in coaching, their enthusiasm will attract others to use it for their own development.

A Tough Referral for Coaching

The difficulties in referring an employee for coaching are illustrated by this story.

In a large financial firm, William was the senior manager selected to guide the resolution of computer security problems. He was chosen for this crucial task because of his outstanding technical skills and his ability to inspire his team to heights of dedication and effectiveness.

A couple of months after this appointment, at lunch with a software supplier, he made an unusual decision to have a couple of drinks. By the time he arrived back at the office, he was feeling good, and began talking to one of his team in a voice that carried throughout the open-plan office. In the course of the conversation, he referred to a particular racial group in a demeaning manner.

No one was expecting this. William was not a big drinker, nor was he known for racist attitudes. A shocked silence fell, and people's eyes locked silently with one another. The question in the air was "Did you hear what I think I just heard?"

After a few minutes William made his exit, and that might have been the end of the situation. But it happened that this organization had recently taken an explicit stand on discrimination, and the president prided himself on it. Furthermore, the multi-racial staff appreciated the respectful atmosphere in which they worked. So it is not surprising that over the next few hours the president received a number of quick visits and phone calls related to the incident.

Before the day was out, he called the director of Human Resources into his office and asked her to take action. She in turn discussed the incident with the specialist who had drafted the organization's anti-harassment policy.

One thing became immediately clear to them: they were in a serious bind. Not only was William considered an extremely valuable employee, but with the clock ticking and with their computer system vulnerable to hackers, the organization could not afford to lose either his focused attention or his loyalty. So how would they deal with this incident? Ignore it? Offer

William some gentle hints? Discipline him? Fire him?

The specialist suggested coaching. He said that coaching would convey a clear message that William's behaviour was unacceptable and would help him to make whatever changes were necessary. It would also help him to avoid public humiliation and to continue his work unhindered.

The HR director consulted the president, and then asked the specialist to raise this idea in a private conversation with William. Two days later, following the customary pleasantries, the specialist told the HR director about the repercussions of the incident. Not surprisingly, William downplayed it.

"You know me well enough to know that I am not prejudiced," he said. "I'm under a lot of pressure and I admit I made a mistake by drinking too much at lunch. I said some things I'm sorry about. But it's over. Let's not stir things up."

"All the same," returned the specialist, "we need to be sure that nothing like this will happen again. It's too dangerous. We would like to offer you a chance to meet with an executive coach so you can get some help figuring out what happened and why. The coach will provide some guidance and will help you to make whatever personal changes you need. And, of course, the entire matter will be confidential."

"Don't you think you're going a little overboard?" William looked worried. "It was a slip. I'm sorry. Just let it go. Besides, I'm far to busy to add another responsibility, and I will be busy until after this computer problem is fixed."

"William, the president wants this. He is very concerned about the results of your slip. In fact, he is willing to provide extra support if you need it to complete your work. But the bottom line is, he wants you to do this."

"What can I say?"

"Just give it some thought and get back to me."

"Okay. I'll think about it."

Well, no doubt William did think about it. But a week later there had been no response. This time the director of HR called William into her office.

"William," she said, "we need a decision."

"Well, I was going to get back to you about that. I have thought about it, and that coaching idea is overkill."

"I am afraid we can't accept that, William. We're going to insist. We want you to start working with a coach right away."

"Even if it means not meeting deadlines?"

"Frankly yes, even if means not meeting deadlines. But I don't believe it has to come to that. It will require an hour or two per week. If you want extra help, you can have it. But the bottom line is, if you are going to continue to be employed here, you must work with a coach."

William's face turned pale. "It sounds like this coaching stuff is just a gentle hint that I should look for another job. Why don't you just come right out and tell me?"

"Because that's not the case. In fact, it is the opposite. Offering you coaching is a way of saying how much we appreciate you. You are extremely good at your work and we don't want to lose you. Despite what you said that day, we don't think you're a racist. And besides, from a purely self-interested point of view, if you left, you would take away a vast amount of our intellectual capital. Frankly, it would cost a pile of money to replace you. So, for all kinds of reasons, there is no way that we want you to leave."

"Is that for real?"

"Yes, it is for real."

"So what happens next?"

"We introduce you to a coach. You decide if this is the right person to work with, and whether you can make it work."

No one knows precisely what happened between the coach and William over the months that followed. Just after the New Year, William asked for, and received, a one-month extension of the coaching contract.

The computer security work was successfully implemented, a credit to William's leadership and technical ability. Along the way, William sent a couple of signals to his staff. About a month after he started meeting with his coach, he concluded a routine staff meeting by recalling the incident and saying that he knew his behaviour had been inappropriate. He told the group that he regretted what he had said and wished he could take it back. Since that time, there have been no reports of further racist behaviour.

During even the most intense periods of the security work, William never returned from lunch showing any sign of having been drinking.

Making a Successful Pitch for Coaching

In the chapters that follow, we will look more closely at the structure of the magic that enables people like William to make significant changes. But for now, let's note what the HR director and specialist did, as the sponsors, that made their pitch successful.

They started out with the support, approval, and authority of the president. They then suggested the idea of coaching to William in a gentle way, through a person of middle rank in the company. (Later, they concluded that they might have been a little too gentle.) By offering William additional help, they made it clear to him that the organization was willing to make a considerable investment in him. In effect, they made coaching a part of his job specs.

They offered William the opportunity to freely choose coaching. When William failed to respond positively, they stated that coaching was a condition of his continued employment.

Throughout this process, they reiterated their respect for his abilities and their hope that he would not leave the organization. They ensured that he could work with a coach with whom he felt comfortable and reassured him that the coaching was confidential. And they followed through.

When Is Coaching Likely to Go on the Rocks?

Despite its successes, you may wonder if there are situations where coaching is likely to go on the rocks. Is it ever inappropriate? Well, there are a few situations that can make coaching a hopeless proposition.

Coaching could flounder, for instance, if the coach does not possess the specific competencies required for the particular situation, or if there is no senior level buy-in. Sometimes, too, the individual is simply unwilling or unable to change. And when it is clear that the person needs to be terminated, rather than being offered yet another "last chance," then coaching would be a waste of time and money.

Coaching may also be hopeless when the organization is part of the problem. This could happen if the organization needs to change itself but is not ready, and attempts to force change on employees instead. Sometimes organizations talk about change, but conversely reward stagnation. Coaching is probably useless when there is a culture of scapegoating employees, shooting the messenger, or when the proposal of coaching is designed to cover the organization's liabilities while it is actually intending to fire the person.

A skilled coach who understands systemic issues can help management improve the way the organization operates. The coach will need to keep alert and consult with colleagues at this point, as he crosses the boundary temporarily into consulting.

Whose Values Set the Criteria for Success?

Here we return to the perspective of the coach, with all other parties invited to see the coaching process from that viewpoint. Values are implicit in coaching, and each of the parties to the coaching process has individual values. Each will rate certain aspects and results as being of higher or lower value. Because the values of the parties are unlikely to coincide in all respects, some conflict will arise.

One example is the organization that holds collaborative leadership as a high value, while the employee/coachee believes only in getting the job done and using his or her authority to that end. This is a values conflict.

Values tend to be highly complex. The differing values held by each person and each organization compete for attention—and each may hold values that are in conflict with those of others. For this reason, it is necessary for the coach to devote attention to understanding her own values and those of others, as she watches the players' values compete. An important aspect of her job is the management of value conflicts, and it helps greatly to be clear about the players and their needs.

The Players

It is tempting but simplistic to think that the organization speaks with one voice. Senior management expresses its values from the viewpoint of a commitment to big picture success. The sponsors of coaching often express their values from a perspective marked by both professionalism and ambition. The direct manager of the coachee may need more productivity or less disruption. Each will exert some influence on the coaching process, and the coach who is unprepared for these value conflicts may be pulled in different directions.

And then there is the coachee. He may wish to become more effective as a leader. He may have needs for recognition as an important and productive contributor to the organization, and he may believe that he knows better than management what will work best. And—he may value confidentiality as much as the organization values disclosure.

Finally there is the wider society, represented in part by families of the coachee's team members. Their values may include the wish that fewer people got upset or confused at work, taking out their distress on those around them. The local community or municipality needs the coachee to contribute to organizational success, so that the entire community is enriched. The parents of the coachee want to see the coachee recognized for his strengths and gently challenged to improve on his weaknesses. And spiritual organizations wish to see the coachee reach his fullest potential, not only in technical skill, but also in how he treats other people and the environment.

The Impact of the Coach's Values

While the coach attempts to reconcile conflicting values within her coaching engagement, she also holds a commitment to be true to the values arising from her professional commitments, and she may hold other values that pull her in other directions. (Some of these are outlined in Chapter Three.)

From the standpoint of earning a living, and at the level of ego satisfaction, she will value success, so she will need to keep gaining new coaching assignments. This value could lead to an internal conflict, because the value of pleasing her sponsors is set against the value of following her own professional standards.

Also, she may face value conflicts generated by her own history. For example, a coach with a strong background in human relations and the human sciences may focus on building interpersonal skills, and she may therefore miss the goal of helping the coachee to learn how to work with those "impossible" financial statements. The coach who has a history in financial management may underplay the coachee's need to improve those "too subtle" team skills.

The Danger of Hidden Agendas

Since values influence our agenda for coaching, the coach must be particularly alert to the possibility of hidden agendas on the part of either the organization or the coachee.

The Organization

The organization may have multiple ambitions for the coaching engagement. One of the most extreme is a wish to ease the person out of the organization. If there is any suspicion of this, the coach will need to find out whether it is true, and if it is, to refuse the assignment. While this rarely happens, it is a scenario often suspected by coachees, and for that reason the coach will need to be assured of the facts.

As well, organizations sometimes believe that coaching can transform the coachee into a model employee. A dangerous example is sending the employee to a coach for the purpose of learning time management. Time is, of course, notoriously hard to manage. While most people can learn to manage their use of time better, in many situations they are already working at maximum efficiency, and squeezing more work from them will ultimately harm them and deplete the organization's resources.

Or, without intending to do so, the organization may be trying to change the individual's values to fit short-sighted organizational needs. In that case, coaching may still be valuable, but as a diagnostician the coach will need to help the organization shift its priorities.

The Coachee

The coachee may also have a hidden agenda. Coachees who are at loggerheads with management may hope to find an ally, someone who will help them to win their arguments.

Sometimes a coachee who has hired his own coach may be looking for help in leaving the organization, using the coaching to build the confidence required to quit and to develop strategies for career development. There is nothing wrong with this desire, but it is essential that the coach understand the agenda.

Contracting Models

There are three types of contracts, each with advantages and disadvantages:

1. IMPLICIT CONTRACTING

This contract takes place silently in the minds of the participants. They assume that they know exactly what the other intends. Frequently this is because they know each other well or have experience in contracting together. They believe, sometimes correctly, that they do not need to say much about their run-of-the-mill expectations.

Problems typically arise when the coaching engagement turns out differently than they expected. The result is often a sense of betrayal that might be expressed as, "You knew what I had in mind!"

2. VERBAL CONTRACTING

Contracting out loud is more time-consuming. It sometimes gives the impression of nit-picking, again as in "You know what I mean!"

But requiring yourself to commit your expectations to paper makes it more likely that you will address the unexpected. It is wise to make sure that contracts include a commitment to consult if problem issues arise.

3. PAPER CONTRACTING

This is the most time-consuming and often the most irritating form of contracting. Once people start down the paper route, they have a tendency to become verbose, crossing every *t* and dotting every *i*. But the benefit is clarity and completeness. The contract written on paper is usually more comprehensive in its vision of the coaching engagement than any conversation.

What Should Be Covered in a Contract?

A contract should specify

- the intention for coaching, in specific or general terms
- an outline of services to be provided
- a description of what will occur during the Assessment Phase, as well as the Development and Integration Phase
- the circumstances under which investigative modes such as interviews and 360-degree feedback might be employed (see Chapter Seven)

- the agreement of the organization and coachee that coaching is part of coachee's job description
- a clear description of the meaning and limits of confidentiality
- all time and cost issues, including an enumeration of services to be invoiced, payment of retainer, and the timing of installment payments
- the cancellation policy
- how the contract is to be consummated: by original, fax, or e-mail?

Limitations of Contracting

It is important to be realistic about the effectiveness of a written contract. While it can clarify expectations wonderfully, no document can restrain people from behaving in ways that they conclude are to their advantage.

Rarely will parties to coaching wish to retain counsel or go to court over the terms of a coaching contract. As a result, if the contract is to be worth more than the paper on which it is written, it must be based on full discussion.

We have provided the sample contract below to help you think about the issues that could arise from the coaching perspective. It makes no claim to be adequate from the point of view of law, and certainly not for the particular jurisdiction in which you work. So be certain to consult with a lawyer as you develop your own standard contract.

FIGURE 5.2 **SAMPLE CONTRACTING LETTER TO AN ORGANIZATIONAL SPONSOR**

Confirmation of Coaching Contract

Dear _____ :

This letter is to confirm a contract for coaching services to be provided by [coaching company]. A form is provided at the end for your acceptance, but we welcome in advance any changes or clarifications you suggest. Coaching is intended to assist the person, whom you have designated, in making changes that will be of value to [your organization] and of personal value to the coachee.

The work with the designated person will begin with an Assessment Phase, in order to develop a mutually acceptable and productive course for the coaching engagement. Following the Assessment, the Development and Integration Phase will begin. We will work with the designated person face-to-face, by phone, and/or by email, using appropriate instruments and in-depth interviewing techniques. Our aim throughout is to use coaching as a brief intervention resulting in effective change.

Provided that the designated person is willing, and that there is clear value in doing so, we are prepared to interview other persons in your organization, to conduct 360-degree feedback, to attend meetings, to facilitate effective delegation of responsibilities, and to mediate conflicts. These can be in consultation with you and/or with the supervisor of the coachee. These methods will allow the coach and the designated person to continuously monitor information that will assist in maintaining a focus on goals, accomplishing the desired behavioural changes, and reinforcing learning and growth.

(continued)

FIGURE 5.2 **CONTINUED**

Time Commitment

[Your organization] agrees that during the course of this coaching engagement, the person designated will be encouraged to regard coaching as part of her or his current work responsibilities. The organization will not expect coaching to be conducted during off-duty hours, nor will it regard coaching as an interruption of the individual's legitimate work.

Confidentiality

Ultimately, we are accountable to [your organization] in this contract. As a matter of effective practice, however, we will treat the designated person as our client. Coaching is in essence a confidential relationship, and for that reason we do not reveal the content of interviews except to the extent that the designated person desires. The sole (and rare) exception is when a person appears to pose a significant danger.

We understand that the coaching process may leave us with proprietary information that your organization considers private. We guarantee that any such information we glean from this work will be held in strict confidence.

Costs

Each Coaching Package provides for up to [number] hours of service, during a [number]-month period commencing with the date of the first interview with the designated person.

"Service" means contact with the designated individual, team members, supervisor, other associates, and/or representatives of the contracting department (whether face-to-face, by phone, or by e-mail). Also included are the following: planning time, materials preparation, report writing (where agreed to by the designated person), travel time (calculated at one/half actual time), and scoring of instruments.

[Your organization] agrees to pay [coaching company] for one Coaching Package at the rate of [amount] plus materials (if required), and taxes. A non-refundable retainer of [amount] will be invoiced at once and is payable within 15 days. The remainder will be invoiced upon completion of the coaching and is payable within 15 days.

Cancellation Policy

If the designated person ceases coaching within one month of the first meeting, actual time used will be calculated at a rate of [amount] per half day, and we will issue a final invoice for the amount by which that cost exceeds the non-refundable retainer.

Medium for Contracting

The parties agree that this contract, if concluded by facsimile transmission, is of the same force as if concluded by paper transmission.

I trust that this letter of contract conveys our agreement. Again, if it differs in any way from your understanding, please let us know at once and we can amend it. If this proposal is suitable as it stands, please confirm that you agree to these terms by signing and dating the acceptance below and returning a copy of the entire document.

(continued)

FIGURE 5.2 **CONTINUED**

Yours sincerely,
[Signature, position, date]

Acceptance
I accept and agree to the terms of the above proposal on behalf of [organization].
[Signature, position, date]

Pricing Models

Most external coaches agonize over their fees. If they charge too much, they fear that they will not get the work. If they charge too little, they may give the appearance of not being a mature and skilled practitioner. How much you should charge for coaching depends on a wide variety of factors: your location, what others are charging, your level of expertise, and who is paying the bill.

Coaching does not lend itself to the typical consultant's billing pattern, which is based on per-day or per-half-day fees. Coaching work is usually provided in sessions of one to two hours. A half-day rate is likely to work only in the rare case where you can schedule two or three individuals from the same organization into a morning or afternoon.

Fee setting is difficult, and the day after the coach reaches a firm decision about what to charge, she undoubtedly will hear about another coach who is doing well because she is charging more, or less. The most reliable sources of information are fellow practitioners in your local area. If you belong to a community of coaches, the members will generally be interested in discussing fees and other difficult matters with each other. Three pricing models follow:

1. PACKAGE PRICE
For a flat fee you can offer a certain number of hours of coaching to be used during a limited period of time. An example could be twenty hours over three months. If an extension is needed, it is generally negotiated based on the average hourly rate implied by the flat fee. (This style is the basis of the sample contract above.)

2. HOURLY FEE
If you decide to contract for an hourly-based fee, most employers will want to establish checks and balances to make certain that your invoice does not go beyond the amount they have budgeted. This is an area where all parties will benefit from open and frank initial discussions culminating in a clear contract.

3. MONTHLY FEE
You may establish a monthly fee if, for instance, you are coaching a management team or other group. In that case, you limit the amount of work you perform each month to roughly correspond with the value of the time involved, averaging it out over the period of the contract. Your contract may have a provision that additional fees can be pre-approved for retreats or other special events outside the organization's offices.

FIGURE 5.3 **SAMPLE DOCKET**

Docket for: [name]

DATE	START	FINISH	TOTAL	CUMULATIVE	CODE	NAME	EXPENSES

CODES: **IN**dividual Visit, **ME**eting with more than one, **PH**one Call, **CO**rrespondence, **RE**port writing, **PR**oviding training, **PL**anning and Preparation, **TR**avel Time (valued at 1/2 actual time)

Avoiding the Perils of Careless Docketing

A docket is a summary that tracks your use of time with each coaching client. Some coaches find themselves overwhelmed by the demand to keep an accurate account of time spent, relying on scraps of paper and inadequate notations in their day calendars.

The straightforward solution is to tape a docket form to the inside cover of the file for each coachee, and make entries at the same time as you make your notes immediately after each session. You will also want to docket phone conversations that exceed five or ten minutes, correspondence, report writing, training, planning time, and travel. (Since your travel time is unproductive for the organization but does save the coachee from having to travel to you, the rate suggested here is a compromise: half your hourly rate.)

Your docket form should provide all the information you may need in the future to validate an invoice, including space for

- date
- start and finish time
- total time for the session
- cumulative time for all sessions (so you remain aware of how much time is left in the budget)
- how the time was used
- name of person you spent the time with (coachee, supervisor, etc.)
- out-of-pocket expenses such as mileage or parking

THE COST OF DOCKET DIFFICULTIES

Many lawyers who are being coached reveal problems keeping their dockets-up-to-date. When they fall behind, they report the same problems that coaches may experience, such as impaired cash flow, uncertainty about the accuracy of their billings, and more frequent disputes with those who pay the invoices.

That First Meeting with the Coachee

As the formal Contracting Phase draws to a close, you may meet with the coachee for the first time. There are several requisite bases you will want to touch:

1. REMAIN CONFIDENTLY TENTATIVE

Even if a contract has been signed with the organization, do not assume that the contract is firm. If this is the first time that you and the coachee have been alone together, it is appropriate to regard it as your private contracting meeting. It will mean a great deal to the coachee if you position the meeting as an opportunity for him to see your work up close and to decide whether he wishes to proceed.

Your obvious comfort with the ambiguity and uncertainty of this session demonstrates inner strength. Because you are secure within yourself, it actually encourages the coachee to view you as someone with whom it would be safe to proceed.

Coach: … so I would like you to be the one who decides whether I am the right person for you to work with. To make that decision easier for you, I will act as though we are going to be working together over the long term. I'm going to ask a lot of questions and get to know you as well as I can during this first session. But if at the end of the session, or at any other point, you feel that someone else would be better suited to be your coach, I want you to tell me that. It won't hurt my feelings, and in fact, I'll appreciate your honesty. Is that OK?

2. OUTLINE THE COACHING PROCESS

It is often helpful at this stage to make certain that the coachee understands the meaning of coaching. To that end, you may wish to explain some of the unique factors that make coaching valuable. The coachee will be able to cooperate with the coach and receive the most value from the coaching if the coach is clear about the underlying structure. Describe the sequence of phases: Assessment Phase follows the Contracting Phase, then Development and Integration Phase, and finally the Completion Phase. Explain the intent of each phase and the kind of action you will be taking to make it effective.

It is better at this stage to provide too much information than too little. No matter how obvious it may seem to you, this is new ground for the coachee. Ask frequently if the coachee understands, or has any questions.

3. SPEAK EXPLICITLY ABOUT CONFIDENTIALITY

In the first session, almost without exception, coachees wonder how far their words will go and whether you are making a secret diagnosis that might be passed on to the sponsors of coaching. Let your coachee know that you understand how crucial it is to the success of coaching that his confidences remain with you. Let him know, too, that you will not disclose to others any proprietary information you may glean from your conversations with him, so that he does not feel that he has to constantly curb his tongue to protect the organization.

4. WORK OUT THE STYLE FOR COACHING TOGETHER

Rather than making assumptions about how the coaching will proceed, find out how the coachee would like to work with you. Small course adjustments at this stage can mean a great deal to him. Questions you may ask include

- Do you have any preferences about how you would like us to work?
- Do you see what we are doing as a secret, or would you like it to be open knowledge among your co-workers?
- Would you like me to conduct 360-degree feedback or interview others to fill out the information you give me?
- Would you work better with a female or male coach?
- Is it best for us to meet in your office, my office, or at another location?
- Do you wish to know more about the contract or fees for coaching?

5. COLLECT ESSENTIAL INFORMATION.

The following chapter on assessment will provide a more thorough guide to this first session. You, however, will find it valuable to begin by asking about the experiences of the coachee. Some of your questions may be

- Have you ever experienced coaching before?
- What is the change or issue that led you to consider coaching?
- What are your objectives?
- What are your organization's objectives for you?

6. SHARE INFORMATION ABOUT YOURSELF

Your willingness to talk about yourself briefly provides a helpful model of openness, setting the stage for the self-revelation that is essential to coaching. If it seems appropriate, for instance, you may talk about why you like your profession.

This is a time of testing, no matter how compliant the coachee may appear to be. He may also appreciate hearing some clearly non-confidential details of similar situations or organizations with which you have worked. The coachee may wish to know whether there are specific types of issues you deal with and any specialties you may have developed. He may want to know whether you employ staff that may have an impact on him, for instance, a secretary with whom confidential information may be left.

By inviting questions in this session, you indicate that the coachee can interrupt the process at any point to inquire about you and your practice.

7. CLOSE THE INTERVIEW WITH CLARITY

It will speak well for your practice of coaching if you bring the first interview to a conclusion pointing clearly toward the future. If you have spent the session largely collecting information, now is a good time to share some of the very tentative conclusions you are reaching. To do so is both generous and graceful. For instance, "Based on what we've talked about today, here's what I think you can realistically expect with regard to your goals… ." You may also ask further questions to help the coachee reach decisions, such as

- Is there anything further I can explain?
- Have you made a decision about whether you wish to continue this coaching relationship?
- How will you make that decision?
- Is there anyone who can help you?
- Are there any unspoken concerns that I could address for you now?
- How will you let me know? Would you like me to call you?

Such questions reveal that even though you have a high tolerance for ambiguity yourself, you are interested in providing him with as much clarity as he may need. If the coachee decides to proceed, you will wish to discuss where and when you will meet next. Make sure he enters this into a day calendar, or hand him a business card or appointment card on which you have written the information.

Providing Printed Information to the Coachee

Many people recall better what they read than what they hear. In a situation as stressful as meeting a new coach, the individual is likely to forget half of what he hears. So it is helpful to provide a written handout summarizing the information you have provided orally.

You may use the summary below as a guide for your discussion of the parameters of coaching.

FIGURE 5.4 **WELCOME TO THE COACHING PRACTICE OF [NAME]**

The Beginning of Coaching
Although you may initially have been referred for coaching by your organization, this is the point when this process takes a significant turn, becoming a private and confidential relationship between you and your coach.

Benefits of Coaching
Leaders tell me that the coaching process has helped them to become more effective, confident, and aware, and they report greater job satisfaction and recognition. Organizations say that they view the person's participation as evidence of flexibility and commitment. In my view, coaching is not judgmental or disciplinary, but designed to provide a safe place where you can maximize your potential in ways that make sense to you.

The Phases of the Coaching Process
1. Careful contracting.
2. A thorough assessment of the coachee.
3. An extensive period of development and integration.
4. A completion stage that provides for dealing with problems and the possibility of slippage.

(continued)

FIGURE 5.4 **CONTINUED**

Being Frank

You did not hire a coach to indulge in flattery or a lengthy academic diagnosis. I assume that you are not faint-hearted, while I am resolutely results-oriented. My commitment is to provide you with forthright feedback right from the start. I will help you to discover what is working and what is not, and I will help you to design changes.

At times, what I say may surprise you. But I understand that is why you invited me to work with you—to help you to achieve a fresh perspective on your work life.

My Limits

My job is to be your coach—to challenge, to stimulate, and to help you to see around your blind spots. But I do not carry the ball. After all, you already know more than I ever can about your business. So I will not attempt to replace your hard work or specialized skills.

My job is to help you to uncover your own wisdom, to stand alongside you, to ask the right questions, and to help you to do the work of adding value in your career.

How Long It Takes

I will work with you for as long as there is positive movement and a business benefit. But ultimately it is my responsibility to work myself out of a job. So I will not attempt to create a dependency, nor stay around a moment longer than you find valuable.

Confidentiality

I operate within a context of confidentiality. I will report back only information to which you have agreed. With this assurance, I find that most people can confront and resolve personal issues without feeling any risk of humiliation or loss of privacy.

I believe that the data required by the organization to measure the success of the coaching will be provided by visible improvements in the client's performance. If, however, you authorize me to reveal information to the organization, I am willing to do so, with the stipulation that you review written reports in advance.

If, in the rare event I discover that you, as my coachee, are likely to harm someone, I will exercise my responsibility to alert the proper authorities. Your organization deserves and will receive fair treatment and respect from me. I will guard any proprietary information that I have become aware of through the coaching.

The Cost of Coaching

My fee will be precisely as we agreed ahead of time. There will be no hidden costs, no surprises.

Questions

Most people have some questions, anxieties, or concerns when they begin the coaching process. If you do, feel free to raise them with me. I am used to people feeling a bit uncomfortable at first, and I will provide frank answers.

Although the coaching process may seem a little intimidating at this point, please remember that it is intended to respond to your needs, not mine. So please do not hesitate to let me know about any changes or additions that you would like to make.

In the Assessment Phase that follows, the planning and discussion with the organization described here will be transformed into a powerful, private investigation of the coachee's perspective.

HOARDING THE DIAGNOSIS

A visit to the dermatologist highlighted the weaknesses of the prevailing medical model of assessment. The patient asked the doctor to check out a couple of bumps on his skin. Looking at the first one, the doctor said, "It might or might not be a problem. I'll dab it with liquid nitrogen anyway."

Having treated it, he looked at the second one. "That's not a problem," he said, and turned to write his notes.

The patient interrupted, "I wonder if you should treat it, too. I'm worried about irritating this one. Maybe it could cause problems later on."

The reply was laconic, "I don't think so," and the doctor ushered the patient from the room. No further explanation. Nothing about how one lump might be different from another. Inwardly the patient growled. Another reminder of why the medical model attracts so much criticism. Another reason for coaches to feel mighty uncomfortable in their roles as diagnosticians.

What Do We Mean by Assessment?

With an agreed contract for coaching, the Assessment Phase begins. Assessment is an exploration undertaken by the coach and coachee to discover all the data relevant to their quest. Only after a thorough assessment will they possess the information they need to work effectively in the following phase of Development and Integration.

The Assessment Phase includes the systematic discovery and collection—in open collaboration with the coachee—of all available information relevant to the coaching process. This includes, as well, a clarification of the goals of all parties. Sometimes information that may not seem relevant at first later turns out to be applicable and important.

Because it is the quality of the assessment that fuels the coaching task, you will find that this chapter covers the topic of assessment in general, while Chapter Seven offers cautions and describes three families of tools available for an enriched level of assessment.

Why Assess?

Coaches who have good intuitive powers are occasionally tempted to skip the formal assessment process. They are used to picking up important information as they go along, and they are generally very good at it. So they may hesitate, thinking, "I don't need to make this conversation awkward by prying and collecting a lot of possibly useless information."

But contrary voices come from professions drawing on centuries of accumulated experience assisting human beings with their health and personal growth. Their numbers include doctors, paramedical professionals, psychotherapists, and social workers. They are unanimous about the necessity of a thorough preliminary assessment.

How many organizational redesigns, plant reorganizations, mergers, or acquisitions have foundered because they were built on an inadequate investigation of the relevant pressures, costs, and other realities? If coaching did not include a commitment to thoroughly assess, it would have to be abandoned as a risky business conducted with vague or useless interventions, a careless tinkering with the human spirit, a costly trip through the dark without map or headlights.

Benefits of a Well-Designed Assessment

Assessment is central to the leadership coaching process. The more complete the assessment, the more successful the coaching. It is always better to collect too much data than to discover later that you have missed the very item that could be restraining the coachee from growth. The lack of adequate assessment is a fundamental source of failure in change projects of all kinds, including coaching. A sound assessment

- provides basic information for communication and contact, such as, name, preferred salutation ("Would you like me to call you Ms. Smith, Deborah, or Deb?"), phone, e-mail, hours of work, and location of office
- collects information to acquaint the coach with the context. Who works for whom, what is the job description, where is home, who are the significant others in the coachee's life, what previous experience does the coachee have of formal growth experiences?
- elicits information about the coachee's level of self-awareness. How well does she understand herself, what are her leadership skills, how does she handle conflict, how do others see her strengths and weaknesses?
- pinpoints for both parties the coachee's areas of development and the objectives for the coaching engagement. "I understand that you're on the fast track in the organization," says a coach. "I was asked to help you get ready for more responsibility. So let's talk about where you see the need to develop."
- identifies the strengths—some may be scarcely recognizable—that will support the person through the hard work of making changes. These might include inner strengths

(being flexible or having a good support network) and workplace strengths (being able to delegate or envision the future)

- identifies factors that tripped up the coachee in the past or might derail the coaching process
- clarifies whether the coachee's issues and concerns can be appropriately handled through coaching
- determines existence of any limitations to progress, such as environmental, physical, or psychological problems
- clarifies when the work can be considered complete.

The Scope of the Assessment

A number of specific techniques can be used to support an assessment:

1. THE GUIDED INTERVIEW

The central, irreplaceable core of any assessment is the guided interview. Not only does it provide the raw information you will need as the coaching develops, but the process of working your way through it has a hidden benefit: it enables the coach and coachee to develop a deeper relationship. The structure of the guided interview is so important that it deserves to be dealt with at length. (See Chapter Seven.)

2. STANDARD TESTS OR INSTRUMENTS

Tests are an excellent means of eliciting more focused information about such important topics as conflict styles and leadership practices. The best standard tests offer the benefit of a very clear format, asking just the right questions and providing a report that is clear and helpful. Most tests require only the coachee's response, providing excellent insight into how that individual regards herself. (See Chapter Seven.)

3. MULTI-SOURCE OR 360-DEGREE FEEDBACK

The use of questionnaires addressed to those around the coachee—supervisor, peers, internal customers, and direct reports—is called 360-degree feedback. It broadens the scope of information available, providing fresh and unanticipated data, along with suggestions for change from the very people who know the coachee best. (See Chapter Seven.)

A POIGNANT SELF-ASSESSMENT

During her coaching assessment, the CEO of a midsize transportation firm accepted a homework assignment to describe in point form how she felt others saw her as a leader, that is, her persona or image in the organization.

Here are the words she chose: "Great expectations, cool-headed, all-powerful, visionary, all-seeing, all-knowing, change agent, creator, planner, teacher, fighter, winner."

Part two of the assignment was to describe how she viewed herself. And how the description differed! "Child, learner, lonely one, risk-taker, lover, parent, searcher, friend, uncertain one, scared one, heavy with responsibility."

As you can imagine, her response to that single assessment task was sufficient to delineate much of the work she needed to accomplish in her coaching. The exercise was particularly powerful because, although the coach suggested the task and provided guidance, the CEO did the homework herself and, in collaboration with the coach, developed her own map for the coaching engagement.

Because she did the work, she trusted the outcome.

A word of encouragement for coaches: the description of the assessment process that follows may seem overwhelming at first, and you may wonder how you can ever cover the topics suggested here and in the chapter that follows. The short answer is, don't worry, give yourself time, and you will master the assessment process. However, becoming comfortable with assessment does require greater dedication to planning than you may be used to.

To develop skills and confidence, beginning coaches have to work hard to approach a professional level in their assessments, but over time, they discover a growing intuitive ability to make effective assessments. Increasingly, coaches will notice familiar patterns encountered in other coachees. On reflection, they realize that they already possess a preliminary understanding of how to manage these situations.

Assessment Leads to Positive Growth

In this hard-sell age, we are increasingly suspicious of people who offer us prepackaged solutions. Whether we are stressed or overweight, whether we should save for retirement or need better computer facilities, there are thousands of people who would like to tell us exactly what we need and where to get it. In contrast, during the assessment process, the coach has no such agenda and no prepackaged solution for the issues faced by the coachee.

By following the sometimes-labyrinthine process of assessment, the coach demonstrates an attitude of respect and a commitment to deal with the actual issues the coachee faces. The coach's support and guidance enable results that the coachee will recognize as valid. The coach's basic assumption is that many solutions are already available within the coachee, even if temporarily obscured. *The task is not to provide solutions but to help uncover them.* The responsibility of the coach is to pay attention to the person and to the context, to the ways that people actually think and act, and to physical and psychological reality.

To clarify how an assessment leads to positive growth, following is an example of a simple moment of assessment by a coach with no specific training but an ability to ask the right questions.

SIMPLICITY OF ASSESSMENT

Sheila, a sales rep, had run into difficulties. To her supervisor, it seemed that she was stubborn, and that she was dragging down the department's efficiency with her unwillingness to make the transition from paper records to computer files. Eventually, the boss was prepared either to fire Sheila or to sideline her.

Then he had a brainwave. A salesman named Dan popped into his mind, a guy who had successfully made the transition to computer use. Dan was no computer genius, but he had a reputation as a good listener. So the supervisor asked him to have a chat with Sheila, a last-ditch effort to see if she could turn around. "But don't twist yourself out of shape," he cautioned. "If it isn't going to work, back off and let me know."

The newly appointed coach took Sheila out of the workplace to the cafeteria, where they spent a few minutes talking over coffee. Dan led off with a simple question: "What's holding you back?" Sheila replied that she was terrified of failures with technology.

Dan was easy to talk with, so Sheila described how, as a teenage driver, she had collided with a car that had turned into her path. As though it was yesterday, she could remember the relentless slide along an icy road into the side of the other car while she was standing on her brakes, angry at her failure to anticipate the other vehicle's turn and the impossibility of undoing that mistake.

So what solution did Dan propose to Sheila? Medication? Driver training? A year or two of psychotherapy? A few months' intense coaching in computer software? Of course, it was none of the above.

Dan simply walked Sheila back to her computer. "There's a way to make sure that you never have to fail with your computer," he said as Sheila looked at him incredulously. "Have you ever noticed the Undo command at the top of the screen?"

"Oh no!" replied Sheila in a panic. "One more thing I have to master!"

"In fact, it's not," said her coach. "It's simply a reminder that any mistake you make, you can fix at the click of the button."

It took about half an hour of coaching, consisting of a twenty-minute assessment (otherwise known as a good chat) followed by ten minutes of experimentation, to put Sheila firmly on the road to productivity.

Assessment from Start to Finish

What happens as we assess? First we are gathering enough information to enable change, and while doing this, we are also building psychological awareness and assessing the cultural context. This information provides the basis for developing a working hypothesis as a foundation for the coachee's assessment. Throughout, we share the results with the coachee.

Assessment Step 1: Gather Enough Information to Enable Change

Even when a coaching relationship has begun on more formal terms than Dan and Sheila's, a new coachee will not always expect a formal Assessment Phase. So, once the contracting is concluded, it is helpful to offer an introduction like this:

"I can imagine that you're eager to get started on making changes. I'd like to suggest that we lay a solid foundation for that work by collecting some information. I don't know you very well, and this will help me work with you more intelligently. It's not difficult; I'll just ask you a lot of questions.

"I expect you'll find the process helpful. Most people say they come to know themselves better than they did before, because some of the information I'm looking for comes from a different angle than they are used to thinking about.

"So, would it be all right with you if, for the next couple of meetings, I ask you a series of questions?"

At this point the coach may wait for permission. Although our coachees have not often wanted to discuss assessment, so far we have never been turned down in this request. After the coachee agrees, it is valuable to add a couple of procedural explanations.

"I won't be making as much eye contact with you as I normally prefer while we're doing this, because I need to write a lot of notes. But I want you to know that I will be listening intensely to everything you say." (In fact, the coach should make an effort during the assessment to raise his eyes to the coachee as often as possible. You do not want her to think for a moment that you consider what you are writing to be more important than the person across from you.)

You can add, with a little humour, that given the state of your memory, the taking of notes is essential.

OUR ENCYCLOPEDIA

As coaches, we find that we return often to our notes, looking for impressions and pieces of information. It might be something as simple as the person's birthday or the name of her supervisor, or the way she originally phrased the presenting issue. By the time we have completed the assessment form, it has developed into our guide, our encyclopedia, and a map for the coaching relationship to come.

AIDING MEMORY

Coaches need help remembering the vast amounts of data they gather. During Assessment, take plenty of notes on the spot. As you move into the Development and Integration Phase, you may find that you take fewer notes, and may even delay at least some of the note taking until after the conclusion of a session.

Especially during training, coaches often audiotape sessions. There are three benefits to this:

1. They hear themselves as coachees hear them.
2. They hear what they may have missed the coachee saying the first time around.
3. They can play back the tapes (with the permission of the coachee) for their coaching supervisor in order to get specific direction about their work.

Coaches sometimes use videotape, as well, which offers the coachee a chance to see how she sounds and looks. Videotape is external feedback with no bias. A caution: practise using the videotape without a coachee in the room, until its use is easy and automatic. Otherwise, it will cause more disruption than it is worth.

ASSURANCES OF PRIVACY

Before we begin the process, we make certain to tell our clients: "I will be asking you questions that touch on many aspects of your life. But there is nothing that you must answer. It is fine for you to say, 'I'd prefer to move on,' and I will respect that."

Finally, although we have already discussed the issue of confidentiality during the

Contracting Phase, we remind the coachee of what we promised then. At this point, when we are actually sitting across from her with clipboard and pen in hand, she will find those reassurances much more relevant.

Once she is ready, we begin with a series of straightforward, unthreatening questions that can be answered factually. As the interview builds a greater sense of familiarity and trust, we can move into areas that are more personal and require more self-revelation. This gentle evolution allows the coachee to grow in confidence before facing deeper questions, which will provide a unique perspective on the coachee's development.

Assessment Step 2: Build Psychological Awareness.

To clarify the meaning of assessment, we will examine it as practised by two very different professional coaches. The first coach has no training in psychology; his prime credential is a profound knowledge of the workplace. The second coach relies, as well, on his background in psychotherapy for the benefit of the client.

How deeply to probe into psychological areas is a matter of debate among coaches. Our preference will be no surprise, when you know that our earlier careers were as psychotherapists. We use that expertise, wherever it is relevant, to move to the areas affected by the family of origin, the emotions, and the unconscious, as well as intimate relationships.

But while we believe that a formal understanding of psychology and agility in exploring the undercurrents of human behaviour are valuable skills, there are many excellent coaches who lack this kind of experience. Here is an example of what can happen when a coach with no formal psychological background but an unfettered willingness to probe, develops an assessment—in this case for a young supervisor who is floundering.

AN ALIEN IN THE WORKPLACE

Rita had been in her new job for only five months, and it was not going well. Her responsibility was to supervise a dozen bright young technicians, but she realized that she was entirely lost. As she put it, she felt like an alien. For instance, when she gave directions to one man, she would be ultra-cautious not to make any undue demands. His response would be to simply ignore her suggestions and go his own way. With another person, she would make her demands very firmly, and that person would react as though Rita was a hostile visitor from another planet.

Rita had no idea why all this was happening, but knew that she had to get a handle on it quickly. Fortunately she found herself a coach who relied on the use of a guided assessment to inform the development process. The turning point came in their second meeting, when the coach reached the Previous Work Experiences stage in his interview schedule. He asked whether Rita had ever been a supervisor before.

"That's what's so confusing," Rita replied. "In my last two positions, I was a technical supervisor the same as here, and in both cases I was seen as having a natural talent for the job. In fact, that's why I was recruited for this one. I don't get it."

At that point, the coach might have simply noted Rita's uncertainty and moved on to his next question. Instead, he set aside the assessment guide for a moment and began to probe. Was Rita absolutely sure that she had been effective as a supervisor in the past? Had there been any covert problems on the job? Had she ever experienced anything remotely like the reactions in her current office? Rita squirmed a little as she searched her memory—for there is no supervisor on earth who hasn't confronted problems, and none who has not made mistakes. But the problems she had faced before were routine, much like those of other supervisors. Nothing like this.

On a hunch, the coach asked for the names of the companies where Rita had worked before. He thought he recognized one of them. "Isn't that a union shop?" he asked. "And what about the other one?"

"Yes," replied Rita, "both of them."

"And this job?"

"There's definitely no union here."

"What does that mean, 'definitely'?"

"Well, as far as I can tell, the owners try to run the place in a way that will make a union unattractive to the employees. They offer stock options, they consult about changes, that kind of thing."

The coach decided to probe further. "So what would happen in your other jobs if you ran into problems with staff?"

"If they were serious, we'd end up going head to head with the shop steward. Of course, we'd do almost anything to avoid that, so if you knew that a certain employee was prone to going to the union, generally you'd be very careful around him. So either you handled people with kid gloves, or if things got bad, you'd push very hard."

"And how does the management here deal with those kinds of problems?"

"I'm not so clear about that. It's different, but I can't put a finger on it."

"Maybe you need to figure that out. What would you think about making that a priority for our next meeting?"

"It's a good idea."

"How would you do that?"

"I'm not sure—unless I just start asking some of the other supervisors."

"Sounds like a plan to me," replied the coach.

So over the next couple of weeks, Rita made it her mission to find out how her peers related to their direct reports. She discovered that the employees were used to regulating themselves most of the time. But to do that effectively, they required more and better information from their managers than she was used to providing. She also found that when attempting to find solutions to problems with employees, the managers generally used consultation and discussion rather than resorting to her familiar system of kid gloves or intense opposition.

On the suggestion of her coach, Rita then widened the scope of her inquiry, taking advantage of casual conversations to ask employees directly about how they perceived her. She discovered that when she thought she was being cautious or delicate, they found her vague. And when she put her foot down over an issue, they saw her as harsh. What they wanted from her, they said, was more communication and more willingness to listen.

Because her coach conducted these and other elements of a careful assessment, Rita quickly gained a fine-grained picture of what she needed to do next. Because the coach shared his insights in a tentative way, Rita was able to "own" and control the assessment process, rather than respond in a passive way to the coach's questions. Her involvement as an equal partner encouraged her to devote herself to the task of learning about herself and taking calculated but enriching risks.

Furthermore, Rita was a quick and motivated learner, unafraid to experiment with changes, so in only a few weeks she found herself more at home, and more effective, within the culture of her new firm.

Now let us examine assessment from another perspective, looking at a situation where coaching with a strong psychological component enabled a leader with excellent technical skills to retain her job, to improve her conduct, and to stop hurting the people around her.

HISTORY TRIPS UP A STAR

Jodi was a talented marketing executive in her mid-thirties, known and admired for her ability to get the word out for her clients and to bring revenues to the firm. She was, however, equally renowned for her vicious temper. As a result, morale was plummeting among her victims, primarily those who reported to her.

After an angry encounter with Jodi, employees' productivity would plunge as they invested all their energy in putting themselves back together again. The more Jodi harassed her staff, the less they dared to expose themselves to risks. So they played it safe, which meant that their productivity sank and there were even more triggers for Jodi's temper. The office was caught up in a negative spiral that eventually got the attention of the senior partner.

Jodi's boss was plenty worried. Terms like "harassment" could be heard increasingly around the water cooler. "Labour law," he realized, could not be far behind. He called in a coach.

But when the coach met Jodi, he found not the monster he had heard about, but a bright, hard-working executive. She told him that she was skeptical and frankly surprised that her boss had referred her to a coach because of the way she talked with staff.

"I don't get it," she said. "That's my style. It's who I am. They pay me well precisely because I'm aggressive in the marketplace. Now they want me to tone it down at the office?" Her voice trailed off, she looked confused. "And I'm not that bad. If people can't handle being told when they screw up, they shouldn't be in the workplace."

As the coach worked through a guided assessment interview, Jodi was open and frank when asked for information about the workplace. Questions about her personal background were answered politely but without enthusiasm. That got the coach's attention. Evidently Jodi saw the work world and her personal life as two utterly distinct regions.

Gently exploring this contrast, the coach discovered that Jodi had experienced a very difficult childhood. Both her mother and father had been tragically addicted to alcohol. He probed further and discovered that, like every child of addicts, she had suffered terribly. Poverty, violence, and chronic instability had marked her childhood. It appeared to the coach that, despite her initial hesitation, Jodi actually seemed to find some relief in having someone to talk with about those secrets. What made it easier was that because of his previous experience, the coach was comfortable travelling with Jodi through this difficult personal terrain.

During the following interview, the coach asked, "Did it ever occur to you that having alcoholic parents has an effect on your present-day relationships with people?"

Jodi looked genuinely puzzled. What did her personal life have to do with the workplace? "Not at all," she replied. "In fact, I don't think I'm much different from most people."

"I agree that in many ways you're like everyone else, but in some respects you are also unique. The reason I asked the question is because I think you're on the edge of a development that could have a huge benefit for you. But it's not something that I can do for you. In fact, what I'm proposing is that you and I become partners in a journey of discovery. The destination we'd both be working toward is to better understand yourself and your relationship with your workplace."

"I don't know what this will be like," replied Jodi. "But you've definitely got my attention. I guess we can see what happens."

She and her coach went on to spend the next coaching sessions exploring two mysteries.

First the coach helped her to understand the past. By asking questions about those troubled years, he helped Jodi discover that the rage she sometimes displayed had its origins in the frustrations of a troubled childhood. Anger had built upon disillusionment, disappointment, pain, loss, shame, and frustration—until it became chronic, a fixture of her personality, as natural and unremarkable to Jodi as breathing.

Second the coach helped Jodi to understand the present. She began to comprehend the impact her temper had on her direct reports, people whose well-being was her responsibility. This part was particularly difficult to wrap her mind around, because she had learned nothing about empathy from her troubled parents, people too damaged to focus on the needs of others—including Jodi. She began to realize that not only had her parents shown her no empathy, they had been relentlessly harsh.

Yet they were pathetic creatures, and in order to insulate herself from their pain-wracked lives, she had learned to distance herself from the feelings of other people.

This was a powerful exploration, even for a tough woman like Jodi. Her eyes were sometimes damp as she talked.

But coaching is not psychotherapy, and as Jodi began to understand the perceptual twist she had inherited from her childhood experiences, she and the coach plunged actively into scenario planning. Jodi would sketch out an office situation in which she was likely to blow up, and they would plan alternative tactics to help her to avoid trouble and remain calm. It was a relief to know that she could do something practical, rather than simply complain about the effects her early life had on her.

They covered the map of her work life from morning to night in their search for solutions. She began to deal with workplace problems before they got too big. Sometimes the most fruitful tactic was to rush out of the office and take a walk, rather than chew out one of her reports. Her coach suggested that she consider additional methods for dealing with her history, including selected reading, joining a personal-growth group, or entering psychotherapy.

Jodi's first decision was to buy—and read—a book written for the adult children of alcoholics, her first self-help book ever. In doing so, without necessarily recognizing it, she had agreed to maintain an ongoing self-assessment process that would outlive her relationship with the coach.

At every session, Jodi and her coach discussed which of her new tactics had worked and which had not, fine-tuning her ability to keep her cool. By the time the coaching assignment ended, Jodi's treatment of her direct reports had improved considerably.

Months later her boss told the coach that the changes Jodi made had stuck. The atmosphere in the office was lighter. There was no further talk of harassment and Jodi's reports seemed less fearful, were taking more responsibility, and were producing better results.

In Jodi's case, only an assessment that attended to her personal psychological state could have helped her to understand and to deal with the roots of her behaviour. After the coaching ended, she continued reading self-help books on occasion and briefly used psychotherapy, wanting to improve other aspects of her relationships, as well.

When our coachees, many of whom are successful leaders, become stalled, it is almost without exception a sign that they have hit a psychological wall. Senior people are savvy, action-oriented folks with plenty of technical skills and options in their briefcases. Otherwise, they would not have risen to their positions. If the key to their problems was a lack of enthusiasm or problem-solving ability, they would get that fixed in a flash. They want effective help, and to rely on a limited bag of tricks or the management-model-of-the-month will simply not help. It will treat symptoms, rather than causes.

The first step for individuals hoping to accelerate their performance from the acceptable to the excellent is to understand what is holding them back. Corporate coaching, as a nascent profession, is unlikely to become consistently effective until coaches embrace the idea of underpinning a profound understanding of business with thorough training in human development.

DISPARATE COACHES

As part of a recent panel of coaches, we were struck by the vastly different backgrounds represented. The one with a clinical background was seated between a former organizational development consultant and a former marketing expert. Because we had each chosen to work in our areas of expertise, and because we were all committed to a process of continuous learning, we were all successful as coaches.

Coaching is a young field. To date, the major criticism levelled at its practitioners is that its results are sometimes shallow: enthusiastic but simplistic solutions to complex problems. While one may hope that this is more perception than reality, coaches have more than once been described as behaving like cheerleaders on the sidelines of a battlefield. At the root of this problem, we believe, is coaches' general discomfort in dealing with the intricacies of human psychology.

We urge coaches, no matter what their background, to commit themselves to a developing understanding of psychology as it applies to the workplace. Admittedly, it is a big undertaking. The coach must become familiar and disciplined in dealing with the family of origin, the emotions, the unconscious mind (memories, assumptions, beliefs, and values), and the impact of intimate relationships.

Assessment Step 3: Assess the Cultural Context

The coach has more to assess than the individual. Our context, community, and culture—the demands they make and the ways we behave in relation to them—have a huge impact on our success in the workplace. Consequently, the coach who has developed an ability to think not only in psychological terms, but systemically, as well, has a great deal to offer coachees who may be unaware of the influence of context.

THE TRUTH ABOUT SWOAP

In my late teens I (the male author) joined the air force reserve. I wasn't eager to go to war for my country, but the armed forces had offered me a job as a public relations trainee. Knowing I would get great opportunities to practise writing and broadcasting, I signed up. Before I got to the good stuff, however, I would have to undergo basic military training, along with a few hundred green officer cadets. During boot camp, the greatest challenge we faced was learning to march in unison.

The only practice many of us had in making precise moves in unison had led to our stepping on our dates' toes at the sock hop. And that's where Sergeant Swoap came into the picture. "Left wheel!" he'd bellow at us, and half of us would wheel around to the right, bumping into other platoons, creating disorder where order was meant to rule.

"Not that left," Swoap would scream sarcastically, "the other left!" Then he'd assign the out-of-condition miscreants to twenty push-ups.

Intellectually, we thought that Swoap's job was to prepare us to march briskly into enemy territory. Emotionally, we feared that he had been sent into our lives to terrorize and punish us for past sins. The truth, of course, was that it would never matter how well we learned to march. Swoap had been assigned to indoctrinate us into the authoritarian culture of the armed forces.

I think of Swoap sometimes when I work with a client who is wheeling to the right while the rest of the organization wheels to the left. Remember Rita, the supervisor who felt like an alien in a new company? The only serious flaw in her skill set was that she did not pay enough attention to the company's culture. An assessment provides the opportunity to uncover information about how any coachee has adapted to his or her work context. Often it requires only this simple question to reveal the truth: "How do you fit in around here?"

THE DIRTY WORK EXPERT

Betty, a senior manager who was stalled in her career, was so intrigued by that particular question that she responded with an essay. She wrote:

I've been trying to figure out why I was passed over for a promotion. I think part of the problem is that I tend to respond to the demands of work as they come along, rather than understanding and confronting the politics.

But what I find especially confusing is the fact that people show a lot of appreciation for my willingness to do the dirty work around here. I'm the one who makes difficult decisions and takes unpopular stands.

So sometimes they see this as valuable. After all, most of our people are complacent souls who creep into change. They're evolutionary at a time when we desperately need revolutionaries. Anyway, I get some praise when they need my particular talents. But the rest of the time, I'm like a fish out of water. I know a lot of people here but I wouldn't say I've made many friends.

Much of Betty's work during the Assessment Phase of her coaching consisted of understanding her organization's culture in greater depth. Building on that in the Development Phase, she experimented with making better connections, and gradually she cultivated a handful of relationships with people who had shown some appreciation of her and offered support. She eventually realized that the understanding of culture and its impact on the people who work in an organization is essential preparation for dealing successfully with the rough and tumble of corporate politics.

ASSESSING THE WORKPLACE

Effective coaches use the assessment to learn as much as they can about the impact of the workplace on the coachee. Here are some factors you will want to explore.

* The well-being of the organization, both strategically and fiscally, can have a huge impact on the confidence and morale of its people. That is why it can be useful to ask for an executive summary of the auditor's report.
* Within the organization and in its relationships with other organizations, you will want to know about any corporate changes that may affect the coachee.
* Cultural attitudes are crucial. Look for ingrained prejudices against women (or, in rarer instances, against men), people of various gender orientations, cultural minorities, the disabled, people who perform certain kinds of work (labourers, for instance), and against those in management positions who lack higher education.
* Examine the relationships among people, attitudes up and down the ranks, and the impact of union or non-union status.
* Assess the impact of the physical environment as a whole, as well as the coachee's work location.

Depending on rank, there may be few factors in the workplace environment that the coachee has the power to reverse single-handedly. But in some cases the coach may be invited to provide feedback about these issues to the leadership, and then the benefits of this aspect of assessment may ripple out to others.

It is always valuable to the coachee when the coach understands the impact of the work environment and helps to develop strategies to deal with any aspects that hurt her.

LOCATION, LOCATION, LOCATION

When a coachee moved recently from the windowless basement of his building to a floor with a view, his energy and enthusiasm for his work lifted at once. In half a day, he became more productive.

Organizations cannot give everyone a window, but a coach can sometimes nudge executives into seeking out low-cost ways to improve the atmosphere for those who work without windows or other physical amenities.

Assessment Step 4: Develop a Working Hypothesis

The value of an assessment is not in the assembly of a pile of raw facts, for facts are essentially passive. Its power is that the coach and coachee can sift through those facts together, discovering the patterns and connections between them. This is like the work of a detective who begins with many unrelated bits of information, jettisons some as irrelevant, and assembles the rest to reach conclusions about motive, method, and perpetrator. In the coaching assessment, we are searching for a set of conclusions that is greater than the sum of the facts. These conclusions form the basis of our working hypothesis.

The singular term "hypothesis" may be misleading, implying only one conclusion, but as a coach, you are likely to reach dozens of conclusions, some major and some minor. You may use one conclusion as the centre of your work in a particular session, and the next day you will be following up some other lead. It is a rich and complex process, and you will be grateful that you kept notes every session so that you can recall all the gems you uncover.

A warning: it is crucial for the coach not to assume ownership of the assessment. Its results are the property of the coachee. They identify her strengths and weaknesses, her relationship with the corporate culture, and her potential for growth. As you will see from the example below, the coach has a responsibility to oversee and maintain their database, but the process is always a collaboration with the coachee.

PATTERNS AND CONNECTIONS—THE WORKING HYPOTHESIS

A working hypothesis is always tentative. The word "hypothesis" suggests an unproven theory used as the basis for further investigation. In other words, a best guess. It is a "working" hypothesis because we use it not for contemplation, but as the spur to further investigation. This commitment to active learning is at the heart of coaching.

Assessment Step 5: Share the Result

The collaborative nature of assessment, as well as its unpredictable nature, is exemplified in the following dialogue, which occurred after a handful of assessment interviews.

POOLING DISCOVERIES

Coach: So, Jodi, I've asked a lot of questions and you've worked hard at coming up with answers. What's it been like?

Jodi: I guess I was surprised that you needed so much information. It was hard work sometimes, figuring out the answers.

Coach: I could see that. It often is. But as we move on with the coaching, I think you will get a lot back from it.

Jodi: So tell me what you've found out.

Coach: Actually, I was going to ask you the same question!

Jodi: How's that?

Coach: What I mean is that this is a time to pool what we've discovered and come to some conclusions together. The point here is not for me to have a theory about you, but for you to use the questions I asked to get a better picture of yourself, and to see yourself from another angle.

Jodi: That sounds pretty good. So how do we do that?

Coach: Would you be willing to start by talking about what you've learned about yourself?

Jodi: Okay. Let's see. First of all, I never guessed that the way I was raised had anything to do with what's happening at the office. That was stunning.

Coach: How do you see that now?

Jodi: Well, I'm starting to realize that just below the surface, I'm near the boiling point pretty often. So it doesn't take a lot to start me off.

Coach: That sounds right. Anything else?

Jodi: I can sort of see that I don't really know what other people are feeling. It's a bit foggy.

Coach: I think that as we get into the Development Phase, you'll have a chance to experiment with that. The fog factor will shrink.

Jodi: I hope.

Coach: In fact, I'd be willing to bet you have more empathy for other folks than you're aware of. After all, you have plenty in common: they've suffered and you've suffered. We can work on making the connection. Now, is there anything else you've learned about yourself?

(Later)

Coach: ....Okay, now let's see what we've learned about the people who work for you. Some of them seem like they're easy to relate to, and others have some problems.

Jodi: That's for sure. And those are the ones who are complaining.

Coach: It seemed to me that the people who are complaining about you include some who are pretty edgy, and some who are just not performing. Is that right?

Jodi: Yes, although to be honest, I'm not sure if the edgy ones started that way, or if they're like that because of all the tension we've had in the office.

Coach: That's a helpful comment, because I think you're on to something. And I have a feeling that if you can do something to cool down the atmosphere at work, both groups will become less upset and more productive.

Jodi: But that depends on them.

Coach: Maybe partly, but I'm not so sure. It's true that every relationship is a two-way street. But it's not going to be helpful to shift the responsibility for what's been happening from your shoulders.

Jodi: What do you mean?

Coach: Just that you can't control how other people react, but you do have control over your own behaviour. If you treat these people well, and after a period of time they are still hostile, then we should talk about them.

Jodi: Gotcha.

Coach: By the way, I was wondering what you thought when I told you about my interview with your assistant, Tom. For instance, when I said I was impressed with his intelligence and the adventuresome things that he does on the weekends?

Jodi: Because I told you earlier that he's a drone?

Coach: Right.

Jodi: Well, I'm confused. I don't see much contribution coming from him at work. And that's what counts, correct?

Coach: You're right. And it's possible that he's wearing himself out on the weekends, so there's nothing left by Monday morning. But I still wonder, is that all there is?

Jodi: You mean, he might be holding back at the office because of the atmosphere?

Coach: Possibly. In a week or two, you might try an experiment with Tom. Take a different approach and see if he comes through.

Jodi: I don't know about that.

Coach: I'm not pushing that right now. Why don't we talk about it later? Maybe make a plan then if you want to?

Jodi: Okay.

Coach: Now here's something else I want you to think about with me. You know that 360-degree feedback project we did...

(Later)

Coach: ....So do you feel like we've finished gathering and sorting most of our data?

Jodi: I think so. Whew! It's a lot. I'm not sure I can remember it all.

Coach: It's my job to help you remember bits of it as you need them.

Jodi: Good. So what's next?

Coach: We're going to turn now to the Developmental Phase of the coaching. The assessment took us a few meetings. But the developmental work is the major part of coaching. It's where you can integrate these insights into your life. It's what we'll be doing until we're ready to finish.

Jodi: So what do I need to do to prepare?

Coach: Nothing at this point. Just let your mind roam around the things we've been talking about. We will get into homework later, but next time we meet, it would be great just to hear what you have been thinking about our discussion today. Sound okay?

Jodi: Sure, fine. See you then.

Assessment Interacts with the Development Phase

As a formal division of the coaching process, the Assessment Phase concludes, and the coachee's attention turns to development and integration of new behaviour. But while assessment as a distinct phase may conclude, as a process it continues to thread its way throughout the Development and Integration Phase until coach and coachee say their goodbyes.

And at every developmental moment, insights from assessment provide support and drive for the coachee's progress. (See Chapter Eight.)

The formal aspect of the assessment has one significant drawback that falls near the beginning of the relationship and is unavoidable, yet part of its very nature. With trust and self-awareness just beginning to grow at this point, it cannot be expected that every piece of information gained will be entirely accurate or useful, or that every detail that needs to be tabled will be provided. That is why assessment is always tentative, never complete, until the coaching is complete.

Controversy: Assessment Versus Judgment

Despite the opinions expressed here so far, it would not be correct to suggest that there is universal acceptance of assessment by coaches. In fact, some say that the idea of conducting an assessment makes them queasy. They worry that it smacks of superiority or judgment. In their minds, assessment is identified with the psychiatrist diagnosing mental illnesses, the corporate head-hunter weeding out inadequate candidates, or even like St. Peter controlling access to the Pearly Gates. Coaching they believe in; assessment they want no part of.

Many daily events constitute assessments. While it is possible to conduct them from a superior, critical perspective, that is not how most people who strive for professionalism regard their assessment work. They see it as the respectful interaction of one human being who has certain responsibilities with another. In fact, they are careful to ensure that their assessments yield information of value to the other person and with no direct benefit to themselves beyond the satisfaction of a job well done.

ASSESSMENT UNDEFINED

Each coach—no, make that each human being—conducts assessments daily, but usually without the label. For example,

- a child sits down at the breakfast table, and without thinking about it, loving parents look her over to be sure she's healthy and all in one piece
- the vice-principal sees a teenager alone in the hallway and inquires whether he's wandering because a teacher sent him to the office or because his migraine makes it hard to cope with the classroom
- the supervisor asks an employee a few questions to decide which of two assignments she will handle best
- the executive notes that a colleague seems distracted and asks if he's okay

---

More Controversy—Assessment and Risk

Another source of controversy regarding assessments is the question of risk to the coachee. Concerned critics worry about the danger of the coach making inaccurate judgments that could have a lasting harmful impact. We have all read of people who ended up wrongly confined to institutions for years on the basis of inadequate assessments conducted by trained professionals. So these critics ask on what basis a coach can decide whether or not an assessment is valid.

After all, the argument runs, the coach who makes an assessment may be untrained, naive, biased, simplistic, or mistaken. These critics note that our society does not allow even medical practitioners to diagnose ailments until they have had many years of intensive training and have passed their medical boards. Even then, there is always the risk of misdiagnosis.

The solution for coaches, we believe, is to differentiate assessment from the prevailing medical model of diagnosis, which too often keeps vital information safely clutched in the control of medical practitioners and out of the hands of the consumer.

We coaches need to deliberately redefine the meaning of assessment, to make it clear that we do not view it as a diagnostic activity carried out by the coach in his expert capacity, no matter how "professional" he may be. Here is the key point: *assessment is a collaborative process of discovery carried out in partnership by the coach and coachee.*

The success of coaching within the Deep Learning Process depends on our sharing with the coachee both the task of assessment and the information it uncovers. Any assessment to which the coachee does not agree is useless. The coach may, of course, carry his own private view of the coachee, but that is merely an opinion. The assessment is only valid, and should only be acted upon, when the coachee embraces it.

So the coach avoids following any conclusions he may have reached until he has had a full and free discussion with the coachee. While this is a matter of simple respect, it is also practical. It is not usually problematic for a doctor to decide on a treatment and pursue it—to dab or not to dab, to prescribe a drug or not. The patient is often a passive receiver of services.

But it is quite another issue to try to influence a coachee to make changes that she does not agree need to be made, using methods that she does not believe in. An assessment is only valuable when it provides a common sense direction for a coaching team that consists of two people.

No human interaction can ever be without risk. But respectful and mutual attention to the process of assessment minimizes the possibility of doing harm, because it relies not only on the perspective of the coach but also upon consultation with the person who knows the situation best—the coachee.

Addressing Serious Problems—the Coach as Guardian

The coach has one responsibility that cannot entirely be shared with the coachee: to assess whether there are deeper physical or psychological problems underlying the presenting issues. There is a special accountability required of professionals, and it is not erased by the fact that coaches choose to operate in a highly collaborative manner.

Of course, it is not our responsibility to diagnose that a person is suffering from clinical depression or hypoglycemia. But by accepting to work with a person in an intimate way, we undertake to be in a special guardianship position. Even if we are only temporary guardians, we can take a larger view, looking beyond the problems that initially defined our coaching assignment to see whether that individual is in some danger that no one else may be in a position to recognize.

It is important to take on this responsibility, because if such a danger exists, the coachee may be either unaware of it or may be concealing it from herself or others. Working closely with her, observing her intently, the coach may be the first to see critical issues that no one else has observed.

Fortunately, in most coaching situations, there is nothing of this nature to be found. But occasionally, the coach is able to steer the coachee toward physical or psychological healing.

Making Professional Referrals on the Basis of the Assessment

Once in a while an assessment will suggest that the coachee has a worrisome physical, mental, or relationship problem. Remember, in such cases your training as coach equips you not to diagnose but only to refer.

Often your first response to a suspicion that something is wrong will be to consult on a confidential basis with your supervisor, an experienced fellow coach, and/or a specialist in the area of concern. This will provide the opportunity to test your concern in the light of day.

If, after consultation, you remain concerned, then you will want to be explicit in explaining the nature of your concern to the coachee. If at that point the coachee is unwilling to consult with an appropriate professional, it may be your responsibility to press the point, explaining that your concerns are important for her and for those around her.

Coach: I understand that you don't think this issue is very important. And you may be right. But it would ease my mind considerably if you were to consult about it with someone who is more expert in that area than I am. I have a couple of names to offer, if that would be helpful.

Coachee: I just don't want to get caught up in the whole medical whirl.

Coach: I can imagine. That would be pretty upsetting. But in this situation, your health may be at stake. Or not. I'm simply not equipped to decide. But this is something that could have major implications for your family and co-workers, as well as for you. So I'm asking you to set up an appointment to check it out, and then we'll continue with the coaching. In the meantime, I'll be stay in touch with you to see how that's going.

In the rare situation where the coachee continues to refuse to consult with someone else about a troubling situation, you will want to consider whether you can continue to act as coach, for it may be impossible for the coaching to achieve the results promised. Your acquiescence in continuing to coach might suggest that the problems are either not serious or not treatable. Furthermore, on conclusion of the coaching relationship, others may infer that all problems have been taken care of.

A coach never wants to lose a client, but in the rare situation where you have to demonstrate integrity and professionalism in this way, it is better for the coachee, as well as good for your self-respect and reputation.

THE COACHEE WITH INTRACTABLE LIMITATIONS

Coaches are endlessly hopeful, and their encouragement can help coachees shift in ways never before expected. But in some cases, the assessment will reveal that the coachee is limited—physically, mentally, emotionally, relationally—in how much she can accomplish.

The coach must be cautious, then, in raising the coachee's expectations and adapt the coaching work to the scope of the coachee. This does not mean abandoning the hope of coaching, but refocusing on how the coachee's limitations can mesh with the task at hand.

The coach may also have to renegotiate the expectations of the coaching sponsors. This is a delicate task, since he does not want to give away confidential information.

Coach: When we first talked about undertaking this coaching assignment, there was something I missed. I didn't realize that the coachee might be limited in how much she can change. I'm not sure how aware you were....

Sponsor: Well, I guess we had our suspicions. So what have you found?

Coach: I'm not at liberty to talk about that, because of our agreement around confidentiality. But it sounds as though you are not too surprised about this.

Sponsor: Not really.

Coach: I wanted to stay current with you and revisit our contract in that light. In fact, I believe I can help the coachee improve her response to the requirements of her job through more realistic planning. So I'm still eager to continue. But I don't want to impose a change in direction on you. How does that stand with you?

Sponsor: Coaching still sounds useful. I'd like you to keep going. I don't think there's anything else to discuss.

Coach: Actually, there is one more thing. At some point, it might be helpful if I were to convene a meeting between the coachee, you, and her supervisor to explore whether some changes might be made in the workplace to help her to become more efficient. What would you think about that?

Sponsor: It sounds like a good idea. Having you there might help all of us think outside the box.

Coach: Great. Then I will get back to work with her, knowing that I have your support. I'll encourage her to request the meeting if and when the time is right.

PHYSICAL PROBLEMS UNDERLYING COACHING ISSUES

It is important to discover whether people having difficulties in the workplace are the victim of physical ailments and disabilities. Examples are insomnia, migraines, back aches, and other forms of chronic pain, vision problems, mobility problems, degenerative diseases, repetitive strain injuries, hypoglycemia, diabetes, anemia, and mononucleosis.

Problems that combine physical with psychological aspects include eating disorders and addictions to food, drink, gambling, sex, or computers. To uncover such problems, be sure to ask the coachee specifically about her health, her relationship with a doctor, her sleep patterns, weight loss/gain, her use of medication, and her eating, drinking, and smoking habits.

Throughout the assessment, follow up on any information pointing to physical problems. Such problems are not usually the sole cause of the presenting difficulties leading to coaching, but treatment can often make the other issues manageable. For instance, the person who is not eating well may appear outwardly normal but actually arrives at work each day undernourished, without the physical resources either to work consistently at a high level or to absorb changes in the workplace. Once she starts to eat better, she will have new energy to devote to resolving her performance problems. Although nutrition counselling may not be your expertise as a coach, knowing how to refer your client appropriately for diagnosis and treatment should be.

GENTLE HINTS

Often individuals are mentally torn about whether to inform the coach about certain problems.

They don't want to appear weak, fearing that something will go on their record, or worry that talking about it will give it even more power. So they touch on the problems indirectly; they drop a hint.

While a coachee may not recognize it consciously, she hopes that the coach—or someone—will pick up on what has been implied. Because when they feel the ship sinking, most people want to be rescued.

Psychological Problems Underlying Coaching Issues

A more common source of workplace difficulties is psychological problems. These problems may be the causes (or contributing causes) of the workplace issues that call for coaching, and as well, they may result from workplace issues. For instance, a person may feel depressed, with the result that she has little energy for her work. As a legitimate result, she feels badly about her performance and that leads to further depression. Breaking this kind of cycle can have a huge impact on well-being and productivity.

In cases like this, the coach can offer two distinct kinds of intervention:

1. Provide practical assistance to improve the coachee's performance.
2. Make a thoughtful referral to a professional who will help the coachee to deal directly with her emotional condition.

The majority of psychological problems the coach encounters are not profound. They are garden-variety difficulties that most people face at some time, like anxiety, depression, or relationship difficulties. Talking about them calmly and with a sense of hope is key to dealing with them effectively.

PROBING QUESTIONS

Coach: As we talk, I notice that you seem quite low. I've been wondering whether you might be experiencing some depression that is contributing to your problems at work. Would you mind if I ask some questions about that?

If the answer is affirmative, the coach might continue with questions.

Coach: Do you find it difficult to face work in the mornings? Do you feel hopeless about the possibility of making changes? Were you once a lot happier than you are these days? Is there anyone else in your family who has had problems like this?

Depending on the responses, he might offer gentle suggestions.

Coach: I'd like to suggest that you have a talk with a colleague of mine (or the person's family doctor, or someone at a certain clinic) and see whether there is more to this than I can help you with. I don't know exactly what's happening, but it does seem to me that it would be worthwhile for you to find out. And it might make a helpful contribution to our work.

When new information like this emerges from the physical and psychological aspects of the assessment, the coach is able to develop more realistic expectations about the coachee's progress. It is always valuable to know whether there are other factors restraining progress that cannot be changed, for instance, a hostile supervisor or a physical disability. Then the thoughtful coach can help the coachee to develop strategies to cope with the difficulty, without raising expectations beyond the probable.

PSYCHOPATHOLOGY

Unfortunately, there is another class of psychological problems that is generally not easy to treat or to adjust for. These come under the heading of psychopathology, referring to psychological disease or compulsion.

Occasionally an individual referred for coaching will be in the grip of such a pathology. This person will not be helped by coaching. In fact, coaching is sometimes risky in such a case, and often counterproductive, because rather than changing the person's orientation, it may actually teach her how to disguise her pathology under a more socially acceptable facade.

The most frequently encountered problem of this sort is sociopathy, and if we look at it here, it will help us to create a framework for dealing with other pathologies.

DESCRIPTION OF SOCIOPATHY

While most normal people are capable of cruel or self-centred behaviour, our actions are moderated from the outside—by our awareness of societal morality, demands, and laws—and from the inside by our natural empathy for other people.

But the sociopath does not make such humane mental connections.

Sociopathy can be confusing for the corporate coach, because the world of business often rewards people who are single-minded, ambitious, and self-involved. Such people may climb the ladder of success by standing on the fingers of those with whom they share the ladder, achieving very senior rank. They may even be widely admired for their achievements.

This does not mean that they would be clinically described as sociopathic individuals. They may have been ignoring their better instincts, yet are open to learning new ways of behaving, especially if they discover that their jobs are at risk. But a minority of these people may be truly sociopathic, and in such a case, a coach faces a very tricky situation.

The distinction between "normal" and pathological personalities is very difficult to delineate. For instance, the person referred to you may have been treating others in a cruel, detached manner. A firm diagnosis of this condition is far beyond your competence or responsibility. But an in-depth assessment can help a great deal. It provides a period for you to get to know the coachee, and if, by the time you conclude the assessment, you develop a sense that there is something wrong, something missing, even something you still cannot quite put your finger on, then you may be working with a pathological person.

The precise steps you should take in any particular case cannot be prescribed in a book. But this is definitely the time to enlarge the circle of people involved in this situation. Do so for your own legal protection and for the sake of treating the coachee in the best possible way.

- Your first move will probably be to consult with the person you have chosen to supervise your work, so that you can work out a plan of action appropriate to the circumstances.
- You may need to ask more pointed questions of the person who referred the coachee.
- You may also need to speak confidentially to a specialist in psychological disorders to check out your suspicions.
- If your suspicions grow stronger, you may even have to disqualify yourself from work-

ing with the coachee on the grounds that you are in deeper water than you are trained for. If so, however, it is urgent that you do everything you can to make certain that the coachee is not merely jettisoned, but has appropriate professional resources to provide support.

The Coach's Wider Vision and Professional Network

By this point you may be thinking, "This is a lot more complicated than anything I had in mind when I decided to practise coaching. I just want to help people." We can reassure you that severe situations are rare.

But it is crucial to develop a broad network of contacts, professionals, and experts. You will want to be prepared to consult occasionally about situations that are outside your expertise. That does not mean that you must have immediate contacts in every relevant field, but you will certainly want to know how to find them quickly.

1. Have one or more medical doctors you can ask about issues outside your training, or to whom you can refer for diagnosis.
2. Consult with one or two fine psychotherapists, plus an expert in relationship therapy, to whom you can refer without hesitation.
3. Know whom to turn to for information about Human Resources law and procedures, especially in areas that have to do with illness, discipline, and termination.
4. Consult with a social worker for advice, particularly if you learn about problems relating to children.

A good measure of your professionalism is that (1) you know when to turn to other professionals for advice and (2) that you can quickly use your network and other sources of information to find the right people for specific help or advice.

DISGUISED ILLNESS

A young woman complained that every once in a while she would feel a strong desire to act violently with the people around her at the office. Her coach asked a number of probing questions and discovered that the woman was a peaceful and gentle person who was shocked by her own impulses.

Without attempting to diagnose the physical condition of the young woman, the coach picked up enough information to suspect that she might be in grave danger. Rather than calling the police or a psychiatrist, he referred her to a physician, who suggested a day in hospital to be checked out for hypoglycemia, a condition in which the body is unable to maintain normal levels of blood sugar. There, the young woman was positively diagnosed and counselled on how to keep her blood sugar level healthy.

During her tests in the hospital, the doctor informed her that her blood sugar level had dipped to a level so low that people normally slide into unconsciousness and could die. She was unusual in that she had remained conscious and alert even while her body was literally fighting for its life. This instinct for physical survival was revealing itself in violent thought patterns that interfered with her peaceful nature.

But the solution was simple. Once she learned to keep her blood sugar levels stable, she no longer had the urge to fight with other people, and the need for coaching was at an end.

You cannot be expected to be up-to-date on every physical or psychological condition you might encounter. The key issue is to hone your instincts and pay attention to them, and whenever you are in doubt, to consult with your supervisor for guidance.

Rewards of Collaboration in Sleuthing

The process of developing a working hypothesis through assessment offers profound rewards. It allows two people the satisfaction of working together to create a whole that is greater than the partial understandings each of them might separately provide. Assessments turn up valuable and often unexpected information.

Best of all, an assessment does more than improve the prognosis during the period of coaching. It raises the likelihood of success at work for the coachee in the long term. And it leads the coachee to a more profound understanding of herself as a human being.

The ultimate treasure it can bestow is a life lived in full awareness, as opposed to a life so many people experience—buffeted by unseen interior forces.

FIGURE 6.1 EXERCISE: ASSESSING YOUR ASSESSMENTS

1. Review your notes from a recent coaching assignment and list all the areas in which you assessed the coachee, either in a formal Assessment Phase or during the Development and Integration Phase.

2. Answer these questions:
   - Did you miss anything early on?
   - What new information arose during the Development and Integration Phase?
   - At the end of the assessment, what did you communicate to the coachee about the results?
   - What did she or he have to tell you?
   - On a scale of one to ten, how accurate did the coachee consider your contribution to the assessment?
   - Were there any conclusions you decided to keep to yourself? What was your reasoning?
   - How would you do it differently next time?

Each practitioner conducts the Assessment Phase in a unique fashion appropriate to his skills and experience. Although this chapter has provided information about the basic requirements for assessment, coaches should be aware of additional tools that may help them to work more efficiently and to provide more options for the coachee.

An introduction to the use of instruments, including 360-degree feedback, and a sample outline for the assessment interview appear in the next chapter: Enriched Assessment.

This chapter introduces the in-depth assessment interview, the use of 360-degree feedback, and other valuable assessment instruments to assist the coach to conduct an effective assessment. A well-designed guide to the assessment interview provides further aid for the coach in exploring the life and times of the coachee in a thorough manner. Using a 360-degree feedback survey helps the coachee to gain a panoramic view of how he is viewed by those who know his work best. Other instruments are designed to focus on more specific but narrowly defined areas such as the coachee's relationships with his world, skill in leadership, conflict management, and other topics that may have been raised during the Contracting Phase.

Risks in Enriched Assessment

It is possible to perform a cursory assessment without using any of the tools described here, and although such an assessment may lack some depth, it carries less danger. There is a risk in using these instruments; the close inspection of the outer and inner life of the coachee could make him more vulnerable. Most people have had the experience of being blamed and shamed when they allowed someone else a close-up view of their lives. As a result, particularly in the organizational world, most people tend to be pretty cautious about self-revelation. There are three risks:

1. The questions asked might tend to be negative, creating an expectation of criticism and a response of defensiveness.
2. The coachee may become consciously aware of aspects of himself that he finds disturbing. The result may be increased anxiety, even the onset of despair.
3. The coach may find herself dealing with matters of personal psychosocial life for which she is unprepared. If she is clumsy in her use of the results, they could harm the coachee.

Limit Assessment to Your Level of Competency

For the above reasons, you should use these powerful instruments with great care. Be honest, and limit your use according to your ability to apply them.

Fortunately you will find there is a wealth of guidance available to you. Use the suggestions here as a starting point, then check the books and courses listed in the Resources section that provide detailed descriptions of assessment tools and point toward training opportunities.

And talk to the experts. You probably already know coaches and consultants who are experienced in their use. In addition, as you become familiar with these instruments, you will want to stay in close communication with your practice supervisor or fellow coaches.

Presenting the Use of Assessment Instruments to Coachees

Introduce the use of instruments to your coachee with gentleness and caution. Be sure you probe for any concerns he may have, so that he does not think you wish to use them because he is outside the boundary of normalcy.

Coach: ...so I'd like to use a test that measures the style in which you generally lead your people. How would you feel about that?

Coachee: Okay, I guess.

Coach: Do you have any hesitation?

Coachee: Not really. I suppose this is what you do with everyone, right?

Coach: I make a different choice with each person I work with. I choose specific instruments that are relevant to the particular individual. But you seem a little concerned.

Whenever the coach proposes heading in a direction that is new to the coachee, it is tempting to take the first sign of acceptance as agreement. But the result of this may be negative. The coachee is still carrying significant concerns, and may feel as if he has been talked into something he doesn't quite understand or agree with.

Here the coach pays attention to anxiety that is just below the surface, and persists in addressing it so that the coachee gets the information he needs and, if he decides to go ahead, will be more committed to the project.

Coachee: Well, the idea makes me nervous. Tell me again why you want to do this?

Coach: I'm looking for a way to shine some light on the issues you've said you're concerned about. For instance, you seem to understand your own personality pretty well, so I'm not going to suggest we do a personality test. But since you said you're having some difficulties in leadership, I believe that this test could help you understand yourself as a leader. It may suggest some changes that you'd like to make. How does that seem to you?

Coachee: I guess I feel a bit like a rat in a lab. You know, being tested for this and that.

A frequent concern for coachees is that they are losing control of their work life and their future. They worry about the coach unleashing forces that could destabilize them. The best response is to normalize both the reaction and the use of tests.

Coach: Lots of people feel that way when they first think about using tests or instruments. But there's a big difference here. You're running the lab. We'll explore only what you want to find out about.

Coachee: So you're not going to do anything unless I want it?

Coach: Absolutely.

Coachee: That's good. But I still don't really know what you're proposing. So tell me exactly how you use this instrument of yours.

We know our instruments, so we sometimes forget how new they are to the people to whom we introduce them. It is always best to provide plenty of information and to check whether more is needed.

Coach: It's not complicated. I'll give you a questionnaire to fill out. When you've finished, we'll score it, and the results will give us some information that we can talk about. If you then want to make changes in how you lead, we'll start planning new ideas for you to experiment with. Would you like me to say more about it?

Coachee: Not right now. I think it's okay.

Coach: But you said you were nervous before. Has that changed?

Coachee: It's better, but I'm still a little nervous.

Coach: Why don't you tell me about your worst fear?

Why introduce something as unsettling as a "worst fear"? Isn't this conversation sufficiently complicated? What if the coachee should decide that his worst fear is enough to deter him? Simply put—if it is, then it would be better not to go ahead.

If the coachee suggests or implies concerns that are not addressed and the test goes ahead, those concerns are likely to function as an invisible drag on the process. In fact, even if the coachee had responded off the top with, "Sounds good. Let's go," it would still be worth saying, "Most people have some concerns about tests, so would you like to tell me about any that you have?"

Coachee: My worst. Hmm. Let me put it this way. What if you tell me I'm a terrible leader and I shouldn't be in my job?

Coach: I see what you mean. That would be pretty devastating. But I won't do that for a couple of reasons. In the first place, it's not up to me to judge your suitability. You are better equipped to decide that, and you can use the test to provide some of the information you need.

Coachee: So what if I decide by myself that I'm so bad I should quit?

Coach: I can't deny that's a possibility. It's the sort of risk that goes with knowing more about yourself than you once did. The results of any self-exploration can be unsettling. But even in those few cases where coaching has contributed to people quitting their jobs, they've felt in retrospect that they made a good decision. They are generally happy about it.

Coachee: Well, I don't think I'd be happy about quitting.

Coach: I understand that, and honestly, I don't believe there is much likelihood of that happening.

Coachee: So what's the second reason you mentioned?

Coach: I think it is very unlikely that you are a terrible leader. Most people have areas of strength and areas needing change. My job is to help you to build on your strengths and make changes where you need to. I'm used to doing that.

Coachee: So how many people use these instruments?

Coach: Thousands. In some cases, millions. They have been used for many years, and most of the bugs have been shaken out of them.

Coachee: Okay. Let's do the leadership test.

That discussion provides a model for informed consent. But it is even more significant than that. Standing as it does near the beginning of the coaching engagement, it also sets the tone for the work. First, it makes it clear that, although the coach may be enthusiastic about taking particular directions, she will not pressure the coachee. Second, it offers permission to the coachee to raise concerns at any point. Third, it establishes the coach's respect for the coachee as a partner in the coaching. And fourth, in general it establishes the collaborative quality of the relationship between coach and coachee.

Using Appreciative Inquiry

Appreciative inquiry is a growing movement in consulting and coaching that looks for success, strength, and potential in individuals and organizations, as a balance to the negative, failure-focused standards of the past century. (After all, it is easy in problem-dominated organizations to focus on breakdowns in procedure and productivity.)

Permitting a negative approach to dominate is to create a myth that fosters fear and depression. By contrast, appreciative inquiry evokes memories of strengths, inventiveness, and successes—motivating people to work creatively toward a positive future.

As coaches, we help our coachees create empowering myths for themselves whenever we ask unconditionally positive questions. For that reason, we should examine both formal instruments, and our day-to-day conversation to make certain that appreciative forms of inquiry dominate. (For more about appreciative inquiry, see *Organization Development Journal* in Resources.)

The Guided Interview for In-Depth Assessment

The key ingredient of each assessment that we conduct is a guided interview—a detailed discussion about the person with whom we are about to work. Presented in outline below, this interview has been designed to cover most of the bases that will require attention if we are to truly understand the coachee. It also encourages the coachee to begin thinking about areas that may have been hidden until now.

As you examine what follows, remember that it describes a guide and not a master. The coach should control the outline, not the reverse. That means, for instance, that you are unlikely to ask every single question on your guide in any given coaching engagement. There are always some questions that are not relevant to the person you are coaching.

Furthermore, it is not unusual to skip from the beginning to the end and then backwards to the middle, or to take some even more complicated dance through the guide. From time to time, you will need to discuss and take notes on important topics not appearing on the guide at all, but that may arise spontaneously during the interview.

FIGURE 7.1 OUTLINE FOR GUIDED INTERVIEW

1. Coordinates
- All relevant contact information
- Occupation and role
- Relevant organizational relationship chart (may be presented visually as box with the heading "Organization Chart." Ask the coachee to place his name in the centre and then add those who have an impact on him and those on whom he impacts.)

2. Context for Coaching
- Person who made the referral
- Information provided by referrer
- Whether coaching was mandated or voluntary
- Presenting issue: what situation or triggering event led to the coaching contract?
- Objectives for change as seen by the individual and the organization. (These may be different.)
- Gap between present reality and objectives
- Factors blocking change, internal and external
- How will we know we have succeeded?
- Coach's initial impressions (trust your instincts enough to commit them to paper, then decide over time whether they were accurate)

3. Workplace Issues
- Any recent changes in the workplace and how they affect the coachee
- Quality of work relationships: with supervisor(s), peers, internal and external customers, direct and indirect reports, others
- How the coachee "fits in" with the organization
- Performance appraisals and other forms of available feedback. (Ask coachee to provide copies or to authorize HR to provide them.)
- Employment history
- Has the presenting issue ever shown up in other workplaces?

4. Values and Value Conflicts
It is useful to create two columns in this section, one for the coachee's values and the other for values of the organization. Note especially any areas where the values are in conflict. Not all of these topics will be relevant to the particular coaching situation; be sure to cover those that are.
- Leadership
- Productivity
- Hard work
- Use of time
- Compensation
- Relationships
- Family
- Commitment

(continued)

FIGURE 7.1 **CONTINUED**

- Sexuality
- Empathy
- Loyalty
- Consultation

5. The Coachee and the Workplace

- What rewards does the coachee get from work, and how does it meet his or her values?
- Coachee's personal strengths and abilities as seen by the coachee and by the organization
- Coachee's perspective on leadership
- Outside of work, three values that are most important to the coachee

6. Relevant Personal Information

You may not wish to collect all the information listed below, but be aware that any of these topics may present unexpected leverage for change.

- Education
- Birth date, place
- Areas where the coachee lived prior to the present home
- Parents, siblings
- Current partner, children
- Relationship history
- Social/cultural identity
- Activities outside the workplace and home
- Peak experiences in the coachee's life

7. Health History

It may be risky to collect information about the use of illegal substances, even though they could have a direct impact on the workplace and on the coaching. Your knowledge and any notes you make could place you in a position of legal obligation to break confidentiality. We can offer no ready solutions to this dilemma. Consult with others in your jurisdiction to discover the most satisfactory way to deal with this.

- State of health
- Relevant medical history (significant changes, sleep, weight, surgery)
- Relationship with family doctor
- Medication (including contraception) and any known impact on the coachee
- Use of alcohol
- Use of cigarettes

8. Assessment Homework

These tasks may be assigned early in the coaching.

- Write your life story in under two pages
- Keep a diary of a day in your work life

(continued)

FIGURE 7.1 CONTINUED

- Write notes on how others in the workplace see you. How do you see yourself?
- Bring to the next interview any additional documentation that we should look at together

9. Preparing for Successful Coaching
- What will enable the coaching process to succeed?
- What can we do to make sure that success factors are in place?
- What might make the coaching process fail?
- What can we do about those factors?
- Do you have any items of "unfinished business" (secrets, unresolved relationships, legal problems, other difficulties still in process) inside or outside your business life? How could they hold you back in your development process? How could you deal with these situations?

10. Previous and Future Coaching Resources
- Past experiences with coaching, training, counselling, psychotherapy
- Which instruments might be useful to deepen the assessment?
  Use a check box here to guide your use of assessment tools.
  - ❐ 360-degree Feedback
  - ❐ Myerpe Indicator
  - ❐ Leadership IQ
  - ❐ Leadership skills
  - ❐ Negotiation styles
  - ❐ Conflict management
  - ❐ Other tools with which you are familiar

11. Selecting Activities for the Development and Integration Phase
This check box section is a menu from which you and the coachee can choose items for the third and major phase of the coaching engagement. It does not limit the possibilities that may emerge in weeks to come, but it provides an immediate sense of structure.
  - ❐ Interpretation of instruments used in assessment
  - ❐ Further in-depth interviewing
  - ❐ Guidance in self-understanding, discovery of unconscious motivation for behaviours
  - ❐ Teaching components customized to coachee's needs
  - ❐ Analysis of actual events in coachee's daily work life
  - ❐ Action-planning for the workplace, experiments followed by evaluation
  - ❐ Simulation of real-life events
  - ❐ Video recording and playback
  - ❐ Written exercises
  - ❐ Selected reading materials from bibliography
  - ❐ Shadowing in the workplace
  - ❐ Facilitation by coach of meetings with co-workers

Using the Guided Interview

The above outline covers a lot of ground, and you may wonder whether it is valuable to devote so much time to gathering information. While we operate at the more exhaustive end of the scale, for other coaches less information is sufficient. They may, for instance, be dealing with less difficult issues, or they may be constrained by a culture that defines personal information as irrelevant to the workplace.

It generally requires two or more interviews to complete a guided interview of this length, but it is time well spent. You will get to know the coachee in a way that deepens and strengthens your work, and the coachee will become more prepared for an effective coaching relationship.

With a guide as full as this, there are many choice points along the way, and with each question, you can make a decision whether to ask for more details, ask the next question, or give it a pass.

Finally, for those coaches who would not be comfortable or skillful talking about some of the personal issues listed above, we suggest that they avoid them. That way they will responsibly maintain their work within the range of their capabilities, and the coachee will be protected from clumsy use of such information. If you feel unready to approach intimate personal issues, you are probably right not to.

If the coaching situation is an emergency, you may wish to gather only the few most essential details before setting to work on the Development and Integration Phase. Once the emergency has eased, it is usually not difficult to return to the assessment interview.

If you are intrigued by the possibility of going deeper than you currently feel able to, do avail yourself of training and development of the kind described in Chapter Three, The Person of the Workplace Coach.

The 360-Degree Feedback Assessment

The most exciting development to enrich the world of coaching is probably 360-degree feedback. While the perspective of the coachee and his supervisor has often limited traditional coaching, 360-degree feedback broadens the canvas, because it provides information from many directions. If you picture the individual being assessed as holding a compass, that person's peers are responding to the survey from 90 degrees, the direct reports from 180 degrees, internal customers from 270 degrees, and the supervisor(s) from 360 degrees. It expands the very private coaching relationship into a wider and more realistic forum, providing frank evaluation by direct reports, peers, and others.

The result is new motivation and direction for the coachee, and the coaching can move toward its goals more quickly and with greater precision.

The General Value of Feedback

Before we look more closely at 360-degree feedback, let's understand feedback in general. For most people, "feedback" refers to the squeal you hear when a live microphone is placed in front of a speaker. Tiny sounds are magnified to the point where you cannot ignore them.

Interpersonal feedback is similar. Things people might say about you so quietly that you don't hear them are made so clear that you cannot ignore them. You end up with new knowledge about yourself. Additionally, things you have always known and accepted about yourself often appear in a new light.

Feedback has always been part of the workplace, generally with the emphasis on critical feedback. Someone described this aptly as "feedback between the eyes." Everyone is familiar with supervisory appraisals that contain no positive guidance and situations where peers will "freeze out" a fellow employee.

Recently, however, there has been greater recognition of the cost of careless, unbalanced feedback. We now know that performance can suffer as a result, commitment to the employer may waver, and the system may harm itself by handing out rewards to the wrong people (typically those with the right political connections and the wrong work ethic), while ignoring others less well connected.

The good news is that properly designed feedback mechanisms encourage our coachees. The expertise that has been developed in the use of 360-degree feedback has resulted in an excellent body of knowledge for effective use. Good feedback tells individuals where they are doing well, and points out where they could improve. So it provides a reliable road map to added value. As coaches, we often watch people respond with surprising eagerness to information that helps them see themselves, sometimes for the first time, as others see them.

People may express an initial fear of being assessed by their co-workers. But once they have actually experienced it, many say they prefer to be assessed by a group whose members see their performance from a variety of perspectives, rather than from the limited perspective of their supervisor.

They see 360-degree feedback as more accurate and fair than that derived from only one perspective. In one survey, a massive majority of workers said they most valued feedback that came from both supervisor and co-workers. Only a small percentage said they preferred to receive feedback from one or the other.

FEEDBACK ABOUT THE COACHING

Feedback is also valuable to coaches. Useful questions for opening the door include, "How are these sessions working for you?" and "Is there anything you'd like us to do differently?" By modelling openness, you help the client to see the value of feedback. Sometimes what looks like feedback for the coach can turn out to be information about the coachee. The way one coach described such a situation is shown below.

While working with a coachee, the coach often felt that he was angry with her. She asked him how he was feeling at the moment, but he said he didn't know (as people often don't).

So she asked the coachee if he would like to know what she was experiencing. When he replied yes, she gently and compassionately told him that she felt that he was angry with her.

She told him what the clues were (sighs, rolling of eyes) and he was shocked. What emerged was that he was extremely frustrated with himself and his "imperfection."

This alone was important information, but even more powerful was his recognition that his frustration with himself was leading to behaviours that others might interpret as anger toward them.

Since this coachee was someone of whom the staff was generally afraid, the discussion helped him to recognize immediate changes he could make that would pay off at the office.

FEEDBACK PHRASES

When you offer personal feedback to your coachee, it is crucial to be both kind and direct. Here are some examples:

- Can I offer you some feedback?
- I noticed that you set yourself a goal, but what you are actually doing is different. Have you noticed this, and what does it mean to you?
- You've climbed a mountain that originally you seemed to think was insurmountable. Yet it seemed like it actually turned out to be pretty easy for you.
- You've said you're going to do that before on a few occasions. Yet you haven't done it. I expect there is a very good reason for this that we haven't discussed, so I wonder if you would you like to talk about that.
- Do we need to revisit your goals for coaching?
- Does this happen in other settings?
- Have you ever received feedback about this before?
- Although that was a pretty intimidating task you undertook, you pulled it off successfully. I've been noticing that when you put your mind to something, you can do it.
- I'm getting the impression that you are uncomfortable being here. Would you be willing to talk to me about that?

Why 360-Degree Feedback Shines

There are many kinds of assessment instruments available, but most of them share the flaw that they ask the coachee to describe himself from his own limited perspective. That, of course, does not convey the whole picture. It is just human nature that when we are asked to reveal ourselves, we run all our responses through a filter.

What emerges from the filter is usually whatever the coachee believes is relevant and safe. So when we ask him to complete a questionnaire, he is likely to alternate between answers that accurately describe his behaviour and beliefs, and answers that he perceives to be "correct" or "acceptable," or that describe how he would like to see himself. As a result, both coach and coachee find themselves working with only part of the information they need to generate change.

Here is where the 360-degree feedback survey shines, providing information with wide horizons. In this context it is important that the coachee also completes the survey, so that he has a standard to compare with the responses of others.

DISCLOSURE: 360-DEGREE FEEDBACK IS OUR BUSINESS

It started with the desire for coaching excellence. Our enthusiasm for 360-degree feedback began when we found it to be a highly motivating aid to navigation for our coaching clients. But because we hated the paperwork, we invented an automated, Web-based tool —one of the first 360-degree instruments available on the Internet: *Panoramic Feedback.*

GAINING OBJECTIVITY

Accurate feedback is rarely what leaders get. People tell them what they think they want to hear, rather than what they need to hear. That's politics. But because multi-source feedback comes anonymously, it provides executives with exactly what they need—the straight goods. It helps them to assess their effectiveness through the eyes of those who know them best—their colleagues and reports. And as an adjunct to a carefully designed coaching program, it can provide powerful motivation for self-development.

A vice-president asked Simon, one of his directors, to meet with a coach. The reason: although much of Simon's technical work was excellent, his people skills were not at the same level.

Up to that point, Simon had remained utterly unaware of any significant problems. He agreed to see a coach to please his supervisor, rather than because he saw the process as creating real value. "I know I'm not a perfect boss," he told the coach in an early visit, "but I communicate pretty well with my people and I think they like working for me."

In theory, he said, he was more than willing to make changes. But to be utterly frank, he was baffled and skeptical about the concerns his supervisor was expressing.

The coach recommended 360-degree feedback as a research tool to provide them with more information. So with the agreement of his vice-president, Simon asked several staff members and colleagues to complete a survey.

Within days, a paperless questionnaire about his leadership was available to them, via a special Internet site. They found it quick and easy to fill out, and some chose to complete it after hours from the privacy of their home computers.

As well as answering questions that evaluated Simon's competencies, they were generous with unstructured narrative comments. (As you would expect, computer-based feedback systems provide many more of these valuable comments than the old hand-written forms.)

It took only a week to get all the replies in, and Simon saw the results the next day.

He was stunned to read the anonymous comments of those who knew his work style best. They described him as technically brilliant and inventive. They also said he was frequently uncaring, self-involved, and hurtful.

A set of charts based on the organization's Core Competencies reinforced those perceptions. Responders rated Simon high on capability, intelligence, and strategic planning, but low on communication, team building, and self-knowledge.

This unexpected response initially shocked him. But Simon was an effective and confident executive, and resilience was one of the qualities that made him a success. He moved quickly from self-pity to a passionate commitment to improve his leadership abilities.

Thanks to 360-degree feedback, he really did get it. Within a few weeks, it was clear to everyone in the department that Simon was showing himself to be more appreciative and communicative. Productivity increased as people spent less time nursing hurt feelings and recovering from bruising encounters. These changes did wonders for Simon's credibility and had a positive impact on that of the management team as a whole.

Introducing 360-Degree Feedback Instruments

A 360-degree feedback instrument is essentially a questionnaire to which typically eight or more people respond. The questionnaire asks whether, in the view of each responder, the behaviour of the person being assessed corresponds with the core competencies required for his or her job. Typically those core competencies provide the headings that guide the responder through the questionnaire.

On average, there are five to ten headings, and under each of them several behaviour descriptions, usually totalling twenty-five to thirty-five, in order to keep the survey to a manageable length.

Responders are asked to note to what extent they agree that the person being assessed behaves in the ways described, marking their responses on a scale. Some systems allow you to choose the length of scale you prefer.

FIGURE 7.2 EXAMPLES FROM 360-DEGREE INSTRUMENTS

1. Example of a ten-point scale

Strongly Disagree		Disagree			Agree			Strongly Agree	
1	2	3	4	5	6	7	8	9	10

2. Example of Core Competencies from a 360-Degree Feedback Survey
- BUSINESS SKILLS AND EXPERIENCE
- PROFESSIONAL AND TECHNICAL KNOWLEDGE
- DEPARTMENTAL REQUIREMENTS
- ENTREPRENEURSHIP
- DECISION-MAKING
- CUSTOMER ORIENTATION
- TEAMWORK AND LEADERSHIP
- COMMUNICATION
- DEVELOPMENT POTENTIAL
- INTEGRITY

3. Example of Behaviour Descriptions from a 360-Degree Feedback Survey
Core competency: BUSINESS SKILLS AND EXPERIENCE
Behavioural descriptions:
- Understands the business requirements and financial policies of the organization
- Formulates strategic goals and objectives
- Is proactive, responding to opportunities, solving problems, planning for action
- Makes wise tactical decisions and sticks with them
- Puts in extra effort as required to attain objectives

UNSTRUCTURED COMMENTS ENRICH THE FEEDBACK
In a 360-degree feedback survey, there is usually space for unstructured comments from the responder. Comment boxes may follow each set of behaviour descriptions and appear at the end of the questionnaire, as well. These spontaneous comments are generally a rich source of insight.

Once everyone has responded, results are compiled and presented (with great care and in a carefully anonymous way) to the coachee in report form. A good 360-degree feedback service can provide reports immediately, allowing maximum impact.

Exploring the report directly will usually require at least two coaching sessions. But throughout the remainder of the coaching engagement, the survey will provide a deep well of material from which the coach and coachee may draw.

Designing and Developing the 360-Degree Feedback Process

You can design a 360-degree feedback survey using paper responses, but many coaches find the process of collating the responses time-consuming and subject to errors and confusion. As comprehensive as any 360-degree instrument may be, its contribution to development is only as good as the preparation of the organization and its people, and that is your job. Here's a list of the most crucial issues to attend to:

1. DEVELOPMENTAL STRATEGY
Wherever possible, 360-degree feedback should be integrated into the organization's strategy for leadership development, not deployed in isolation. Otherwise the coachee may find himself more isolated. Consider these factors:

* Are opinion leaders convinced of the business benefits of leadership development and the cost of not making changes?
* Is there a commitment to being a learning organization?
* Are supports in place, such as coaching, mentoring, training?

2. CULTURAL READINESS
Before you start a 360-degree feedback program, make sure fertile ground is prepared for feedback.

* Does the culture currently support honest feedback provided informally?
* Are employees likely to believe you when you say it's safe to be frank?
* Are leaders aware that 360-degree feedback may result in initial instability by revealing unexpected requirements for change in culture or procedures?
* Multi-source feedback encourages openness and raises expectations, leading people to believe that the organization values continuous learning and honesty

3. ENCOURAGING BUY-IN AND COMMITMENT
* If possible, have the competency list developed by a representative group.
* Be clear about who will and will not have access to reports.
* Help the coachee to select the most valuable responders.
* Provide a brief training opportunity for responders, assuring them of their safety and anonymity, suggesting how to provide feedback so it can be "heard" by the coachee.
* Design the survey around observable behaviours and performance, rather than values or opinions. Because it focuses on specific observable behaviour, the survey assists subjects to buy in to the process.

4. PRESENTING REPORTS

Receiving their reports is a time of high vulnerability for people being assessed. Reading the results in isolation can demotivate and discourage, even if most people say the coachee is doing a terrific job. So make sure good supports are available.

* Hand over all reports to the coachee in person.
* Reports are crammed with information, so provide graduated help in comprehension.
* Help the coachee focus on compliments, not just critiques.
* Provide assistance and encouragement in action-planning; some systems provide workbooks for recipients of feedback.

Using Other Instruments for Coaching

Once the coach has developed her own interview guide and is familiar with 360-degree feedback, she possesses the most useful tools to conduct coaching at a deep level. These quickly become as essential as a hammer and saw to a carpenter.

There are, however, a number of other instruments (the chisels and pliers) that can enable her to assess the coachee's skills in areas where he shows specific needs. Each instrument provides its own framework, a useful and specialized vocabulary, and a set of measurements. Each assists the coaching team to work with precision and clarity in particular areas.

The Differences Between 360-Degree Feedback and Other Instruments

The strength of 360-degree feedback is that the standards are local and relative. There are literally tens of thousands of 360-degree surveys, each differing from the other, each reflecting the needs of a particular workplace.

These "360s" have a local reference, meaning that they do not measure the person being assessed against the world, but only against the expectations of those with whom he or she works. The best 360-degree instruments make no pretence to universality, no claims that certain scores are normative. The challenge they present is to be or to become the best you can in the situation you find yourself in.

In fact, 360-degree feedback can be dangerous if it claims to be based on normative standards, or if coachees are told, in effect, "You should score seven on this question to be considered acceptable." Such an approach will result in discouragement. So it is intriguing that the strength of most other coaching instruments is that they have the opposite quality. They rely, in fact, on time-tested standard questionnaires. They compare or correlate the individual to literally hundreds of thousands of other people.

The *Myers-Briggs Type Indicator,* for instance, will tell you that you share your personal characteristics with one or six or fifteen percent of the population. The *Leadself Test* will describe the circumstances in which you are an effective leader. The *Thomas-Kilmann Conflict Mode Instrument* assigns you to one of five universal conflict management styles. The *Negotiating Style Profile* relates you to one of five universal negotiating styles.

Because these are standardized tests, the authors have carefully written them to minimize negative comparisons, reducing the possibility of their being used in a discouraging, comparative way, while highlighting the strengths of each type or style.

Selecting Instruments for Coaching

With the exception of the first instrument, which is described below, shorter tends to be better. When a questionnaire has a highly focused topic, like conflict or leadership skills, less than fifty questions can usually provide enough data to assess the coachee. Needless to say, the shorter the test, the greater the likelihood that the coachee will complete it without delay.

So let us examine a handful of standard instruments that provide valuable guidance in precisely delineated areas. In some cases, only coaches who have taken specific training can employ them.

1. The Myers-Briggs Type Indicator

The "Myers-Briggs," as it is called, is a fine all-round tool for helping individuals develop greater self-understanding. It enables them to see themselves within a simple psychological framework. At the same time it is sufficiently complex that it can describe accurately the many combinations and permutations of people's thinking.

It is based on the century-old typology theory of Carl Jung, which provides a structure for understanding similarities and differences among people. It was developed by Isabel Myers and her mother Katharine C. Briggs in the middle of the twentieth century. Since then, it has undergone intensive research, is widely used, and has endured the compliment of being copied and adapted. It measures the preferences of the coachee, that is,

- where they like to focus their attention
- how they like to take in information
- how they like to make decisions
- the way they orient themselves to the outside world

The Myers-Briggs Categories

- *Extroversion/Introversion*
  Where you focus, get, and give energy:
  E – focuses on the outer world of people and things.
  I – focuses on the inner world of ideas and impressions.

- *Sensing/iNtuiting*
  How you perceive or observe:
  S – is a focus on the present, on information gained from the senses ("concrete" information).
  N – is a focus on the future, on patterns and possibilities.

- *Thinking/Feeling*
  How you judge and make decisions:

T – uses logic and objective analysis of cause and effect.
F – uses values and subjective evaluation of person-centred concern.

* *Judging/Perceiving*
  Attitude in the outer world
  J – is planned and organized.
  P – is flexible and spontaneous.

USES OF MYERS-BRIGGS

The Myers-Briggs is valuable in a variety of situations.

* In leadership development: helping leaders to understand themselves and others, and to develop skills and behaviours enabling them to be effective with different types of followers
* In team development: helping work groups to better understand one another, to appreciate their differences, as well as their similarities, to manage conflict and decision-making, and to solve group problems
* In coaching with difficult individuals: helping them to gain greater self-awareness and to develop in areas needed to cope with their problems
* In career counselling: guiding individuals in their choice of occupations and work settings, and examining the "fit" between their personality type and their work setting and role
* In training: developing different teaching styles, curricula, methods, media, and materials to meet the needs of different learner types

2. Situational Leadership

Situational Leadership—developed by Paul Hersey and Kenneth Blanchard (1977), then adapted by Professor Marilyn Laiken to incorporate the group development theory of Bruce Tuckman (1977)—provides a practical perspective on team leadership. Professor Laiken's integrative model demonstrates how the leaders' style must be constantly adapted to the skills and commitment levels of the people they wish to lead. (See Resources.)

Rather than proposing a single set of competencies that leaders should possess, Situational Leadership recognizes that there are stages in the development of every working group, and that an effective leadership style corresponds to each stage.

The *Lead Self* tool (see Resources) enables leaders to assess themselves according to the categories below, relying, as do all self-assessments, on the subject having a clear self-view.

FIGURE 7.3 **HOW LEADERSHIP ADAPTS TO GROUP DEVELOPMENT**

Stage of group	*Corresponding leadership role*
Forming	Telling
Norming	Selling
Performing	Participating
Adjourning	Delegating

3. Leadership IQ Questionnaire

Emmett Murphy's self-test (see Resources) poses intriguing questions about leadership and proposes surprising answers. This includes a series of tests challenging conventional intuition and stimulating leaders to rethink everything they thought they knew about their trade.

4. Negotiating Style Profile

The Negotiating Style Profile was developed by Rollin and Christine Glaser to assist leaders in the negotiating and mediating aspects of their work. The Glasers recognized that the negotiator is concerned simultaneously with two aspects of each negotiation: the relationships and the substance of the negotiation.

The instrument enables leaders to see how their predominant approach to negotiation is influenced by concerns about relationships and substance. The five styles it identifies are accommodation, compromise, withdrawal, defeat, and collaboration.

While each style may have benefits in certain situations, the Glasers propose that the leader whose strength is in collaboration is likely to negotiate results of higher quality most of the time.

5. Thomas-Kilmann Conflict Mode Instrument

When conflict is in the air, most people instinctively want to duck. If forced to face it, say Kenneth Thomas and Ralph Kilmann, they generally depend on a well-worn response style: to compete, collaborate, compromise, avoid, or accommodate.

Each style has its strengths and weaknesses, depending on the situation. So this self-scoring questionnaire guides the coachee to reflect on the impacts of his or her behaviour and describes situations in which each style can be useful.

FIGURE 7.4 EXERCISE: DESIGN YOUR ASSESSMENT INTERVIEW

This task will help you to clarify your own approach to assessment, while providing a valuable tool that you can use with every new coachee who enters your practice.

1. With the guided interview outline given earlier in the chapter as a starting point, create your own assessment form. Be sure to adjust it so that it fits your style of coaching and covers all the bases in your practice.
2. Lay it out so that you have plenty of blank space to add notes.
3. The first time around, print up only a handful of copies.
4. Revise the outline, reprint, and keep on revising.

You may be alarmed at the length of your guide. Rest assured that in this case, more is better. Speaking personally, if we didn't have such a guide, we would feel as if we were looking at our clients without our glasses.

> FIGURE 7.5 **EXERCISE: DESIGN YOUR OWN 360-DEGREE FEEDBACK**
>
> **INSTRUMENT**
>
> Here is a task that will help you to develop your comfort with assessment and clarify your use of 360-degree feedback. You begin by creating a core competency list.
>
> 1. Think about a current or recent coachee.
> 2. Based on your knowledge of his or her job, list five or six of the core competencies required to perform it effectively.
> 3. Under each competency, list two or three descriptions of how she or he would behave to be congruent with that competency.
> 4. You have now created the skeleton of a 360-degree feedback instrument. Start talking to clients about the possibility of developing a 360-degree survey collaboratively to enrich your work with them.

> Coaching instruments harness the accumulated wisdom of their developers and strengthen you in your task of coaching. The big winner, of course, is the coachee. People never forget the gems they learn about themselves and others through these tools, and as a result they become better managers and more insightful guides to others.
>
> As the Assessment Phase reaches a conclusion, the coach guides the coachee into the Development and Integration Phase. This is the subject of the next chapter, the most extensive and exhausting phase of coaching, and the one that will generate the greatest personal changes.

Mechanisms that Generate Change

The first two phases of the coaching engagement are a prelude or foundation for the main event: the Development and Integration Phase. In this phase—the longest of all—the coachee is very active, performing experiments in self-development and integrating new behaviours into her repertoire.

Throughout this Development and Integration Phase, the coach and coachee use a process of action and reflection to develop solutions that are practical, self-reinforcing, and sustainable, and that take into account the forces posed by the organization's culture.

Acting as cornerstones of the coaching engagement, ensuring that every phase of the coaching edifice stands true, are four developmental concepts: an increasing self-awareness and ability to reflect; developing new skills and behaviours; retaining this learning; and engaging the power of evaluation. The reason these cornerstone concepts work so well is that they are essential supports for every form of learning. It is during the Development and Integration Phase of coaching, however, that their steadying influence is most evident.

1. Increasing Self-Awareness and Ability to Reflect

Reflection interrupts the unproductive cycle of action and reaction. The coachee who is most likely to make progress is the one who has become more self-aware through reflection. As we have already seen, nothing triggers a deeper understanding of the self than the process of assessment and inevitable self-reflection. Fortunately that process persists throughout the Development Phase.

Causal and historical links hidden in the darkness of unawareness are the factors most often limiting people's growth. That is why the excavation of personal history is so powerful. Confronting such personal history helps the coachee to assert control and ownership over these factors, some of which may have arisen only during the previous week while others may date back several generations. Reflecting on the link between current behaviour and one's past allows one to develop the freedom to constantly make choices.

Another potent means for growth in awareness is the person's relationship with the coach, which serves as a prototype for future work relationships. By talking with the coach about her changing relationship with him, the coachee prepares to tend other relationships, behaviour that will have great potential for stimulating future growth.

2. Developing New Skills and Behaviours

A key objective of coaching is to develop new skills and behaviours. This happens in logically linked stages.

- Setting of reasonable and challenging goals
- Detailed planning and rehearsal of the actions required
- Trying out new skills or behaviours in real time—often with some anxiety
- Analyzing trials to discover what worked, what didn't, how and why
- Creating new plans to produce even better results

3. Retaining the Learning

Learning styles that fail to provide a stimulus to retention often look good in the moment but ultimately disappoint. Those who use coaching show a satisfying tendency to continue to demonstrate their new behaviours and skills. Here's how it works:

- As the coaching team (coach and coachee working together) deliberately reflects on the effects of experiments, they are mapping new options and reinforcing positive behaviours for the coachee.
- Retention is supported when the coachee seeks and receives ongoing feedback from others or uses other objective ways to measure changes in productivity.
- As the coachee recognizes that the end of the coach's reinforcing relationship is approaching, she shifts gears and begins to establish a self-sustaining system of reinforcement.
- The coaching team also develops ways to prevent relapses and how to cope with setbacks.

4. Engaging the Power of Evaluation

To evaluate is to make a judgment and to assign a value. The coaching team continually returns to the coachee's daily experiences to analyze successes and to mine failures for their hidden riches. Then, assigning differing values to what they have learned, the team will choose what to ignore for now and where to devote the coachee's immediate energy.

Such a process should be happening as a matter of course every single day in every workplace. But most people are too close to their successes and failures to see them clearly, and usually are so familiar with their habitual patterns that they hardly recognize them.

The power of deliberate evaluation is that it radically changes our perspective, the more so when employed in a coaching team context. It transports the coachee from the depths of the valley to the top of a hill, helping her to apply greatly increased clarity and wisdom to the project of self-development.

A benchmark supporting this process consists of the objectives set at the beginning of coaching. This is like a fixed point on the horizon to which the coaching team can frequently turn to make comparisons between those expectations and what has actually happened since.

Another benchmark consists of the coachee's developing hopes for the future. Although at first they may be less distinct, they too provide an evaluative mark helping her to distinguish what needs doing and with what urgency. They imbue the original objectives with a more immediate reference.

The Benefit of Working from an Outline

Taking into account the forces posed by organizational culture, our challenge as coaches is to help our coachees to develop solutions that are practical, self-reinforcing, and sustainable. Beginning with structured meetings provides helpful limits and guidance. Such structure ensures that the coachee's most successful experiments are transformed from isolated events into reliable habits. By reinforcing good solutions with repeated use, these solutions are sustained and become resistant to those aspects of organizational culture that would otherwise wash them away.

Although we attempt to describe a typical session in the Development Phase, we admit that there is no such thing as a typical session. Each has a unique structure, depending on the needs of the coachee, the responses of the coach, and the external environment. So we invite you to view this not as a template to be applied arbitrarily to your work, but as a stimulus to help you to discover the appropriate structure for each of your sessions.

And although the individual components of a session are listed below as if they were distinct items presented in a fixed order, the reality is different. You will find in practice that these components often blur and blend into each other. Some will be missing from a particular session; others unnamed here may appear. And their order may change. All of this is entirely normal.

Yet there is a huge benefit in working from an outline. It provides you with a crucial sense of location. So even when you decide to veer in another direction, it remains within sight as a fixed point to which you can return at any time to get your bearings.

Structuring a Coaching Session from Beginning to End

Here is an outline of a session in the Development and Integration Phase:

1. Greeting and news
2. Agenda building
3. Reflection on experiments with new behaviours
4. Celebration of successes
5. Addressing difficulties and blocks
6. Teaching segment
7. Commitment to developing new skills and new approaches
8. Action planning
9. Conclusion

Let's put some flesh on that skeleton outline by examining the session components individually. We begin each component with a description of what it aims to accomplish, and then use case examples to provide a view of the component at work. The first case in each component, entitled realistically "The horrible example," shows how this section of the coaching interview can be rendered powerless or destructive by the coach's clumsy handling. The second case in each component, "Getting it right," shows how the component can be used in a creative and positive way. For the sake of continuity, for most of this chapter we'll follow the case of Cary, a female executive with a pharmaceutical firm. We will also look, more briefly, into coaching sessions with other managers.

THE PROBLEM WITH CARY

Superficially, when the coaching began, there was nothing disastrous about the way Cary did her work. She was successfully hitting her numbers, and the president of the company indicated satisfaction with her productivity. But from the first day she admitted two serious problems to her coach.

The first was that she was having trouble concentrating on her job. In fact, that was the issue that initially pushed her to work with a coach.

The second problem was that she never found time for those aspects of her position where she could best add value, for instance, networking with customers or helping to develop the organization's vision.

Cary was fortunate to have a very capable staff. As the coaching began, she asked them to complete a 360-degree feedback survey so we would have more material for a good assessment. In their responses, several staff members said they were frustrated because Cary did not delegate tasks that would allow them to be creative or to deal with sensitive issues.

"That's because it's my responsibility to make sure those jobs are done right," she explained ruefully at the time. "It's a lot of work for me, but I guess it's the price I have to pay."

According to her staff, Cary wasn't the only one paying a price. These capable people often saw their talents wasted on work they could perform in their sleep.

We will see how Cary dealt with these issues by examining a session with her coach. To begin, like most encounters, a coaching session is initiated quite simply with a greeting and an inquiry about the other person.

1. Greeting and News: Warming Up the Session

The first few minutes of a coaching session have the vital purpose of helping the coachee to make a transition from the tensions of the outside world into a coaching relationship, warming up the atmosphere, and building empathy and engagement between them. This segment invites input from the coachee, important information that will begin to impose a helpful structure on the session, enabling coach and coachee to develop their agenda together.

If handled badly, the first few moments of a session can create tensions that cripple the coaching. The "horrible example" below is fictitious but based on real, if deplorable, events from our experience and that of other coaches.

Whoever said that first impressions are lasting was right on the mark. In fact, the first few words of the session set a tone that will either send it soaring or force it to a crash.

THE HORRIBLE EXAMPLE
Coach: Hi, Cary. How're you doing?

It's a conventional greeting. It's comfortable, friendly, unthreatening. Problem is, the coach is positioning his relationship with Cary as just the same as that of the mail boy, the cafeteria helper, or her boss. There's nothing here that implies the helpful work of a disciplined, professional coach.

Cary: Just fine, thanks.

It's the conventional response to a conventional greeting. What else can she say?

Coach: Great. Me too.

The coach just reinforced Cary's fear that we're committed to staying on the surface here.

Cary: Hmm.

The coach is becoming worried that it's going to be really hard to get anything significant done in this session. But he's not going to say so, because at this point we've established that we're definitely not talking about feelings.

Coach: So, Cary, everything's okay?

In other words, please say yes.

Cary: Yeah, things are pretty good.

She obliges.

Coach: Right. Glad to hear that.

The coach is feeling really stuck. If everything's "okay," what exactly are we doing here anyway?

Cary: Hmm.

That's precisely what Cary's wondering, too.

Coach: So what do you want to talk about today?

In other circumstances, that sentence might imply that the coach is willing to share responsibility for the direction of the session with the coachee. But here, it means just one thing—desperation. Maybe the coachee can rescue us from this mess.

Cary: Hmm. I'm not sure.

Unless something huge and heavy is happening in her work life, something so dramatic that she can't help talking about, she's not going to rescue the coach.

Coach: Right.

Message received. Now what do I do?

Cary: Hmm.

This is becoming very awkward.

Coach: So how about we talk about that meeting you had scheduled....

Frantically, clumsily, the coach begins to push for something a little deeper. But because he blew the opening of the session, this is going to be tough sledding. Most catastrophically the ownership of the agenda has become his, not hers. So if she is the slightest bit uncomfortable, Cary will keep shifting the responsibility to the coach, making his work even more difficult. Soon he will begin to feel a little irritated about that, and as he does, Cary will pick it up subliminally, increasing the distance between them.

HOW TO MAKE THE GREETING AND NEWS SECTION EFFECTIVE

- Open the session, building comfort
- Set the stage by revealing yourself honestly
- Model frankness and transparency
- Encourage the coachee to self-reveal
- Empower the coachee to lead with what is important
- Handle feelings without discomfort
- Develop an agenda to propel the session

CONVENTIONAL GREETINGS CAN PREPARE THE COACHEE FOR WORK

Coach: Hello, Cary. I've been looking forward to seeing you today. How are you?

As simple as that looks, several interesting things are happening here simultaneously. First, the coach is greeting the coachee in comfortable conventional terms. He may shake hands, if shaking hands is Cary's preference. He may move a chair to make it easier for her to sit down. He's expressing a positive feeling about seeing her and about the session the two of them are about to develop together.

These few words create a sense that this session is within the bounds of normal behaviour. That's comforting for a coachee, who may be feeling vulnerable and anxious.

But he is also using his voice to subtly deepen the encounter, thereby making it easier for Cary to do some of the more difficult self-development that she is facing. "I've been looking forward to seeing you today," is not flirtatious. It's not just a compliment. But it is mildly self-revealing. Within clearly professional bounds, it conveys warmth and safety, and allows Cary to feel cared about.

In these first few minutes, a crucial task of the coach is to set the stage for what will happen next. He needs to present himself honestly. If, in the previous session, the coachee placed problems on the table, it is sometimes better to begin by saying, "I've been concerned about you," or "I've been wondering how that meeting you told me about worked out," or "I must admit I've felt some nervous anticipation, thinking about the issues we agreed to talk about today." It can even be helpful to say, "I've got a headache today, so if I seem like I'm in pain, I want you to know that it's not you, it's me."

GETTING IT RIGHT: MOVING TO AN APPROPRIATE DEPTH

If you model frankness and transparency, you give permission to your coachee to be equally open. If you model a moderate amount of depth in the opening moments, then the coachee will be attracted to depth. Otherwise the session is likely to get sticky right from the beginning.

Cary: I'm okay.

Cary isn't offering much to start. She hasn't yet changed gears into coaching mode. But that doesn't stall the situation, because the coach has prepared for this session and knows where to go with it.

Coach: I've been wondering what's been happening since we met last. Any successes, any challenges you'd like to talk about?

This tells the coachee that there is a warm concern for her, that it is focused, that the coach is interested in both her successes and problems. Unlike more defensive corporate situations, unlike her relationship with her boss, it is both safe and expected here that she will have positives and negatives to report on. And she has permission to talk only about material she wishes to reveal.

Cary: It's been a pretty good week, but I've been puzzled about ...

She is presenting her feelings with a positive spin, but when she says that she is puzzled, she's beginning to experiment with the possibility that she can open up to the coach. As the relationship matures, she will be able to say right out, "It's been a tough week, and sometimes I felt like a failure." Or, "I'm so proud of myself."

> ### SHARED LEADERSHIP
>
> When the coach provides graceful leadership at the beginning of a session, rather than taking a vague or laissez-faire approach, it is not long before the coachee is leading the conversation toward the next place it needs to go, in this case, agenda-building.
> So who's in charge here?
> Both are, each in their appropriate sphere.

In certain circumstances, the coach will wish to spend longer on the greeting section.

Cary: I guess I haven't told you that my uncle died last month.

This news may call for a simple expression of condolence, or it may be a signal that there's more to discuss here. The coach who avoids grappling with emotion may respond with, "Gee, that's too bad. So, what's been happening since we met last? Any successes, any challenges?" In other words, he may miss the whole point of the session, plus an opportunity to help Cary to develop her workplace skills. In the example that follows, the coach is not afraid of the possibility that he will encounter feelings.

Coach: I'm sorry to hear that. What was that like for you?

He makes certain that Cary knows that she was heard. And the question is diagnostic.

Cary: It's been difficult. He was a guiding light to me.
Coach: It must be rough, being under pressure at work when you've lost someone that important to you.
Cary: It is. I also lost a friend in the spring, and my dad a couple of years ago.
Coach: So it sounds like you've been reeling with losses for a couple of years. People you were close to....

It's just a suggestion, an open-ended question, and if Cary replies, "Yeah, but it's okay, I can handle it," the coach can mentally file the information, and keep a watch out for the possibility that it will become relevant later.

But the coach knows, from breadth of experience, that deaths and other serious losses almost always have a negative impact on people's well-being, their behaviour, and their productivity, as they come to terms with grief. In other words, he's open to the possibility in every session that there may be a need to change or at least adjust the contract between them.

Cary: I find it hard to concentrate sometimes.
Coach: Do you think it's those losses that are distracting you from work?

Again, it's just a suggestion, a tentative probe allowing Cary to go deeper or not, as she chooses. For some people, no matter how safe and confidential their relationship with the coach is, discussion of personal matters in the workplace is out of bounds. Others will welcome the opportunity.

Cary: It could be. These days I'm never sure who I might lose next.
Coach: Do think that's part of why your boss suggested that you work with a coach?
Cary: Maybe. I know I used to be a real star around here, but I'm not nearly as productive these days.
Coach: It takes time for that kind of loss to heal. I know you'll start feeling better as time goes on, and you'll work more effectively, too. But that may be hard for you to believe right now. Does your boss understand why you've been less productive?

Based on experience, the coach is able to be reassuring without glossing over the pain. He's "normalizing" her situation. Equally, he is recognizing Cary's need for extra support.

Cary: Not really.
Coach: Would there be a benefit to telling him?

Once again a suggestion, but it is truly a question. Listen closely for the answer.

Cary: I don't think so. He sometimes says that our personal lives have no place here at the office.

Had the coach made that suggestion about talking with the boss in a more forceful way, it could have initiated a no-win power struggle between him and a frightened but rebellious Cary. Instead, he decides that he's been given information to store for now. There may come a time when an open discussion about the benefits of Cary talking with her boss will be appreciated. Till then, he can let it sit.

Coach: What's it like for you to not be accomplishing as much as you used to?
Cary: Sometimes I feel badly about it. But after what you said, I think I shouldn't beat myself up. I'm still adding lots of value around here.

In truth, just opening the topic with the coach will likely result in Cary becoming more productive and less anxious. It's human nature.

ON THE POSSIBLE EXISTENCE OF FEELINGS IN THE WORKPLACE

Notice how the verb "feel" pops up in these dialogues. Feelings—the emotions—play a major part in how people manage their work. Joy, enthusiasm, peace, anger, grief, all make their appearance in the workplace.

But it's a rare workplace where feelings are easily talked about in a helpful, positive way. Depending on organizational culture, the prevailing attitude toward feelings may range from "Don't exist" to "Very scary." The coach who can talk about emotions without frightening the coachee will help to harness the power of feelings for the coachee's benefit.

ANOTHER EXAMPLE: JACK'S ATTITUDE TOWARD EMOTION

You will want to keep a close eye on the kind of language you use to describe emotions. Let's leave Cary's session for a moment and look at what happened in a session where the coach tried to talk about emotion with his coachee Jack.

Coach: So, Jack, how did you feel when your boss said you're not performing?

The coach is unaware that, like many males, Jack doesn't talk about feelings, doesn't really understand his own feelings.

Jack: I just told him he was way wrong.

So Jack avoids talking about how he felt, and instead tells the coach what he did.

Coach: But you must have felt something.
Jack: I just thought, "You jerk!" and left it at that.
Coach: Sounds like you were feeling vulnerable and angry.

Jack didn't ask to be analyzed, and he doesn't talk easily about emotions. He's quietly resentful of having words put in his mouth. This is beginning to look like a car accident where the coach keeps insisting he has the right of way but loses the contest with an oncoming truck. It can be a big mistake to insist on hearing about feelings, even though the coach may be certain that they are the key to this situation. Here's a more effective approach:

Coach: So what did you think about that?

For many people, "think" is a much safer word than "feel."

Jack: That he was being pretty unfair, not really counting my contribution to the department.
Coach: How did that hit you?
Jack: I nearly walked out. Don't forget, performance appraisal time is coming soon, and I don't want to lose my increase.

As the coach adjusted his language to Jack's habitual way of communicating, the result was that Jack identified his feelings without actually naming them: anger ("nearly walked out") and fear ("performance appraisal time"). He communicated a lot without literally mentioning feelings or emotions.

In response at this point, the coach may still be tempted to ask, "How can you manage your negative feelings so you don't lose out at work?" That would probably be a mistake. Instead, a sensitive coach may say something just as probing but less likely to distract his client.

Coach: So it sounds like you're working on a problem: how to manage your relationship with your boss so you don't lose out at work. Have I got that right?
Jack: You sure have. Even if I'm pissed off about what happened, he's still my boss and I respect him for that. So I've got to figure out how to keep what happened from getting in the way of our relationship.

Jack has eventually used an emotion word—when it felt appropriate for him, rather than when the coach forced the issue. Like most people, he's willing to talk about feelings, but only on his terms.

 At the risk of oversimplifying and/or stereotyping, men are usually more comfortable talking about anger than other emotions. Women are more likely to admit to fear, sorrow, and anxiety.

2. Agenda Building: the Agenda Is a Flexible Map

Those first few minutes of greeting provided the raw material to build an agenda for the rest of the session. Viewed from the surface, coaching may seem like a rambling conversation that sometimes doubles back on itself or leads up blind alleys, like the path of children playing aimlessly in a park. It may appear that its direction depends on the shifting interests of the two parties at any given minute. This appearance can create a considerable sense of worry and discomfort in the coachee. After all, he or she has chosen to be coached by a professional because of an acute need for development, and wants assurance that time is not being wasted.

In the hands of an experienced coach, however, even the most "rambling" session is a carefully guided conversation with aims that are absolutely clear. The coach knows where the coachee needs to go, follows the conversational cues he or she offers, and at each choice point or intersection, guides the coachee in the direction identified as leading to his or her goal.

How does the coach accomplish this? The compass for the journey is provided by the agenda. Before many minutes of the session have passed, both coach and coachee need to agree on a plan for where the session is to go. Otherwise, the reality will match the appearance, and they will have difficulty staying on track.

Before coach and coachee talk together about agenda, the coach has an unseen initial conversation with himself. This is part of his work of self-management, answering a number of crucial questions about the process:

- Where am I in this relationship?
- How do I feel before I meet with the coachee and when I'm with her after the session ends?
- Do the results we generally get match our objectives?
- What seems to be working right now, and what is not?

Thoughtful answers to these questions will help to develop the agenda by pointing in the direction of whatever needs to be accomplished next. But this does not mean that the coach will impose his own agenda. The idea of agenda-building is not to create a box to restrict the movement of the conversation, but to assist the coachee in aiming at tangible results.

This can be a big challenge to new coaches, for they are especially likely to mistrust both the wisdom of their coachees and their own listening skills. Instead of entering a collaborative discussion about where the coachee needs to go, they may attempt to drive the session in a direction they have—in their anxiety—already determined.

A CLEAR VIEW OF THE COACHEE

Student coaches sometimes keep their class notes handy during telephone coaching sessions, leafing through them as they talk, to find the "best model" to apply to the session.

But while frantically flipping through their notes, only a fraction of their mind is actually available to the coachee, to attend, to support, and to guide.

The key to good coaching is to attend fully to what you hear, see, and feel in your relationship with the coachee. Contradictory though it may seem, models, tools, and techniques are most reliable when used by coaches who don't need them.

EVALUATING PROGRESS

As well as checking in with himself, the coach will also ask the coachee to evaluate the coaching process. This should happen several times, even during sessions that are well into the course of coaching.

Mid-process checking enables the coach to fine-tune his work and allows both parties to assess their progress and make necessary adjustments to their relationship and expectations. Questions like "Are we on course?" or "How can we make this better?" validate both change and celebration.

The coach's inner conversation with himself is only the first tool to help guide the conversation about agenda. The next tool is to gather vital information by asking questions of his coachee. It is valuable to find out what she thinks (or "feels," if appropriate) about the sessions so far, how she's been doing in the workplace since the last meeting, and what's working and what is not. Now let's get back to Cary.

THE HORRIBLE EXAMPLE

Coach: So, what do you want to talk about today?

Cary: Well, you're the expert. What do you think is most important?

The coach begins to scan through his notes, trying to find whatever he wrote—or failed to write—about the last session, desperately wracking his brain for memories.

Coach: Well, I'm not sure. Wait a sec till I find that note I wrote... Do you remember what you decided to do between sessions?

You'd be amazed how many coaches either don't make notes (during or after their sessions) or fail to review them before the upcoming session. As they bumble their way through agenda building, their coachee's faith in the value of the session plummets.

But let's assume instead that the coach has actually written and checked his notes and knows what is happening. This situation needs to be handled with grace and delicacy.

Coach: Cary, I've been thinking about what you said about your relationship with your boss last time we met. Today we should focus on developing better communication with him.

The coach has a legitimate instinct about what needs work here. But he makes a serious tactical error by trying to impose his expectations on the agenda. If he should succeed, his expectations will inhibit the coachee. After all, the coach's truth is not necessarily the coachee's truth. Yet, if the coachee disagrees and argues with his choices, the coach will lose credibility.

Cary: Okay. So what do you suggest?

Good move, Cary. If the coach is so determined to take over, let him do all the work.

Coach: Well, let's see. Um, you could ...

By apparently taking control of the session and making suggestions, the coach has actually thrown away most of his power. He's been reduced, self-reduced, to a problem-solver, when he could have functioned as a visionary guide and catalyst. And because he's an outsider, not in the middle of the office situation, his solutions stand a good chance of being valuable only in theory. And that is bound to lead to problems in this relationship.

KEYS TO AGENDA BUILDING

* Guide, imply, but don't impose.
* When asked to take the lead, don't swallow the hook.
* "Track" the coachee, for she knows where she needs to go.
* Show your trust in her wisdom by picking up on whatever she has said.
* Tell stories that inspire.

GETTING IT RIGHT:
AGENDA-BUILDING THAT'S VALUABLE TO THE COACHEE

Coach: Cary, what would you like to get out of this session by the time it ends?
Cary: I'm not really sure.

Big opportunity here for the coach to jump in and impose his own agenda. But wait, there's another way to use his instincts.

Coach: Last time, you talked about your relationship with your boss. It sounded to me as if you were concerned about it going off the rails. Is that something you'd like to focus on today?

The coach is tentative, respectful of the coachee's desires. And at the same time, he is assertive, feeding back diagnostic information that she herself provided earlier, helping her to make a decision.

And why would she need such help? The answer is that although the human mind has an incredibly powerful filing system, it will often hide the very things we are most anxious about. Cary may or may not have forgotten about this urgent issue.

It may seem strange that Cary might forget important aspects of her coaching. But remember how hard it is sometimes to remember the name of a person you met a few minutes earlier? And then how the name pops effortlessly into your mind later on, when you are distracted by making a cup of tea?

A crucial part of the coach's task is to listen very closely to things that are said, to note them, and to raise them when appropriate. Sometimes coaches remind their coachees of things they said months, even years, in the past. Developing that kind of memory may not come easily for the coach in the early stages, but over time it emerges.

Coach: Is that something you'd like to focus on today?
Cary: Gee, I'm not sure.
Coach: It's entirely up to you. Would it help if I told you what I've seen in the past in these kinds of situations?

It's simply an offer. She can say no and move on to other issues that she feels more comfortable working with. A coach less certain about his role might have said, "Well, here are some of the problems I've seen in the past when people don't confront these kinds of situations. First of all ... " He'd have valuable information to offer, but he'd be imposing it on Cary.

That's not only ineffective, it's bad modelling. It is not the kind of approach he would encourage her to use with her reports.

Cary: Sure it would.

Who, when offered a choice, is going to turn down free information from an expert? Not Cary. She'll listen, and she'll decide.

Coach: Well, I was working with a person who...

The coach tells a story, with the characters' identities professionally disguised, that roughly parallels Cary's situation. He makes sure to identify the benefits of creatively confronting the relationship even with a frightening boss.

But he is doing all this to provide information. He is not attached to a particular outcome.

THE CURSE OF ATTACHMENT

Some of the most damaging coaches and counsellors are well-meaning folk who have become attached to certain outcomes. They suffocate their coachees with their need, their hunger for success, and their lust for particular results.

The cause is the coach's insecurity.

The impact on the coachee who doesn't provide this outcome for the coach is that a memory is triggered—that old sense of inadequacy caused by letting down parents, teachers, or significant others.

Coach: ...so that's what happened in that case. But, you know, if you decide not to work on this right now, there'll be another opportunity. Even if you choose never to work on it, that's okay. It would be your decision—and it might even be the best decision. Who knows better than you?
Cary: Well, it makes me pretty nervous even to think about changing my relationship with my boss, but let's talk about it.
Coach: What is it about changing the relationship that makes you nervous?

The coach is "tracking" Cary. That means following in her footsteps, picking up her vocabulary, and letting her lead. But tracking does not imply following every lead she offers. The coach who tracks effectively, tracks selectively.

He shows particular attention to Cary's cues that are most likely to lead toward her chosen objectives. He may ignore or show less interest in those that could detour her.

The coach is consistent about leaving the ball in her court. His job is to give her permission and to help her to focus. Now that she owns the problem and is moving toward a target, she's energized to find her own solutions in her own way.

3. Reflection on Experiments with New Behaviours

Once the coach and coachee have clarified where they want this session to go (a process that generally takes only a couple of minutes), they will usually want to look at the results of whatever experiments the coachee committed to trying out during the last session.

Let's take a detour from Cary's situation to look at a difficult situation that a coach named Greg brought to his coaching supervisor. He was working with an executive new to her job who was constantly undermined by hostile employees and poisonous office politics.

According to Greg, the executive arrived at every coaching session more interested in complaining than in taking charge. His frank assessment: "She wants to whine, not to help herself." He said he wanted either a sense of progress in the coaching or what he called closure. "Lots of people want to whine like that," Greg said. "But I tell them, 'My responsibility is to move you forward to contribute to the organization.'" So the question he brought to his supervisor was whether she should terminate this coaching relationship.

The supervisor observed that one of the most fruitful ways to counter resistance is to reflect out loud on what's happening. Sometimes that process converts whining into progress. It's a way to ignite fresh sources of light into the world of a person who cannot see in the dark.

The reflection aspect of a coaching session returns the coaching team to the original goals they established for the coaching relationship. It permits up-to-date evaluation, with analysis of successes and attention to gaps in awareness. It enables a learning analysis of actual events in work life.

It also contributes to the ongoing assessment process. The coach helps the coachee to discover unconscious motivations for behaviour and to become more self-aware and more aware of the impact of new skills and behaviours on others in the workplace.

In the reflection segment, coach and coachee will not rely entirely on the coachee's reports of what happened. Where available, they will also look together at more objective measures (sales figures, for example), and at feedback from others in the workplace. The provision of feedback may be informal—"collecting feedback by walking around"—or use a formal instrument.

Reflection is a primary contributor to retention of skills and information. The coachee who talks with a trained professional about her experiences is most likely to remember what she did right and to continue doing it. The reflection segment of the session can make a major contribution to reinforcing positive behaviour and helping to prevent relapses.

THE HORRIBLE EXAMPLE
Here's our construction of what might have happened if Greg had failed to seek consultation on managing his coaching relationship.

Greg: Well, Donna, it just doesn't look like we're making much progress here.
Executive: You can say that again.
Greg: So what would you think about us cutting our losses and terminating the coaching?
Executive: Pardon me?

Greg: Well, I'm sure we're both disappointed in your progress so far. And I think you'd agree we should stop banging our heads against the wall.

Executive: Really! Banging our heads? I thought you were supposed to be helping me.

Greg: Well, you see, coaches are sculptors. We're sometimes limited by the kind of materials we're working with.

Executive: Hang on just a minute. Are you saying that I'm not capable of making changes?

Greg: No, of course not. I'm sure you're capable. But so far all you've done is complain.

Executive: So for these three sessions you've been thinking that I was just complaining? Has it ever occurred to you that I'm very frustrated and I'm waiting for some guidance? Why did we hire you anyway? Okay, fine. The coaching is finished, and I'll have a few things to say to our HR director next time he starts preaching about the value of coaching.

REFLECTION CAN BE REVOLUTIONARY

- It interrupts repetitive patterns.
- It enables the coachee to take responsibility.
- It provides a jumping-off point for more effective experiments.

HELPING THE COACHEE MOVE FROM REFLECTION INTO ACTION

Phew! Thank goodness the interchange above did not actually happen. During the supervisory conversation, in fact, Greg decided that although he was frustrated, he would visualize an imaginary shelf on which to place his impatience. Instead of constantly returning to those feelings like someone picking at a scab and worsening the injury, he decided to devote his attention to more easily solvable issues. In doing so, he freed himself up to experiment with the use of reflection.

The supervisor asked him if he had ever been successful working with someone in a similar situation. After a moment's hesitation, he said that he had. So they examined what he and that coachee had done to improve an unpleasant work situation. In minutes, he had increased his stock of solutions and seemed encouraged about his ability to deal with the current situation. Here's how he reported his next coaching session.

GETTING IT RIGHT: REFLECTION WITHOUT DISTORTION

Greg: I've been noticing that every time we meet, you seem discouraged about how your new employees are treating you.

Executive: It's true. It feels like nothing ever changes. I'm getting really fed up, and I'm thinking of applying for a transfer.

That's important information. Donna knows she's fed up. This provides a potentially helpful handle to grab on to when she's ready to make progress. But beyond that, there's even more valuable data in what she's saying to Greg.

She's telling him, without knowing it, that there was a good reason for Greg to feel fed up with the coaching relationship. His client's attitude, like a flu bug, had infected him, as well, and he had begun to feel her unspoken feelings. His mental processes were running parallel to her mental processes. In fact, this phenomenon is called "parallel process."

PARALLEL PROCESS

Parallel process can be a dangerous trap for the unwary coach. Without knowing it, the coach is showing the same symptoms as the coachee. They're at the beginning of a downward spiral.

So how do you find out what you don't know?

Talk with your supervisor about how stuck you feel or how irritating your coachee is. Keep yourself open to the possibility that it's not just him but you, too. Identifying parallel process is like magic. It no longer controls you because you know what's going on. Extra reward: you'll start feeling good about your coachee again.

Although Greg had tumbled headlong into the let's-give-up trap, he did sense that something was wrong and used his supervisory relationship to recover his equilibrium. Now he begins to establish a more healthy emotional distance from the executive.

Greg: Sounds like you've just about had it.

Executive: You bet. This may be a career-limiting move, but I'm finished with them.

Greg : Since you sound a little worried about your career, I wonder if you would like to look a little more closely at the alternatives?

Executive: I guess so, but I'm not sure I have any alternatives.

Greg takes a positive approach, unpolluted by his impatience and frustration, which are safely stashed on a "shelf." He now models the problem-solving, inquiry-based approach that offers the greatest potential for solutions.

Greg: What I'm getting at is that there may still be a way for you to improve your relationship with the people at work. After all, office politics is nothing new, and there are techniques around that people have used with great success.

Executive: Such as what?

Clearly this executive is not an easy sell. But it is simple human nature for her to be curious about solutions, ultimately hopeful, and motivated not to appear a failure. In coaching, as usual, human nature is our ally. So, following her coach, she sets her impatience on her own inner shelf and inquires: "Such as what?"

Greg : Well, I worked with someone who felt he was hated by everyone in his office, but instead of banging his head against the wall by trying to improve relationships with everyone, he decided to focus on a couple of people. His reasoning was that if he had one or two allies, he'd relax and maybe others would be influenced by the fact that some people liked him.

He didn't choose the biggest challenges, either. He wisely picked a couple of people who were only moderately distant to him and with whom he had something in common. He had previously worked with one of them, and he belonged to the same fitness club as the other.

There was no miracle, but a few months ago when I checked back with him, he said he had developed better relationships with both of them and was much more comfortable at the office. Oh, and he said that his team had actually won a couple of the monthly productivity competitions.

Executive: So let me see if I've got this right. His technique was to focus on the possible and leave the perfect for later?

Greg and his coachee went on to explore a number of possible strategies, some of which she decided to put into practice. Gradually, as Greg used the reflecting segment of his sessions to help her look at the results, she recognized that she had boxed herself in by giving in to her impatience. Over time, not only did the coachee achieve substantial progress in her relationships with staff, but she also developed a more strategic approach to all her workplace relationships—up, down, and across.

4. Celebration of Successes: Breaking the Pattern of Criticism

In most workplaces, there is very little celebration. People are asked to work harder or better. They are expected to respond to changing circumstances with personal flexibility. And they will definitely hear about it if they screw up.

There's nothing wrong with any of that in itself, but there is a problem when those reactions are not mixed with an appropriate amount of appreciation and celebration. Staff morale begins to sink imperceptibly. Enthusiasm leaks away without warning. Commitment ebbs like the tide, but unlike the tide, it keeps ebbing and ebbing and ebbing.

A little celebration can change the tide of grief.

DON'T FAKE IT, CELEBRATE IT

- Choose genuine successes to celebrate.
- Catch your client off guard by celebrating the unexpected, unspectacular.
- Avoid the patronizing approach, as in, "You've been a clever guy."
- Don't take on too much responsibility; where possible, incite the coachee to name the successes.
- Use celebration to encourage further development.

OH NO, YOU DID IT AGAIN

For most people, there's a terrible, familiar feeling that accompanies criticism and challenge.

We felt it when we were four, and kept spilling our orange juice.
And at six, when we tried with little success to write our names like adults do.
And in high school, when we caught hell for low marks, knowing we could do better.

Unhappily, that mood is rekindled daily in workplaces around the world. Criticism unbalanced by encouragement and hope has an utterly predictable result: depression, the anticipation of future failure. It may be subtle, it may be subdued, but it continues to sap energy from millions of working people every day. So what's the alternative? To ignore failures and overlook perception gaps? Probably not. When there's a problem, it is best for everyone that it be named and plans be made for overcoming it.

> If criticism is the steering wheel, guiding the individual's inner vehicle around obstacles, then celebration is the fuel that propels it across long distances and up steep hills.

But what is most needed in the workplace is an appreciation of success that balances the regret and fear associated with falling short. And in the world of coaching, when people are moving into the territory of personal change and feeling unprepared and at risk, a little celebration of successes can go a very long way.

Now, back to Cary.

THE HORRIBLE EXAMPLE

Coach: And how are you doing with your problem concentrating?

Cary: It's so much better. I just decided that if I'm going to work more slowly, I'll spend longer at the office. So I've been spending a day here every weekend and a couple of evenings during the week. I'm getting all caught up.

Coach: Wow, that's terrific. So you've really succeeded in beating this problem.

Cary: I think so. Of course, I haven't much time for my friends and I'm pretty tired, but it's one of those times when you just have to make sure the job gets done.

Coach: I'm impressed.

The truth is that Cary hasn't beaten anything. She has substituted overwork for inner healing, and in the short term she's showing results. But the risks to her and the workplace are huge. The coach who doesn't probe beyond the surface is likely to endorse this behaviour and may even carve another notch for success into his clipboard. But he risks the possibility that in a few months Cary may crash and burn.

On the other hand, Cary might have replied like this:

Cary: It's so much better. I've just pushed negative thoughts out of my mind. I've decided to just be positive. I'm taking a course, I'm going to the gym. I'm really over the grief.

Coach: Wow, that's terrific.

FLIGHT INTO HEALTH

There's a term for what Cary has just done: "a flight into health." It means that she is fleeing from the arduous process of dealing one by one with issues that she faces. She's fleeing into "health," because she is choosing to do all the right things. These are certainly not negative behaviours, but the problem is the unrealistic rate of change. Rather than growing gradually into healthy attitudes and behaviour, she has rushed into something that is unlikely to be sustainable. It's just too much too fast.

Old patterns of behaviour are almost certain to recur, and when this happens, the best response is to help the coachee see herself as normal. Encourage her not to waste energy by "beating herself up," but to try again, this time taking smaller steps and going a little more slowly.

The flight into health usually occurs early in the coaching engagement. Coachees are spurred on to premature solutions by their pent-up desire to change and their desire to please the coach.

FLIGHT INTO HEALTH OR RUSH TO A CRASH?

Whenever you sense that a coachee is making progress too quickly, wonder about the possibility of a flight into health.

- Ask some gentle questions about whether she is really ready for the changes she is making.
- Be ready to provide encouragement and support, without judgment, if she cannot sustain the improvement.
- Help to uncover more gradual and realistic ways of changing.

GETTING IT RIGHT: POSITIVE AND GENUINE

Coach: Frankly, I'm a little concerned about how many hours you're working.

Cary: You are?

Coach: Yes. I'm afraid you may be wearing out your inner resources. Getting exhausted.

Cary: Well, like I said, I'm tired a lot of the time. But isn't that what you have to do at a time like this?

Coach: In my experience, people like you, who are dealing with grief, need more rest, not less. You're also likely to need more positive input from your friends and loved ones, not less. So I'm afraid you may be playing with fire.

Cary: Really?

Coach: Yes, really. I think you may hurt yourself, and I'd like to look at some alternative solutions with you. But first I'd like to take a look with you at what's positive in all this.

Cary: Okay. But from what you're saying, it doesn't sound like there's much to celebrate.

Coach: Don't you think so? How about the fact that instead of going to bed and staying depressed, you're still at work every day? Instead of giving up on improving your productivity, you tried an experiment that required hard work and dedication. And instead of trying to go it alone, like many people do, you've chosen to get some support by working with a coach. How do those things sound to you?

Cary: They sound pretty good. In fact, I guess I've felt all those things, I've just never said them out loud.

Coach: Who might you say them to? Who's the most important person to tell?

Cary: Hmm, my boss, I guess. He's the one who seems most disappointed in me. He's the one person I need to satisfy.

Coach: The one person after yourself?

Cary: Right. After myself.

Coach: So you need to affirm yourself, and you need to communicate your successes to your boss. If you did that, what would it be like?

Cary: I think I'd feel really good about myself.

Coach: And so you should. Why don't we think about exactly what you'd like to say to ...

5. Addressing Difficulties and Blocks

The celebration of success should certainly occur in every session, but inevitably each session must also address whatever difficulties and blocks the coachee has experienced. Otherwise coaching will degenerate into cheerleading, and dishonesty will sap its potency.

Attending to problems is no easy task. Failures are frightening. For most people, they loom like the monsters in their worst nightmares. It can be unnerving to confront one's difficulties, no matter how courageous the coachee may appear. It's hard enough in the privacy of one's own thoughts, but tougher still in an open relationship with another person.

> ### LOOSE LIPS SINK SHIPS
>
> The coachee is unlikely to confront weaknesses or failures openly if she believes that information confided to the coach may leak back to a supervisor or to the HR department. That is why it is important for the coach to make a point of clarifying his commitment to confidentiality and the terms of his contract with the organization regarding the privacy of the coachee.
>
> When the issue no longer raises nagging doubts for the coachee, she will be ready for honesty and action.

Despite the fear factor, addressing problems and blocks is in several respects the most rewarding work in a coaching relationship. As the coaching proceeds, the coachee is growing in her ability to self-assess accurately, and she is increasingly able to identify what is below the surface and how to get at the real issues. In this context, to analyze failure in a graceful way teaches the coachee how to achieve success. (Speaking personally, we have learned much more through reflecting on failures than from reading books or taking courses.) A taut little joke conveys this idea:

Elmer: Tell me, how did you become so successful?

Leon: Two words.

Elmer: And what are they, sir?

Leon: Right decisions.

Elmer: How do you make right decisions?

Leon: One word: experience.

Elmer: And how do you get experience?

Leon: Two words.

Elmer: And what are they?

Leon: Wrong decisions.

Why does this process work so well? Because in the majority of cases, there is some degree of success within each failure. So it is very encouraging for the coachee when the coach shines a kindly light on failures, picking up the success that accompanies it. Sometimes the success is simply that the person took a risk, rather than played it safe. Sometimes the person failed in a way so absolutely glorious, so close to success, that it shimmered with potential. It is a rare failure so trifling that we learn nothing from it.

During a practice coaching session in an advanced training course, we were admiring the direct and probing questions that one of the students was asking another student, who was role-playing a coachee. But during feedback afterward, another student, who had been observing, criticized his directness. "The questions you asked were very leading questions," she said. "I would never ask questions like that."

This second student had accepted the myth that good coaches are simply facilitators. She had been led to believe that they don't probe or assess what they are hearing. According to this belief, the coach is available as a friendly figure to draw out the coachee's ideas, to help the coachee express herself, and to make plans for the future.

This role for the coach is passive and undiscriminating, much like that of a cheerleader.

While there is some validity to this description—the coach does definitely provide a safe and protected place to work in—we should not discount the beneficial impact of the intelligence, intuition, and experience that the coach brings to his critiques and challenges.

This myth that good coaches are simply facilitators suggests that coaches really have only two choices. The first is to mutely accept everything the coachee says, and the second is to respond with devastating and brutal honesty. But those choices represent only the two extremes of a broad continuum. The most competent coaches find their most effective place somewhere in between. In dealing with areas where a coachee has fallen short of expectations, it is urgent that the coach be direct. For it is only when both parties can identify a failure honestly that they can plan for more effective experiments. And only in those circumstances will they trust each other to accurately name the successes.

GENTLE DENTISTRY: PAIN MEETS RESPECT

To be effective the coach must be direct and honest in a kindly way. I think about my dentist, who doesn't hesitate to insert a painful needle in my jaw before a filling.

But he accompanies the needle with information and thoughtfulness.

The results are positive: I feel respected and don't fear the drilling as much.

THE HORRIBLE EXAMPLE

Cary: ...so I guess that didn't work out very well.

Coach: Not only didn't work out very well, but it seems to me you've made it far less likely that your department will meet its objectives this year.

Cary: I guess you're right.

Coach: In fact, I don't think it would do you any harm to start polishing up your résumé.

Cary: That seems kind of harsh.

Coach: Well, it's not my job to coddle you. They pay me to call it like I see it. It's the responsibility of a coach to let you know when the emperor has no clothes.

Cary: But isn't there something I can do about it?

Coach: Maybe, but the first thing we need to do is to call a failure by its proper name.

Cary: I was kind of hoping ...

The coach is certainly not coddling Cary. Neither is he providing a safe or encouraging opportunity for reflection and learning. He is simply demonstrating the most common (and destructive) response to failure known to humankind: providing a critique in a harsh and impatient manner.

The result of this kind of treatment is not difficult to predict. No one (child or adult) can learn and grow in an atmosphere of harsh criticism. Cary says she "was kind of hoping ...," but from this point on, she is rapidly losing both hope and faith in herself.

DO AS I SAY, NOT AS I DO

Like parents and supervisors, coaches set an example. After all, the logic runs, if they weren't great with people, surely they wouldn't be coaching. Often without thinking about it, they are providing a model of how someone with more power treats someone with less power.

In the worst-case scenario, a coachee like Cary might believe that this authority figure actually knows what he's doing. The imminent danger is that Cary may use similar techniques on those who report their mistakes at work to her.

THE POWER OF JUDGMENT-FREE EVALUATION

* Acknowledge painful feelings.
* Maintain the dignity of the coachee.
* Hold on to hope, yet do not insist on it.
* Sift data to discover solutions.
* Help the coachee to move from experience into wisdom.

GETTING IT RIGHT: LETTING THE COACHEE MAKE HER OWN POTENT JUDGMENTS

Cary: ...so I guess that didn't work out very well.

Coach: You're the best judge of that, but I'd tend to agree with your assessment.

Cary: I was afraid you'd say that.

Coach: I know. It's hard to talk about this kind of thing with another person. But while I wouldn't minimize what happened, I want to be sure you remember that everyone makes mistakes, and that this kind of mistake is rarely fatal.

Cary: Yes, but I am really worried here. I mean, it's a situation that could cause some permanent damage.

When the coach refrains from coming down hard on the coachee, it encourages her to take responsibility for herself and name her concerns. She becomes less defensive.

Coach: Sounds like you're pretty worried.
Cary: It's difficult. It's affecting me. Most mornings this week I didn't feel like getting up and coming into the office.

Depression is often part of the growth process. To name problems, as Cary and his coach are doing here, can temporarily make her feel even worse. But the potential benefits—sharing the problem and finding solutions—far outweigh the transient cost.

Coach: That's not so unusual. You've had a rough experience, like someone falling off a horse. Most people feel pretty draggy at a time like this....

The coach is letting Cary know that there is nothing abnormal in having depressed feelings when acknowledging a mistake; he won't push her, and he won't expect an instant recovery. For the time being, while she is not capable of doing it herself, he holds on to the hope for her. The famed analyst Bruno Bettelheim once asked a child who had recovered from a dangerous, lengthy depression, what had made the difference. "You hoped for me," she said. "When no one else hoped for me, you did."

When individuals are in bad shape emotionally, they often believe that they're the only person in the world who feels that way. They think of themselves as freaks and are tempted to isolate themselves from others.

By countering those reactions, by positioning the coachee as right in the middle of the normal range, the coach helps her to move through depression, out of isolation, and back into hopeful spirits.

Coach: ...but then most people just get back into the saddle. That's what I expect you'll do. I think that you're strong and that you'll be okay.
Cary: I guess.
Coach: In the meantime, I'll be here to support you.

The coach doesn't insist on Cary's agreeing. He appreciates her right to be skeptical at this particular moment in time. He has offered some verbal reassurance, and he's ready to back it up with something practical.

Coach: You mentioned permanent damage before. Would you like to tell me what you had in mind?
Cary: I'm not sure our department can meet its objectives this year.

Coach: You sound worried.

Cary: I am.

Coach: Would you like to take a closer look at what actually went wrong? Maybe if we do that we can figure out a way to lessen the damage.

The coach is not softening the blow. Something actually did go wrong. But what he is saying, without expressing it in a patronizing way, is that he sees Cary as an adult who is capable of owning up to and coping with reverses. This implied message is very encouraging for someone whose self-esteem is pretty shaky right now.

It should also be noted that, unlike the previous example, the coach is also more interested in helping her to learn from the experience than in proving that he is an all-knowing prophet. He allows Cary the dignity of being the one identifying the damage. And instead of taking a superior position (which, in Cary's unconscious mind, is likely to correspond with the parent who chastises a child), he is joining her as a partner. He says, "We."

Cary: Yes I would. But where do we start?

Coach: Let's start by taking a look at what you were thinking when you made the first decisions that led to this problem....

As they conduct this examination, Cary and her coach will gather the raw data of what actually happened. Then, by examining the impact of events, they will sift and sort this data so that they end up with refined information about causes and effects.

Reflecting on this information, Cary will develop the knowledge to accomplish something successfully. And as she and the coach apply that knowledge, recognizing the repetitive positive patterns in both her behaviour and the workplace, she will develop wisdom that she can apply to other situations.

Because her wisdom transcends the limitations of time and place, ultimately she will be able to apply it throughout her career, even to problems quite unlike the one that she and her coach are addressing right now.

ASSESSMENT CONTINUES IN THE MIDST OF DEVELOPMENT

During the Development Phase, assessment is never far from the coach's mind. Every word the coachee utters, everything she does, is likely to provide new information that, properly assessed, can help to shape the process of change. The alert coach is constantly weighing new information to see whether it might signal a shift in the direction of the coaching. Take Brooke's situation, for instance.

When Brooke began working with a coach, one of several issues she identified was that she sometimes felt flustered and confused for no apparent reason. But during the Assessment Phase, she reported that in the office she was generally relaxed and calm. So the fluster issue, with no solution in sight, was pushed to the back burner, while other issues that she identified received the coach's full attention during the next few weeks.

But after several weeks, a chance remark revealed that Brooke played tennis regularly and that she had a reputation as a ferocious and combative player. When the coach expressed surprise at this self-description, Brooke replied that tennis was a way of dealing with certain pressures in her private life.

Based on this chance piece of information, the coach remembered her describing her apparent calmness at the office. He suggested that they take a second look to begin to understand why Brooke sometimes became flustered.

What they discovered was that when frustrated by events, Brooke had an astonishing ability to "keep going" outwardly, with a smile on her face. At the office she had no equivalent to an active game of tennis to release some of the inner pressure. So the pressure would show up in unexpected, subtle ways, such as losing track of what she wanted to do or say next.

As an outcome of the coaching, Brooke decided she needed to find ways to unload her tension. She began to spend more time and talk more frankly with a fellow supervisor whom she liked and trusted. They sometimes used their private meetings to let off steam, particularly when they were "up to here" with frustration. As time went on, she noticed that her flustered feeling was becoming increasingly rare. The reassessment that took place deep into the Development Phase had made a positive difference for her.

REVISING ASSESSMENTS DURING THE DEVELOPMENT PHASE

Not only is assessment never really finished, but the Development Phase includes the possibility of revising conclusions that may have seemed unchallengeable during the formal assessment. For instance:

In the Assessment Phase, an executive revealed that she had a broad and valuable experience of management. During the Development phase, however, she reported a serious altercation she had had with her president. The topic: the possibility of an unanticipated takeover.

It turned out that despite her extensive experience, the executive had never worked in an organization like this one, which was swirling in the maelstrom of major change.

She realized that she needed to shift her style to respond more quickly to new developments and to show more support for the president. This renewed assessment—in the midstream of the Development Phase—helped the coach and coachee to make a significant change in direction. As a result, their ongoing work became more finely focused.

6. Teaching Segment: Instruction Balanced by Inner Wisdom

A delicate balance: teaching vs. evoking inner wisdom: Much of the time, the effective coach will operate like Socrates in the ancient Agora of Athens, walking alongside his students, asking difficult questions and challenging them to find their own answers. Similarly, the coach opens up questions for discovery and guides the coachee, without imposing his views.

It is essential that the coach not position himself as the main source of wisdom. That approach carries a very high cost. If he does not believe that his coachees possess within themselves an infinite quantity of wisdom, he will, subtly or directly, discourage them from engaging their strengths. He will blunt their winning edge, their sense of inquiry, and their self-confidence, and may even undermine their ability to make independent decisions.

In other words, he will discourage the very qualities that would make them fine leaders. And—another big problem—his coachees are likely to see him as arrogant. That means he has lost the battle for credibility.

But there are always certain areas where the coach has something valuable to teach. To be a good coach does not require that he pretend to know nothing. In some instances the coach may have developed specialized skills and may limit himself to coaching in that area.

A CEO whose organization was on the verge of breaking through to success in its marketplace was facing overwhelming financial pressures. So she hired a coach who had previously held a senior position in a bank.

To make the company credible to bankers, the coach helped the CEO to tailor both the business plan and the way she presented herself.

We can measure the value of this intervention by the outcome: the CEO got the support she needed from the bank.

By contrast, most coaches have a less narrowly defined focus. They are experts in helping people grow. Fortunately most organizations see the need for coaching not so much in terms of specific technical skills (like attractiveness to the bank, the development of a business strategy, or time management), but in the area of self-understanding. Often the greatest cause of executive failure in this highly complex age proves to be the lack of self-knowledge.

That is why, not only in the Assessment Phase but throughout the phase of Development and Integration, the coach who understands human psychology offers added value. He can guide his clients to understand how they operate—at both conscious and subconscious levels. He can help them to reverse their most damaging tendencies and to activate unrecognized strengths.

THE OPPOSITE SEX

When we work with men, we often find ourselves coaching them in skills that come to women more readily—typically the relational and self-management skills, for example, building a high-performing team, expressing the fact that they value their employees, mentoring their employees, rather than just telling them what to do. These are skills increasingly valued as organizations view their future in terms of alliance, collaboration, relationship, trust, and partnership. Men's experiential learning on their own is sometimes not sufficient to convey these skills. They may need the coach to offer them some direct teaching, as well.

Although women often have a head start in these areas, they can usually benefit from learning and practising certain of the so-called male skills. As a senior woman executive recently described the situation to us, women need to develop greater confidence in the areas of assertiveness, decisiveness, and clarity. In addition, they can benefit themselves and the organization by more effective self-marketing, letting others know that they combine two varieties of ability in potent combination: people skills and strategic skills.

Again, the best way for women to learn how to do this is often through teaching combined with experience.

Those are gender generalizations, of course. To fine-tune their work, effective coaches customize the teaching components of their work to the actual needs of clients, whether male or female.

THE HORRIBLE EXAMPLE

Coach: Sounds to me like you're not very good at being decisive. Don't feel badly. Women usually aren't.

Cary: You mean ...

Coach: Right, they're scared to come out and say what they mean. Men are better at it.

Not true, of course. It's a vast overgeneralization.

Cary: Oh.

Her heart is sinking.

Coach: But women can learn decisiveness. It's pretty simple. Here are the four stages....

GETTING IT RIGHT: THE SUBTLE SKILL OF EFFECTIVE TEACHING

Coach: So what went wrong originally was that you were vague when you suggested that your employee take on that task?

Cary: That's right. I kind of implied that he should do it. He didn't see it as a priority, so it never got done. And the executive committee was furious. With me, of course.

Coach: So can we talk for a moment about delegation?

Cary: Sure.

Coach: Being decisive about delegation is a mystery to most supervisors. In the first place, it's usually not easy to tell people what to do. And to add to the confusion, most of us have suffered from bad delegation. Sometimes we've been told what to do by authoritarian people who barked orders, rather than consulted. Yet people sometimes delegate to us in very confusing ways. Okay, so far?

Cary: I'm with you.

Coach: So, faced with a limited number of models to follow, supervisors either tend to bark orders or—because they're more sensitive human beings—they tend to "kind of suggest that it might be nice" if so-and-so were to "maybe" do this or that. You can see the problem here for the person being supervised.

Cary: Yes. They're not exactly sure what to do, where the buck stops, or what the consequences are.

Coach: Exactly. And when we're uncertain what to do, what do we usually do?

The coach knows that he can't teach effectively if he simply recites a stream of facts. One of the most powerful mechanisms for generating change is the relationship between student and teacher. So even in teaching mode, the coach makes sure that their relationship and communication are fluid.

In order to be an effective teacher, the coach

- shows empathy for the coachee
- connects with her
- behaves the same way as he is suggesting that the coachee behave
- offers support and warmth
- shows a willingness to offer challenges
- and, yes, imparts appropriate new information

To be more precise, he usually helps her to see what she already knows, but from a new and practical perspective, and in a well-organized form.

Cary: They do nothing. I get that part. That's exactly what my employee did. But wait, if I was in that situation, the next thing I would do is to start asking questions, so I could gather enough information to get myself back into motion.

Coach: Right, and that's why you're an executive today. But not everyone has that get-up-and-go quality. In fact, it can be dangerous to assume that they do. From what you're saying, it sounds like it's really important for you to increase your clarity when you're giving directions, so they know exactly what's being asked of them. Now I've got a hunch.... Can I ask you something about your family background?

Cary: No problem.

Coach: When your father needed something done, how did he ask for it?

Cary: Uh-oh, I think I know where you're going with this one. He yelled at us, we were pretty scared, and we jumped to do it.

Coach: What about your mom?

Cary: Well, she had to cope with him, so she became pretty indirect. Let's say we were at the supper table. The potatoes were out of reach, and she wanted more. She'd say, "Jimmy, would you like more potatoes?" My brother would have hardly touched the potatoes on his plate, but still she'd ask him if he wanted more. We'd catch each other's eyes and almost break up. But she'd never ask for herself, just wait till someone caught on to the fact that she'd run out of potato.

This coach has already undertaken a thorough assessment near the beginning of the coaching relationship. But this new information illustrates that assessment is never complete. Information emerging during the Development Phase can be used to empower the coachee to make changes.

Coach: And you know where I'm going with this?

Cary: I think so. My dad taught me a lot. But because I didn't want to be like him, I took the opposite approach, and now I'm more like my mom—not too direct about anything that I need!

Coach: In fact, there's nothing particularly unusual about your story. It's the same problem for many people, which means that we need to learn how to ask for what we want done. We need to learn to delegate decisively.

It is not unusual for people to think that once they have described themselves, they are stuck with the description, powerless to change. It is crucial that the coach be clear with Cary about why he is exploring this issue.

- Her knowledge is her power.
- Her power enables her action.
- Her action leads to change.

Cary: So it sounds as if I'm stuck with this problem.

Coach: Actually no. The things you've been saying are not an admission of defeat, just preparation for a change. In other words, if you know your enemy, you know what tactics you need to defeat it.

Cary: So you really think I can make changes in how I delegate? Because I haven't a clue where to start.

Coach: Yes, I have an idea of where we could begin. Would you like to look at four steps I've identified to help people delegate more decisively?

The coach is definitely leading this segment of the session, but much of what he is accomplishing comes from asking the right questions and being open to what he hears. As you can imagine, this would be an easy time to push Cary into a corner, criticize her parents, and unleash a defensive reaction. The skilled coach evokes all the information the coachee needs to express without putting her on the defensive.

Cary: At this point I don't think there's any doubt!

Coach: Okay, so why don't I list the stages, then we'll go into them in more detail. Before we finish, maybe you and I can try role-playing them.

First, make sure you state the need clearly.

Second, find out whether the other person is actually able to take on the task.

Third, assuming that they are, clarify deadlines and expectations.

Fourth, ask the other person to summarize what they've agreed to, either on the spot or later on paper. How's that, so far?

At this point, the coach is in a very traditional teaching mode. But he has built up to this carefully, and you can be sure he'll stop lecturing the first chance he gets. He will soon offer his coachee the chance to practice some skills before she returns to the office.

7. Commitment to Developing New Skills and New Approaches: Turning Reflection into Promise

It is very satisfying as a coach to watch one's coachees grow in courage. They begin to reach toward the previously unreachable. They see themselves as resilient—capable of recovering from reverses and increasing their range of options. While some modes of growth are legitimately contemplative, coaching is not. The public has become fascinated with coaching because they see it as making an unmistakable difference in people's behaviour.

Inherent in all coaching is the question "What am I going to do about the things I am learning right now?" It is a spur to action. Until this point in the coaching session, there has been a call to reflection. Now it is replaced by the call to action. As the session moves toward its conclusion, it is the responsibility of the coach to encourage the coachee to begin making some commitments.

But this does not mean that the coach has to identify what those commitments should be, nor present a plan for action to the coachee. As much as possible, the coach should avoid interfering in the coachee's selection of commitments. The very best predictor of success at this point is whether the coachee has made an unqualified commitment to a particular plan.

Unfortunately, both in management and in coaching, this is a truth often forgotten. Whenever coaches ignore it, trying to impose their own ideas, either they will run into massive resistance or they will discover that the coachee is devoting only half her energy and imagination to the task. Why? Because she feels that the coach actually owns the idea.

THE HORRIBLE EXAMPLE

Coach: So I see we're near the end of this session. Here's my suggestion for what you need to do this week. …

To be honest, it isn't common for a coach to be this gauche. Generally coaches jump into a controlling stance like this only if they feel insecure or have just received an inquiry from Cary's supervisor asking why she isn't making better progress.

The suggestion the coach has to offer here might actually be quite helpful. The problem is that he wants to impose it. Whenever a coach thinks he has to tell the coachee what to change, it is pretty clear that he has painted himself into a corner.

An opposite but equally ineffective approach is taken by this coach:

Coach: Well, okay, I notice we're just about out of time. So listen. Think about what we talked about. And hopefully we'll return to it next time.

It sounds so friendly, so casual, so unthreatening. Yet there's an unspoken message here: the coach has run out of ideas, he doesn't think the coachee is capable of change, or he simply doesn't care what is happening in the workplace.

Reading between the lines, the coachee begins to lose faith in the coach and discount the process. She entered coaching because of her difficulty undertaking necessary changes. The last thing she needs is a coach who colludes with her in not committing to new behaviours.

GETTING IT RIGHT: SUPPORTING THE COACHEE TO TAKE THE INITIATIVE

Coach: At this point, you seem to understand much better what's behind these problems. So would you like to look at experimenting with some changes?
Cary: Well, yes, I suppose so. But I'm not that confident that I can actually do things differently.

Notice that the coach is not taking over. He offers a choice even at a time when he's pretty convinced that it's time for commitment. He's making plenty of space for Cary to name her ambivalence. Rather than impose his agenda, he's going to permit her good sense to lead her to whatever commitments she is ready for at this point.

Coach: I can see that. It's impossible to predict what will happen, isn't it? And you've been burned before. So what do you think we should do?
Cary: Well, there's part of me would like to take a few more weeks to think about it! But I have a hunch that I'll never be any more ready than I am today. And I have gained some insight into why these things happened. So maybe I'm ready to try something new.
Coach: Why don't you tell me what you'd like to do differently in the week to come?

Note that the coach is unmistakably nudging Cary to make a commitment here. But he's doing so based on Cary's self-assessment that she will never be more ready than today.

Because Cary knows that the coach is not going to take over, she makes her own suggestion.

Cary: Okay. I don't think there's any use trying to do anything right now about the person who didn't complete the report for the executive.

Coach: That person is a pretty big challenge to start with, isn't he?

Cary: For sure. Too difficult for right now. But there is someone else I've been delegating to recently in a half-hearted way. I wonder if I could focus on him....

THE POWER OF DECISION

The coach encourages Cary to make her own decisions. She is not passive—far from it—but he is careful not to take the initiative away from her. If she feels that she "owns" the process, she is likely to throw herself into it and succeed. And when she runs into the inevitable glitches, she is likely to explore what she can do differently next time, rather than blaming the coach.

8. Action Planning: a Technique that Supplements Commitment

Action planning results in new behaviours, which can lead to outcomes that may or may not be expected. These in turn demand reflection so that new theories can arise to be applied through renewed action planning. This is the cycle of coaching because it is the cycle of much human learning:

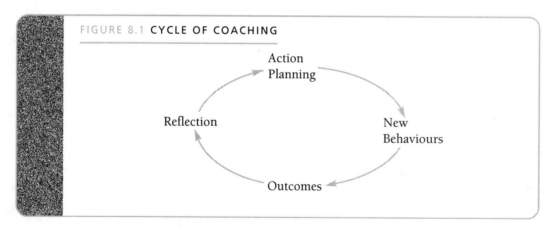

FIGURE 8.1 **CYCLE OF COACHING**

Properly executed, the action-planning segment of a coaching session sets the stage for changed behaviour. These changes will inevitably lead to a variety of outcomes, some of them predictable, some not. Some will be pleasing, some disturbing, and a few may shake the very foundations of the workplace. But all of them will provide grist for the mill of reflection, which will form the early part of the next session between coach and coachee, thus completing the circle.

ACTION-PLANNING STEPS

The making of an action plan involves precision about
- objective (precisely what coachee wishes to accomplish)
- actions (exactly what needs to be done to get there)
- additional resources needed (and where to find them)
- outcome (which will prove that objectives have been achieved)
- time frame (when to begin the process, timing for specific aspects, time of conclusion)

THE HORRIBLE EXAMPLE

Coach: So, Cary, what's going to happen this week?

Cary: Well, I'm going to try to delegate some stuff to Matt.

Coach: I guess at this point you don't know exactly how or when?

Cary: No, I guess not.

Coach: Oh, well, I'm sure you'll figure it out when the time comes. I have faith in you. Anyway, good luck.

Cary: Thanks.

It's nice to have faith in people. But it's far more empowering to provide the tools to back up the faith.

GETTING IT RIGHT: HELPING THE COACHEE PLAN FOR ACTION

Coach: So, Cary, what would you like to accomplish this week?

Cary: Well, I think the most important thing is to start delegating and build up my confidence.

Coach: Sounds like a promising objective. Maybe this is the time to introduce you to my action-planning form. It's a simple guide that helps people make action plans that actually work.

Cary: Good idea. Let me see how it works.

Coach: Okay, first write in your objective here. Next to that is a space to sketch out exactly what you need to do in order to accomplish that.

Cary: Well, basically I need to try to delegate some stuff to Matt.

Coach: Right. But that's fairly general. Why don't we take a look at exactly what you'll do?

Cary: You mean, what I'll actually say to him? I don't really know that yet. It depends on the moment.

Coach: I understand that. But let's start at the beginning. First of all, are you absolutely clear with yourself about what you want to delegate?

Cary: Hmm, maybe not. Maybe my first step is to write a description of that for myself.

Coach: Good idea. So getting back to actually talking to Matt, what would you like to say to him? What could you communicate to give him the best chance to pick up the ball and run with it?

Cary: Well, I could ask if he'd like more potatoes!

Coach: Terrific. I can see we've made a lot of progress today.

Cary: Okay, seriously, I'd tell him exactly what I'd like him to do and ask if he's able to do it.

Coach: What if you run into a roadblock? Like he doesn't really want to do it, so he says he's too busy.

Cary: Well, I can't think of anything he's doing for me that couldn't wait a couple of days till he finishes this. I'd tell him that.

Coach: So you know what you're going to do. And by the way, you sound pretty certain, pretty determined. Still, doing this without any backup could be hard. Are there any outside resources you could look to for additional support?

Cary: I'm not sure. I thought this was pretty well up to me.

Coach: Sure it is, in the long run. But if your boss could support you, or if you could read an article about delegating, or if you could do something else to boost your confidence, it might help.

Cary: Well, actually I do have an article that I've been meaning to read. I'll take it on the bus with me. But as soon as you said, "boost my confidence," I suddenly thought about my exercise class. Whenever I go to the gym, I feel so good and sure about myself. Maybe I should make a point of getting up early and getting to the class on the way to work.

Coach: Both those ideas sound practical. So now, if your objective is to increase your delegation skills, how will you know that you've accomplished that?

Cary: Well, if I was sure that I had been clear with Matt, I'd be happy. That would be a definite start. But it will take more than one success to get used to being direct with people about what I expect from them.

Coach: Sounds like you're keeping your eye on both short-term and long-term outcomes. Is there anything else that will convince you that you've succeeded in the short term?

Cary: Yeah. If Matt actually does what I ask him to!

Coach: Okay. So let's look at some time lines. Why don't you write down when you'll write up Matt's task, when you'll talk with him, and when you'll know that he's done the job you asked for. Oh, and how about adding a long-term date, too, for when you think you might be able to say, "Overall, I'm now doing a pretty good job of delegating."

THE POWER OF A PAPER GUIDE

A simple but valuable way to guide a conversation about behaviour changes is for the coach to offer a one-page action-planning guide. Such a guide is useful for designing any sort of change initiative, because it enables the coachee to examine briefly but directly each of the major issues she will face in real time. Coaches often keep a supply of these forms available for use at the end of each session. That way the coachee can carry away a concrete reminder of what she is undertaking.

FIGURE 8.2 **ACTION PLAN**

Action Plan				
Objective (Specifically what do I want to accomplish?)	Actions (What do I need to do to accomplish the objective?)	Resources Required (Material, interpersonal support, etc.)	Outcome (Exactly how will I know that I've achieved my objectives?)	Time-line (Start, middle, end.)

9. Conclusion: How "Goodbye" Empowers

In those final moments at the conclusion of each session we do a lot of business. We

* use conventional, socially comfortable ways to say goodbye
* express good wishes
* leave a snapshot of the relationship in the memory of the coachee, and
* empower the coachee to move decisively forward

THE HORRIBLE EXAMPLE

Coach: Oops, I just noticed the time. Gotta run. Supposed to meet someone on the third floor ten minutes ago.

Cary: Oh, I was hoping …

Coach: I know, I know. So let's meet next week. Same time, same station?

There are plenty of ways to blow the ending of a coaching session; this is merely one example. Coaches accomplish the same end by being vague about the timing of the next meeting, fiddling with their briefcases or forgetting to make good eye contact with the coachee as they say goodbye. Here the coach has ensured that, even if ninety-nine percent of the session was valuable, what Cary will carry away is not pragmatic optimism but a muddle of confusion and disappointment.

GETTING IT RIGHT: CONCLUDING BY FUELLING THE RELATIONSHIP

Coach: We have a couple of minutes left. Is there anything else we should cover?

Cary: I don't think so. I'm pretty clear on what I want to do.

Coach: Well, you've picked a pretty interesting challenge for this week. I'm really looking forward to our next meeting just to see what happens.

Cary: I'm a little nervous about it. But I'm okay.

Coach: I know you are. If you should want to call me this week, before or after you talk with Matt, I'd be glad to chat with you. It's hard to do this alone the first time.

Cary: Thanks, but I don't think I'll need to call.

Coach: Well, even if you don't need to, call if you want to. Okay?

Cary: Thanks

Coach: You're welcome. And good luck!

Cary: See you next time.

What was the outcome of this particular coaching engagement? Cary did experiment with delegating more challenging jobs to her staff. Increasingly she asked them to run with the ball and to consult with her whenever they were uncertain about how to proceed.

"Frankly, I was terrified," she related at a follow-up session. "And at first they made some pretty interesting mistakes. Plus, I know I interfered too much. But I'm amazed at how able they've turned out to be. Now I'm handing them more sophisticated work all the time."

Needless to say, the morale and creativity of Cary's department is on the rise. A new generation of managers is becoming better prepared for succession to senior positions. And Cary herself is beginning to look more promotable as she demonstrates her ability to add vision and value, rather than simply keeping the wheels turning.

AU REVOIR, NOT GOODBYE

An effective conclusion to a coaching session has the same impact as the end of a chapter in a novel: it makes the reader want to move to the next chapter, to engage again with the characters, to discover the further adventures.

The coachee needs that kind of encouragement, for she is facing great challenges, exploring parts of herself never before examined in any detail. A strong conclusion helps her to feel enthusiastic about the experiments ahead and about the next time she will meet with her coach.

UNFORESEEN DEVELOPMENTS

The Development and Integration Phase is by far the longest and most challenging part of a coaching assignment. During its course, the coachee must

- develop new skills
- evolve a new relationship with herself
- integrate new behaviours
- learn to use unseen strengths
- prepare to continue without the coach
- become a more committed continuous learner

No one can foresee with any exactitude what the outcome of coaching will be. We enter it because we have faith in the power of one human being guiding, challenging, and encouraging another.

Nor can we know for certain how much time it will take to complete the work. A coaching contract provides only a rough guide, for this is an art, not a science. But as your coachee develops, it will become clear that he or she is approaching the end of this journey.

Nearing the conclusion of the Development Phase, you will find yourself saying to the coachee, "When you're finished coaching ..." and "When you and I aren't working together any more ... " In this way, you will be preparing the ground for a new, independent phase in the development of the coachee.

FIGURE 8.3 EXERCISE FOR THE COACH

1. Survey your past coaching relationships to see which of these themes showed up most often:
   - Individualized skill training to increase effectiveness
   - Developing a more productive management style
   - Resolution of values conflicts

   Based on your experience, would you add other themes to the list?

2. Read your notes from a recent coaching session. Chart the structure of the session and compare it with this suggested outline:
   - Greeting and news

(continued)

FIGURE 8.3 **CONTINUED**

- Agenda building
- Reflection on experiments with new behaviours
- Celebration of successes
- Addressing difficulties and blocks
- Teaching segment
- Commitment to developing new skills and new approaches
- Action planning
- Conclusion

Note *how* your session differed and *why*.
Write notes on what you would do differently in hindsight.
Write notes on the strengths of how you handled the session.

3. Design a structure for a session that you will be conducting soon, based on your previous session with a coachee and on what you already know about the situation. Use your design as a guide during the session.

4. Once you have held that session, compare what you planned with what actually happened. What were the differences? What led you not to follow your plan precisely? Were your deviations from the plan beneficial or not? What made them so?

5. Develop your personalized version of the standard structure above and use it to guide future sessions.

In the next and final chapter, we'll examine the Completion Phase of the coaching process. We will discover how to complete a coaching relationship in a way that helps to cement the coachee's learning, and how to deal with predictable pitfalls, so that the result will be remarkable success.

The Opportunities of the Completion Phase

Saying goodbye sounds simple. Yet this can be a complex and difficult interchange, and in the coaching relationship it requires both grace and caution. Although it involves assessing the work performed during the recent weeks or months, the Completion Phase has more to do with the coachee's future than the past. The Completion Phase begins when the coach and coachee prepare for the conclusion of the coaching, the challenge of continued growth, and the successful management of obstacles.

This is a moment of great potential. Your managing style will have a significant impact on how the coachee remembers the events and outcomes of the coaching relationship. Handle it carelessly, and the coaching may soon slip into a vague recollection, a formal intervention half-recalled from somewhere in the shadowy past. Handle the Completion Phase carefully and thoroughly, and the impact of coaching is likely to persist as an ongoing force—ocean waves rolling repeatedly onto the shoreline of the individual's life.

FEEDBACK: REWARDS FOR THE COACH

Coaches conduct evaluations at the conclusion of a coaching engagement because they are personally committed to continuous learning. They want to know how they can do better next time.

But in a calling that demands so much of us, requiring that we become involved with coachees at a personal level, there is frequently an additional, heartwarming benefit to an evaluation. Sometimes it reads like fan mail. "I could never have come as far as I have if it had not been for our discussions in coaching," wrote a grateful coachee recently.

Despite its importance, the Completion Phase typically receives the least attention. It is too easy to simply let the coaching relationship fade out.

Coach: So here we are at the end of our contract. It's been good working with you. Best wishes for the future. Oh, and call me if you know anyone else who needs a coach.

That lame goodbye conveys only the tiniest fraction of what you can accomplish at the conclusion of a coaching relationship. So let's look at what your coachee needs from the conclusion—and what you need, too. For the coachee the Completion Phase is the chance to

- cover areas needing more attention and or requiring a conclusion
- evaluate progress
- plan for maintaining successes to date
- plan for continuous growth
- plan to prevent slippage
- reflect on what worked and what did not work in the relationship in order to help with the coachee's future coaching or mentoring situations
- preparing to release the coaching relationship, let go of the sense of dependency and the supportive friendship with the coach

If life presents an endless series of opportunities for learning, this is the ideal moment to sketch out a map for the future, extending the impact of coaching potentially into the coachee's entire lifetime. Do not ignore the fact that this stage is important to you, too, as a professional, offering you opportunities to

- cover under-serviced areas in the coaching, items of that were temporarily overshadowed by more urgent needs
- satisfy yourself that your coachee has the best chance of maintaining his progress and continuing to develop
- reflect on what worked and did not work in the relationship for the sake of your own continuing development as a coach
- say goodbye properly to someone to whom you have devoted a lot of care
- end the relationship with clarity, leaving a positive memory in the mind of the coachee
- set the stage for the possibility of further referrals from the organization or the individual

Looking at the combined length of the above lists, it becomes clear that the completion of a coaching relationship cannot be left until the last day of coaching. Too much remains to be done. Where possible, you and the coachee should identify the approach of the Completion Phase a few weeks ahead of time and begin working on it together even while the Development and Integration Phase continues.

Mingling the Phases of Coaching

The phases of a coaching engagement are never discrete or linear. Maintaining clarity about what is going on at any given moment is no easier than juggling oranges while steering a shopping cart through the market. Although steeped in the present, you and the coachee are constantly referring backward and forward:

- During the Contracting Phase, you are also picking up vital information that will be a valuable part of the Assessment Phase.
- The questions asked during the Assessment initiate reflection, which in turn can lead to change and to the phase of Development and Integration.
- Throughout Development and Integration, you are refining the Assessment, and particularly toward the end, you are anticipating the Completion Phase.
- And during Completion, you are re-Assessing so that the coachee leaves the engagement with clarity about future areas for development.

To successfully juggle these requires deliberate focus, but it transforms the coaching engagement from a series of unrelated meetings to a unified whole.

Steps in the Completion Phase

The Completion Phase of a coaching engagement should include all of the following aspects, although not necessarily in equal measure. The relative attention you give to each of these tasks reflects the needs of the coachee and the nature of the work you have accomplished.

1. Mutual agreement that the work is complete
2. Evaluation with the coachee
3. Evaluation with the organization
4. Preparation to prevent slippage
5. Scheduling follow-up
6. Planning whether the coach will remain available for further consultation

1. Mutual Agreement that the Work Is Complete

Termination of the coaching engagement may be triggered by a number of events:

- The time agreed to in a fixed contract is almost up.
- The coachee has suddenly been transferred to Moscow, or for some other reason coaching cannot continue.
- Objectives have been met. You may have been working on a contract of indefinite length but one with clear objectives. At this point, most of the objectives have been fulfilled

In the case of the first two events, the coaching may not be entirely complete, that is, the objectives identified in the Contracting Phase have not been achieved, and that makes things complicated. The coachee may not be prepared to let go of the coaching. If you share the coachee's concern, it is legitimate to raise this issue. You are, after all, an independent observer with an objective viewpoint.

EXTENDING COACHING

There is, of course, a problem implicit in saying, "He's not ready to stop yet." It may appear to be in the coach's interest to extend the coaching indefinitely, whether or not she is internal or external to the organization, to keep those cheques or plaudits rolling in. And even if no one objects out loud, the cynical belief may be fed that coaching and consulting contracts can be extended just because the provider of services needs to meet a mortgage payment.

If you are thinking of recommending that a coaching engagement not end at this time, be sure to search through your own motivation before others do. To present yourself as thoroughly professional and to limit the possibility of later recriminations, present the pros and cons of extending the contract on paper. Then prepare to discuss the business benefits for the person and the organization.

PREMATURE TERMINATION OF COACHING

Often coachees feel disappointed as they approach the end of this special relationship. After all, they have had the undivided attention of a supportive, stimulating person who—unlike others in the workplace—held no hidden agenda.

Yet some coachees want to terminate the coaching too soon. Of course, it is normal for people to wish to "graduate" as soon as possible, to demonstrate that they have completed a process and are ready for the next challenge. But sometimes, this may short-change them. If this is true, the coach could raise the possibility that the coachee is terminating prematurely.

Coach: Steven, I know that you've made a lot of changes in our work together. And if we end the coaching at this point, I have no worries about your ability to carry on. But I'm curious to know what your thoughts are about the other issues that you and your boss identified when we began this. [Names the issues here.] Do you think that you've made sufficient progress in them that you'll be satisfied in the long term?

The key is to be gentle. Questions like this can stir up lots of hidden shame. If you ask in a compassionate, inquiring, and non-critical spirit, you will find the coachee generally able to confront even frightening issues.

Part of your tool kit here is your ability to not hold a heavy investment in the outcome of this discussion. "Attachment" to particular outcomes is a dangerous trap for the coach during any phase of coaching. The effective coach will offer her best insights and her care, and then step back to allow the coachee—and in some cases the supervisor—to make the final decision.

Taking a neutral stance does not imply detachment. Permitting the other person to take final responsibility does not connote a lack of caring.

With those cautions clearly identified, note that there is generally no controversy about whether the work is finished. Coach and coachee have been working together so closely that they will both know, more or less, when the coaching should conclude.

2. Evaluation with the Coachee

In this bountiful harvest phase, there are as many approaches to evaluating the coachee's progress as there are coaches. One effective technique is to use an evaluation chart like the one below. It covers the key aspects of the progress of the coachee, with a decided bias toward self-awareness.

To use it, simply copy the chart or create your own version, then invite the coachee to write notes on the paper evaluating his progress in each of these zones:

1. his growing awareness of self and others
2. his integration of the learning into his thinking about his work life
3. his actions in experimenting with and applying new behaviours

With that done, both of you can discuss your impressions, noting the relationship between the three aspects, looking for areas you can celebrate and those requiring close monitoring in the future.

FIGURE 9.1 **EVALUATION TRIANGLE**

AWARENESS
- Self-awareness
- Other-awareness
- Awareness of the impact of self on others and vice versa

ACTION
- Application of learning
- Experimentation with new behaviours

INTEGRATION
- Reflection on learning
- Minimal recurrence of old unproductive behaviours

Use of this chart is not limited to the Completion Phase. It can be employed and repeated at any stage in the coaching work as a means to check the coachee's progress.

Keep in mind that its scope is limited. It evaluates the progress of the coachee in isolation. It should be accompanied by questions like those below, which clarify the effect of the coach and the progress of the coaching relationship—not to mention any bumps in the road.

EVALUATING THE RELATIONSHIP

While saying goodbye, it is good to look together at the relationship that has developed between the two of you. Here are some lines that could help you to initiate the conversation:

- What stands out in your memory?
- What were the highlights of this experience?
- Looking back, how would you describe the process of coaching?
- How would you describe our relationship? (If it had difficult moments, you may need to demonstrate that it is safe to talk about them, such as: Remember when we struggled about...? Am I right in thinking you were angry with me on a few occasions?)
- For me, it's really okay that everything has not been smooth as silk as we worked together. What do you think?
- I'd like to hear frankly what these experiences have left with you in the way of impressions: How do you look at coaching now? How will you remember me as a coach?
- Is there anything else that, if you do not say now, you might regret later?

Because the focus here is on your work as a coach, this is a great opportunity to learn more about your professional abilities as seen by the coachee. But like every other moment in a coaching relationship, this is a profound learning opportunity for the coachee.

The evaluation process permits the coachee to identify the importance of relationship in any growth process. It enables him to look back and to recognize the ways a relationship can shift emphasis and grow deeper. By attending to these questions in a direct manner, you are modelling the importance of taking time and of talking (not merely thinking) about the progress of a work-related relationship.

Also, such questions offer the coachee a golden opportunity to learn by observation how to evaluate his relationship with his direct reports and peers.

BY REVIEWING YOUR RELATIONSHIP FRANKLY AND IN DEPTH

- you make clear that you need to hear the best and the worst (corollary truth—so does he)
- you demonstrate that it is better when uncomfortable facts are discussed, rather than buried—not that they can ever be successfully buried (corollary truth—as it is for him)
- you model how clear, honest feedback in the workplace actually improves the work environment (corollary truth—including his)

3. Evaluation with the Organization

A crucial aspect of most evaluations is a meeting or phone call with the sponsor or supervisor of the coachee. At that time you can request the person to complete a questionnaire, such as the one below, providing you with a record that won't fade with memory. Another advantage to requesting a formal evaluation is that some people are able to be more frank in writing than in speaking.

There is an additional benefit. Your interest in being evaluated will recommend you to the sponsor or supervisor as a professional deeply engaged in the process of continuous learning, the kind of person to whom he may be more likely to refer again.

FIGURE 9.2 **EVALUATION FORM**

Private and Confidential

To: [sponsor]

It would be helpful for my development, and to enable me to serve you better in the future, if you would evaluate the coaching I have been offering.

Please be entirely frank. My aim is to constantly improve the quality of my work. Just select the box below that best characterizes the impact of the coaching, and then add any personal comments below.

❏	❏	❏	❏	❏
Made situation worse	No change	Some improvement	Very helpful	Exceeded expectations

Comments
In a few words, please describe how the coaching process has affected
- the employee
- the sponsors or referrer(s)
- the organization

Please add additional comments about
- the availability/flexibility of the coach
- the coach's responsiveness to your needs
- direct and indirect costs of coaching
- any difficulties with coaching process

Do you have any additional comments?

Please return this form to [your address].
Thank you for your help. Please do not hesitate to get in touch with me if you have any further questions or suggestions.

[Signed]

REPORTING TO THE ORGANIZATION

Life would be easy if only the coach needed feedback. But it is common for organizations to press for feedback from the coach about the progress of the coachee. As the chapter on contracting suggests, the coach must exercise great caution about reporting.

From the beginning, there should be an explicit agreement with the coachee that the organization will receive a report. Then the coach can create a report without compromising his professional commitments. It will describe the coaching engagement in a factual way and refer to the progress made by the coachee—without revealing personal or overly specific information.

A report may suggest further steps that the coachee could pursue, but such information should be offered with great care. If you include explicit information about any ongoing problems the coachee has, there are dangers for all parties. The coachee may be humiliated, experience discrimination, or lose his employment. If the organization takes disciplinary action or terminates the employee based on those comments, the organization may be in legal jeopardy. And finally, the coach may be in legal jeopardy. She may be regarded as lacking in professionalism, having allowed herself to be co-opted by the organization.

It is a sensible caution to mark any report prominently as "Confidential." As well, we make it a practice not to use the name of the coachee in the report, so that if it falls into other hands or is retained in a file, the confidentiality of the engagement is not compromised. (If there is any doubt as to the identity of the person we are writing about, we use a phone call to alert the person to whom the report is addressed.)

So how do you write a report that is not restricted to positive and optimistic comments, one that does not appear to be slanted and self-serving? Frankly, it is difficult. The credibility of a report that lacks any "negative" information, along with the credibility of the coach, may be diminished in the eyes of certain readers. That is why it is important to address this issue during the Contracting Phase. Warning the receiver of the report at the outset about the kind of material that will be deliberately omitted is a good idea, also.

FIGURE 9.3 **SAMPLE COMPLETION REPORT TO AN ORGANIZATION**

CONFIDENTIAL REPORT

Dear [director of human resources],

This is my report on the Coaching and Team Development Contract for which you engaged me. As you recall, the coachee assented to my preparing this report at the time of our original contract, and has now read and approved it. As you and I agreed at the time of contracting, this report will not provide detailed or personal information about the coachee.

Here is a description of the course of this engagement. I met with the coachee on eight occasions for assessment and coaching, as well as having a number of telephone conversations. To cover the team development aspect, I used 360-degree feedback to gain a broader perspective, prepared and presented a report for the coachee, and then facilitated three meetings between him and his team. I devoted several hours to planning these interventions to ensure that each had a reliable design and direction. *(continued)*

FIGURE 9.3 **CONTINUED**

As to the business benefit of this work, I am not the best judge. You and [the coachee's supervisor] are in the most favourable position to assess the impact of coaching on the employee's behaviour and productivity. I would encourage you to continue to monitor developments closely and to maintain a dialogue about them with the coachee.

I have found the coachee to be a person of considerable intelligence and tenacity. Because you and [supervisor] presented a clear picture to him of his need for development, the coachee was highly motivated from the beginning to learn from this coaching process. I found him to be flexible and actively interested throughout.

His commitment to coaching did, however, take a considerable forward leap when I presented the 360-degree feedback report focusing on his leadership behaviour. While the experience was initially shocking and humbling, the coachee rallied with respect, tenacity, and curiosity. He appears to have crossed a watershed during this period, with a deeper commitment to continuous learning.

As for the team, my impression is that they are now more willing to experiment with new behaviours and with building trust. Each person has demonstrated a willingness to take risks for the sake of improved working relationships with the coachee.

In concluding this contract, we have reached a critical juncture. As always in coaching, staying power is the final issue facing us. Now that I am no longer involved in his progress, I believe that you could play a key role, helping him to stay on track by showing interest in his development on an informal, ongoing basis.

Also, I would like to see him supported by a more formal relationship with a reliable mentor from within the organization, someone who could support his ongoing progress. You may be able to encourage this.

In summary, the coachee is a person of superior abilities who has never before experienced such an opportunity for personal and interpersonal development. I believe that this intervention could result in better morale and higher productivity for the coachee and the team. If your organization can manage the situation attentively, they should show continuing improvement.

You will be aware that I have omitted any specific reference to the problems that led to this coaching engagement. Should you wish further information, I suggest that you speak directly with the coachee, who can decide how much he wishes to reveal.

I would appreciate any feedback you may have for me regarding this engagement. Please take a moment to complete the evaluation form attached.

Above all, please feel free to contact me further about this case. Thank you for your interest and trust in the coaching process.

[Signed]

4. Preparation to Prevent Slippage

One of the strengths of a properly concluded coaching relationship is that it prepares the coachee to confront the possibility of slippage and backsliding. Everyone backslides into old behaviours; it is just human nature. The difference between success and failure is what you think and what you do after the slide.

Unless you normalize slippage, it will feel confusing and disastrous to the coachee, and can lead to despair. Contradictory though it may sound, it is important to think of slippage as positive. To slip is both natural and human.

Beyond that, it reveals that the coachee has had the courage to climb to a position from which there is the possibility of slipping down. After all, no one slides downhill from the valley. So you should make a clear distinction between slippage and failure.

Here is a framework for confronting the possibility of slipping. Essentially it asks the coachee how he will fill the gaps when he doesn't have a coach to turn to.

OUTLINE FOR A CONVERSATION ABOUT SLIPPAGE

- Imagine a situation where you might be tempted to revert to your old patterns of behaviour. Describe where you are, whom you are with, and what is going on.
- Imagine the thoughts and feelings that you may be having in this situation.
- For each thought or feeling write down a more constructive thought or feeling that could help you respond in the new ways you have developed.
- List two or three strategies you will use to help you move into your more helpful thinking and feeling.
- Describe your new, more constructive responses for this situation.
- List some people you can talk to for encouragement when the possibility of slippage looms.

You can handle this issue by asking the above out loud, using it as a guide to conversation. Or you can develop a handout, allowing space for written responses, and then discuss the completed form later. The deciding factor is whether, in your experience, the coachee will respond best on the spot or given time to reflect.

Whichever choice you select, it is essential that you confront the possibility of backsliding with compassion and with hope. After all, backsliding represents the coachee's and the organization's worst nightmare.

FEEDBACK: MOVING PAST RESISTANCE

"It was an extremely helpful process, enabling me to continue to move forward and accept changes, despite great difficulties on my part in the beginning. [The coach] was warm, perceptive, honest, gently-challenging, and curious—all of which were vital to my dealing with my situation with integrity and courage, and continuing to trust my intuition."

5. Scheduling Follow-Up

Some individuals are eager to fly solo, but a majority will welcome further contact with their coach. During the Contracting Phase you will have included one or more follow-ups in the budget, so in the majority of cases all you need to do here is to make a specific plan.

Coach: We've agreed to conclude the coaching, and we've looked at the progress you've made. Now it would be a good idea to make some decisions about what you can plan to help you maintain your progress.

Coachee: Well here's what I'm planning to do.... [identifies plans]

Coach: That sounds really solid. Would be helpful if we were supplement that plan by touching base together? For instance, I would be happy to meet with you in a few weeks to hear how you're doing. I'd like to help you work through any unexpected issues that might come up. Would that be useful to you?

FOLLOW-UP MEETING

The purpose of the scheduled follow-up is to deepen the impact of coaching. Also, it provides the coachee with encouragement to continue to develop, a chance to reflect on any problems that have arisen since the coaching concluded, and an opportunity to plan new approaches.

What makes the follow-up so powerful in deepening the coaching is that it has a different quality from the routine coaching meeting. By now, both parties have a little distance from their intensive work. They can look back with objectivity, and they are in a better position to discuss the actual benefits the coachee received. This increase in objectivity allows the coachee to be profoundly honest with himself and to approach issues that may have seemed too threatening in the heat of ongoing coaching.

But to ensure that the follow-up meeting will be fruitful, the coach requires preparation. By scanning her notes, she can make sure that she has a good memory—at a minimum—of the following items:

- presenting issues
- objectives of the coaching
- results of the assessment process
- factors that made it difficult for the coachee to change
- highlights and difficulties during coaching
- relationship between coach and coachee
- plans for further development
- strategies to prevent slippage

With refreshed memory of these issues, she will be able to sit down with her former coachee serenely and confidently. Whenever a coach does not prepare adequately for a meeting, whether during coaching or in follow-up, her mind will be largely and anxiously engaged with a search for relevant memories. Such a situation can stand in the way of any real encounter between the coach and coachee, and could lead to disappointing results for the coachee.

6. Planning Whether the Coach Will Remain Available for Further Consultation

Just knowing that you can be reached means a lot to a graduating coachee. Your willingness to spend a few moments on the phone or at lunch reminds him that he was not just a contract but a person to you. And it allows you to offer resources that are value-added.

In some respects the coach is in a parental role. As all parents have discovered, it is sometimes more important to their offspring that the parents remain available than that they actually see each other. Some coachees will never call again, but they benefit by the sense of support that goes with your willingness to stay in touch. Our experience has been that it is very gratifying to stay in touch with our graduates.

STAYING IN TOUCH

While it is not always possible to stay in touch with a coachee once he has finished coaching, there are plenty of rewards when you do.

In a professional firm with several hundred staff, the coach worked intensively with Daniel, the edgy, difficult CFO. (For finance people, the transition to management responsibilities can be particularly challenging, since their strength and interests don't always lie in the area of human relations.) By the coach's guess, Daniel was within a year of being fired.

"My job is finance, not communication," he brusquely informed her in an early interview. Commanding his troops by demand, favouring his star performers and ignoring the rest, occasionally bursting into public denunciations of his beleaguered staff, he was inadvertently doing everything humanly possible to demoralize his people.

Desperately disorganized, he would demand reports from staff, then lose them in the chaos of an overflowing desktop. Urgently summoning a worker to his office, he would then ignore the person to talk on the phone. He'd arrive late for meetings and leave before they were over. He was, in the words of one colleague, "High maintenance." He required, in the uncharitable description of another, "a lot of mothering."

He was mandated into coaching, and the coach suspects he would have kept her politely at arm's length for the duration of his sentence, except for one decisive factor.

The coach received his agreement to do a 360-degree feedback, sending a questionnaire to every one of his workers, his supervisor, and a few of his colleagues. It revealed in devastating detail the plummeting level of morale in his department and the negative spiral of his business relationships. Receiving that information, he felt upset and frightened about his career, but he was no quitter.

Their work was cut out for them, and with considerable uncertainty, Daniel experimented with treating his people with greater respect. When they fell short of his standards, for instance, instead of publicly humiliating them, he would try to speak to them in private and, without assuming their guilt, inquire about what had gone wrong.

As the coaching proceeded, the coach saw increasingly positive outcomes. Still, she was surprised and pleased when he told her that she had been approached to take on similar responsibilities at a much larger firm in another city.

After half a year in the new position, Daniel phoned his coach to say that his new job was going very well. This was welcome news, because his position had several of the most problematic qualities of the old one—the pressure, the unwelcome surprises, the technical breakdowns. "Someone burps," he remarked laconically, "and I have to get on a plane. In fact, recently I went into the office for a weekend lunch meeting and found myself eating supper in Washington, DC."

He told his coach that coaching had prepped him for dealing with this extreme level of pressure in a more graceful way. He had become increasingly effective, he said. And, as Daniel put it, "Communication is now a large part of my job."

ATTENTION TO DETAIL CONVEYS CARE

The coachee knows that he is not just an assignment for the coach when she uses phrases like:

- remember how you said …
- At one stage in the coaching it seemed to me that …
- Do you recall the difficulty we ran into when …
- One of the most important things I learned about you was that …
- How is your relationship these days with …
- What kind of progress have you made on the issue you identified …

When the coach demonstrates that the coachee is in the forefront of her mind, it is natural that he will feel cared for. It is a simple psychological truth that this will encourage him to continue the hard work of self-development.

OUTLINE FOR FOLLOW-UP MEETINGS

It is impossible to structure a follow-up until you are at that point, but it is likely to cover at least these five issues:

1. Impact of the coaching on the coachee's responsibilities
2. Impact of the coaching on the coachee's work relationships, including the sponsor of coaching and/or supervisor
3. The coachee's evaluation of how effectively he has followed his plans for development
4. How the coachee has dealt with the tendency to slip
5. Plans or revised plans for growth in the future

FEEDBACK: THE PERCEIVED ECONOMIES OF COACHING

"We could have spent much more on a training course than we did on coaching, and the manager would never have had this level of individualized attention."

The Varied Roles of the Coach

And so the coaching engagement comes to an end. Now what do we make of the impact of coaching—on ourselves and on the world? As we reflect back on our experiences as coaches, we have found ourselves in a multitude of moods and roles.

Guide

One day we are mountain guides, leading our coachees to the very edge of the precipice, lending them the courage to peer over the edge at the opportunities and dangers surrounding them in the workplace. Terrified and thrilled, they gaze at distant summits and deep abysses, then demonstrate—with risky and carefully thought-out manoeuvres—that they do possess the courage to move carefully on.

Cheerleader

The next day, we are like cheerleaders, encouraging the faint-hearted. "Go get 'em! You can do it!" We watch our coachees respond with incredulity, then hope, and then, at long last, with action. We are excited. We were right. They can do it.

Failure

And sometimes we feel like failures. We just don't seem to be reaching the coachees. Is it them? Is it us? What's going on here to thwart a coaching process that for the vast majority of coachees is hugely valuable? We wait. We worry. We suspend judgment. Eventually we are given the answer.

Therapist

Sometimes we feel like therapists, helping brilliant people who nonetheless have a serious neurosis to make a new start in their lives. We have learned how gratifying it is to be patient and give them time to grow.

Parent

Often we feel like loving parents, restraining our impatience with coachees' self-defeating habits and awkward relationships, endlessly encouraging them to reach beyond. "Do you see how when you're vague, you lose the respect of your team? Do you think you could find a better way to communicate what you need from them?" Exercising gentle, firm, parental guidance, we nudge our charges through baby steps into emotional adulthood. Coaching is a version of good parenting.

Lover

It is not uncommon for us to feel like lovers. Chaste, even distant, but so appreciative of the coachees that sometimes our eyes well up. How often have we started work with coachees with whom we have little in common and as we work together—as our coachees work, we should say, and as we remain close and supportive—something remarkable changes in the chemistry between us. We are partners, a team; we know what they'll say before they open their mouth and vice versa. We care so much that we have to be sure not to care too much. We discover over and over again that to love someone is not to make them love us (or, indeed, to impose any obligation) but to let them go. We don't burden them with our affection. In fact, we believe that most of our coachees would never guess that what we felt for them was … love.

Sports Coach

Next thing we know, we are sports coaches. "Let's figure out the moves. If they pass the ball to you, what will you do next? If they tackle you, how will you react? How will you stay in touch with your team? How will you know when to pass off to someone better positioned?" At such times, we can almost hear the roar of the crowd!

Skeptic

Or we are skeptics. We hear ourselves saying things like "Sure you could do that, but won't the organization tear you apart? Is it worth swimming against the current so hard, so long? Is it worth the discouragement, rage, and depression that could accompany such long odds? Would it not be better to find a sunnier environment, one where your talents would be appreciated?" It is always hard helping coachees face the impossibility of changing the world around them. So like them, we feel sad, discouraged. And then they act! They move to a different division or a different organization—such relief! Or, very often, they assess their current environment and argue that they understand more than we do about its potential. We are filled with awe in the face of our coachee's insight and courage.

Student

At times we are students. It feels as if we're studying day and night to understand our coachees, their organizations, and their environments. We don't quite get it, we can't rely on our experience to show us the way, so we have to pay closer attention. We are inquirers, asking foolish questions that, because they are so naive, actually help our coachees to help us to understand. And then, surprise! It turns out that a silly question has uncovered a whole library of valuable information that until now had been inaccessible to the coachee. Suddenly the coachee has become brilliant. And so have we. What a buzz!

Spellbinder

We are spellbinders, and at times, storytellers. "Let me tell you a tale about someone who faced a problem a little bit like yours … ." Through our stories, we help our coachees to see how they connect with an unseen host of people. They are not alone, not strange, not perverse, but share in the common frailties and powers of humanity. To our delight, they grasp the stories, grasp those unseen individuals who people the stories, and make them their encouraging friends.

Tightrope Walker

Or we are like tightrope walkers, struggling to maintain that most dynamic of balancing acts: to be honest and at the same time to be kind. "Hang on just a second there. Did you actually believe what I thought I just heard you say? Did you really mean that? And do you understand the impact of your attitude?" Sometimes we are the only people who care enough or feel safe enough to be perfectly frank. It is so much more convenient to be "imperfectly frank," either to gloss over the unacknowledged problems of our coachees or to devastate them with criticism.

Philosopher or Fool

We find ourselves sometimes like philosophers, expressing deep truths about life and work. Or sometimes we are more like evangelists, preaching good news about more effective and happy ways to work. Other times we are prophets, trying to convey to the leaders of an organization challenging information about its culture that they would prefer not to hear. And sometimes we are voices crying in the wilderness, wondering why the world is too deaf to hear us. Or we are the fools, crying in the wilderness when, if we were to stand in the main square instead and only whisper, a few individuals would certainly be intrigued enough to listen.

To be a coach is to take so many roles, to feel so many emotions, to behave in such a bewildering variety of ways, that it is impossible to adequately define the work, whether in a few words or in the pages of an entire book. This much is clear, however: coaching is a fabulous profession!

So we wish for you great satisfaction as you pursue coaching, and we hope that you will not hesitate to plumb the depths of learning that it offers.

www.leaderscoach.com
The Leader's Coach website provides further materials for coaching and information about the co-authors' practice.

Instruments for Coaching

www.blanchardlearning.com
Publishes the *Situational Leadership II* instrument.

HRDQ 1-800-633-4533
Publishes *Negotiating Style Profile*

www.mbti.com
Publishes the *Myers-Briggs Type Inventory* and *Thomas-Kilmann Conflict Mode Instrument*

www.panoramicfeedback.com
Panoramic Feedback is the Internet-based 360-degree feedback tool developed by the co-authors, Bentley and Kohn-Bentley. Click on "Demo" to create a demonstration 360-degree feedback survey. You can respond to it, then view the report.

www.situational.com
Provides the *Lead Self* and *Lead Other* instruments.

www.eiconsortium.org
This is the Web site of the Consortium for Research on Emotional Intelligence in Organizations. The report on developmental guidelines described in Chapter Eleven of Goleman's book (below) can be downloaded from this site.

Training and Accreditation

www.adlerontario.com
The Adler School for Professional Coaching provides excellent workplace coaching training. The school is based in Toronto, Ontario, Canada.

www.coachfederation.com
The International Coaching Federation is an organization of coaches of many varieties.

www.coachu.com
CoachU is a virtual coaching school.

www.peer.ca
Peer Resources, based in Victoria, B.C., provides training for coaches and mentors.

www.thecoaches.com
The Coaches Training Institute provides coaching training.

Bibliography

Coaching

Barer-Stein, Thelma. "Learning about Learning" in James A. Draper, Maurice C. Taylor, Eds. *Voices from the Literacy Field*. Toronto ON: Culture Concepts Inc., 1992.

Understanding the universal processes—including the influence of past experiences, present emotions and concerns—through which each person learns.

Cooper, Robert K. and Ayman Sawaf. *Executive EQ: Emotional Intelligence in Leadership and Organizations*. New York: Grosset/Putnam, 1996.

Based on a slightly different model of emotional intelligence than Goleman's book, this work contains useful tools and techniques to use with clients working on self-mastery and the soft skills required for success in the workplace, whether at the leadership level or below. Each chapter has a section called "EQ in Action." Some of the tools and techniques may be familiar from other sources, but it is helpful to see them interpreted in this particular context.

Crane, Thomas. *The Heart of Transformational Coaching: Using Transformational Coaching to Create a High-Performance Culture*. San Diego, CA: FTA Press, 1998.

A useful book for those interested in the role of the manager as coach or for those making coaching an integral part of their interaction within an organization. There is also useful information for coaching in general, especially the section on the "heart of coaching."

Noteworthy features include

* a detailed process model for a coaching interaction
* a series of chapters devoted to the heart of transformational coaching (including topics such as mindsets, beliefs, communication filters, behavioural styles and coaching)
* a chapter on creating a high-performance organization

Flaherty, James. *Coaching: Evoking Excellence in Others*. Boston, MA: Butterworth-Heinemann, 1999.

This is a text for those who prefer a strong theoretical orientation. Noteworthy features include

* an in-depth exploration of a philosophical framework for coaching
* an extensive discussion of the coaching relationship
* a discussion and outline of coaching processes with different time lines
* an ongoing "coaching case study" to illustrate the points made in the text
* a chapter devoted specifically to the development of the coach

On the method side, Flaherty puts a strong emphasis on self-observation as an integral part of the process, and his appendices contain several examples of self-observation exercises, in addition to sample practices.

Freedberg, Edmund J. *Activation: the Core Competency*. Toronto, ON: HarperBusiness, 1997.

This text is a useful source of simple, practical exercises and tools for use with clients.

Goleman, Daniel. *Working with Emotional Intelligence*. New York: Bantam Books, 1998.

Outlining the importance of emotional intelligence for excellence at work, Goleman also explains in detail how the so-called soft skills required for today's workplace are based on underlying emotional intelligence capacities. Chapter Eleven (Best Practices) contains helpful guidelines for designing training processes to acquire skills with a social or emotional component.

Gallwey, W. Timothy. *The Inner Game of Work*. New York: Random House, 1999.

Here is a self-coaching guide on how to learn and work more productively and fulfillingly. In the chapter on coaching, Gallwey emphasizes the value of coaching in the quest for fulfilling work. Coaches who are either internal or external to the working organization will find the concepts and principles valuable.

Hargrove, Robert. *Masterful Coaching*. San Francisco, CA: Jossey-Bass, 1995.

Here the question "Do I have what it takes to be a masterful coach?" is thoroughly addressed. Filled with useful stories and exercises, and primarily aimed at coaching within an organizational context, the book also offers a section focused on team learning.

Features include

- an emphasis on personal change and perspective-shifting as key to results
- an emphasis on coaching as a conversation
- an inventory of several tools for one-on-one and team coaching

Hargrove, Robert. *Masterful Coaching Field Book*. San Francisco, CA: Jossey-Bass Pfeiffer. 2000.

Written primarily from the perspective of the internal coach or leader-as-coach, here is a field book companion to Hargrove's first book, *Masterful Coaching* that contains valuable ideas, tools, and techniques for external coaches, as well.

Hudson, Frederic M. *The Handbook of Coaching: A Comprehensive Resource Guide for Managers, Executives, Consultants, and Human Resource Consultants*. San Francisco, CA: Jossey-Bass, 1999.

Written for internal and external coaches, as well as professionals from other fields, Hudson's book is directed to those who are adding coaching skills to their inventory. It provides an orientation to the field from the perspective of the coaching model developed by the Hudson Institute, rather than how-to skills. The extensive resource lists cover a wide range of topics particularly relevant to coaching.

Landsberg, Max. *The Tao of Coaching: Boost Your Effectiveness by Inspiring Those Around You*. Santa Monica, CA: Knowledge Exchange, 1997.

Aimed at the manager as coach, this book is based on the "GROW" model (see Whitmore's *Coaching for Performance* below). Noteworthy features include

* handy fact sheets on key points
* illustration of major points (a story running through the text)
* concrete ideas on dealing with different situations
* a set of appendices containing tools to help support the coach in practicing the concepts

O'Hanlon, William and Brian Cade. *A Brief Guide To Brief Therapy*. New York NY: Norton, 1993.

A guide book to brief therapy, providing an overview of its history and theory from its beginnings with Gregory Bateson through Milton Erickson and John Weakland to contemporary practitioners such as Steven deShazer. It concentrates on ways of working with clients that are common to all brief therapies, including framing, pattern, paradoxical, metaphorical, and family interventions.

O'Hanlon, William and Michele Weiner-Davis. *In Search of Solutions: A New Direction in Psychotherapy*. New York NY: Norton, 1989.

O'Hanlon articulates a new, competency-based, approach to helping people grow that is distinctive because of its focus on the present and future. It helps clients move from being dominated by their problem to relying on their own solutions and strengths.

Weisinger, Hendrie. *Emotional Intelligence at Work*. San Francisco, CA: Jossey-Bass, 1998.

Written in a practical style, this book contains dozens of exercises to help you develop and practise emotional intelligence in specific work situations. These exercises provide a great course of ideas for designing practices with clients.

John Whitmore. *Coaching for Performance*. London UK: Nicholas Brealy Publishing, 1996.

This is the classic text on performance coaching. Noteworthy features include

* an insightful discussion of the context of performance coaching
* a detailed account of the well-known "GROW" model (complete with a list of sample questions to use in various phases)
* ideas on a variety of related topics, including motivation, feedback and assessment, coaching teams, and overcoming barriers to coaching

Whitworth, Laura, Henry Kimsey-House, and Phil Sandahl. *Co-active Coaching: New Skills for Coaching People Towards Success in Work and Life*. Palo-Alto, CA: Davies-Black Publishing, 1998.

In his foreword, Whitmore notes that the authors have collaborated to produce a resource for all who aspire to coach, from parents to professionals.

Noteworthy features include

* an outline of three key aspects of coaching, according to the Coaches Training Institute

model: balance, fulfilment, and process
* a handy coach's tool kit, with exercises, forms, etc. Some of the tools are for personal coaching, others for the workplace

Organization Development Journal. volume18, number 2, Summer 2000.
An issue focused on the power of "appreciative inquiry" in international organizations.

Working with Teams

Isachsen, Olaf and Linda V. Berens. *Working Together.* San Juan Capistrano, CA: Institute for Management Development, 1988.
With clear descriptions of the nature of each type of person—using the Myers-Briggs typology—this book describes how to manage the people who fall within each of those specific types.

Laiken, Marilyn. *The Anatomy of High-Performing Teams: A Leader's Handbook.* Toronto, ON: University of Toronto Press, 1991.
A clear and useful way of understanding how teams work, based on the most widely accepted and essential ideas about leadership and the development of teams. Written by an expert who combines theoretic understanding with immense practical experience in guiding teams.

Wellins, Richard S., William C. Byham, and George R. Dixon. *Inside Teams.* San Francisco, CA: Jossey-Bass, 1994.
How twenty very different organizations laid the plans, made the switch, and started their own teams. Each unique story provides a breadth of perspective.

Change Management

Bridges, William. *Managing Transitions: Making the Most of Change.* Reading, MA: Addison Wesley, 1993.
This book is not only how to manage each of the stages of transition, but it also offers a focus on the human impact of change, with true-life illustrations.

Danco, Leon. *Beyond Survival.* Cleveland, OH: Centre for Family Business, 1975.
This book is written for the owner-manager of a successful family business, for the entrepreneur who made it and now wants—somehow—to ensure that the dream survives the transition to younger members of the family.

Dimock, Hedley G. *Intervention and Empowerment: Helping Organizations to Change.* North York, ON: Captus Press, 1992.
Carefully explained here are the concepts and practices of planned change with step-by-step methods for planning, facilitating, stabilizing, and evaluating interventions.

Smye, Marti. *You Don't Change a Company by Memo.* Toronto ON: Key Porter Books, 1994.

You change a company by changing yourself. Essentially this book explains how to reinvent the leader and then invite everyone else to buy into the changes.

Skills for High-Challenge Situations

Deems, Richard S. *Fear of Firing.* Franklin Lakes, NJ: Career Press, 1995.

A pragmatic book about how to handle the task that many leaders consider the most distressing.

Johnson, Barry. *Polarity Management.* Amherst, MA: HRD Press, 1992.

This book explains how to identify and manage unsolvable conflicts. Clear discussions on leadership, decision-making, and the dilemma of individual freedom versus group cooperation are also valuable sections.

Ury, William. *Getting Past No.* New York: Bantam Books, 1991.

You don't have to get mad or get even: Ury explains how to negotiate your way from confrontation to cooperation.

Personal Development

Bernstein, Paula. *Family Ties, Corporate Bonds.* Garden City, New York: Doubleday, 1985.

Explaining how we act out family roles in the office, and how to recognize them, use them, and learn to change them makes this a valuable addition to your library.

Covey, Stephen R. *Principle-Centred Leadership.* New York: Simon and Schuster, 1992.

How do we as individuals and organizations survive and thrive amid tremendous change? This book provides a guide to a more balanced, rewarding, and effective life.

Covey, Stephen R. *The 7 Habits of Highly Effective People.* New York: Simon & Schuster, 1990.

Providing holistic lessons in personal change, this classic book has had a huge impact on the leadership of corporate North America.

Ferner, Jack D. *Successful Time Management.* New York: John Wiley and Sons, 1995.

Ferner is one of the gurus of time management, and this book communicates his belief that we can manage this finite resource with more finesse than we ever dreamed.

Mackenzie, Alec. *The Time Trap.* New York: AMACOM, 1990.

This provides practical guidance for every executive who needs to increase personal effectiveness, from the other time guru.

Murphy, Emmett G. *Leadership IQ*. New York: John Wiley and Sons, 1996.

This book provides not only a personal development process based on a scientific study of a new generation of leaders, it also includes a useful and intriguing self-test referred to in Chapter Seven.

Peters, Thomas J. and Robert H. Waterman, Jr. *In Search of Excellence*. New York: Warner Books, 1982.

This book contains eight basic principles of management distilled from studies of forty-three of the best-run companies in America.

Rogers, Carl R. *On Becoming a Person*. Boston MA: Houghton Mifflin, 1961.

A parent of the human potential movement describes his focus on the growth of human beings through client-centred therapy. Rogers sees his clients as possessing an infinite capacity for development.

Senge, Peter M. *The Fifth Discipline*. New York: Doubleday, 1990.

Senge provides clear and helpful treatment of the five disciplines underlying successful organizations: personal mastery, mental models, shared vision, team learning, and—most crucial—systems thinking.

Philosophical / Spiritual

Della Costa, John. *Working Wisdom*. Toronto, ON: Stoddart Books, 1995.

Helping us to look beyond the search for information and knowledge data, Della Costa sees wisdom as the highest form of understanding and says it is the ultimate value in the new economy.

Eigen, Lewis D. and Jonathan P. Siegel. *The Manager's Book of Quotations*. AMACOM, New York, NY: 1991

Arranged according to topic, here is inspiration, education, and a great source for speeches.

Heider, John. *The Tao of Leadership*. New York: Bantam, 1986.

Lao Tzu addressed this to the most powerful leaders of his day: "In order to lead, the leader learns to follow. In order to prosper, the leader learns to live simply." Heider's book is based on the work of this ancient Chinese sage.

Sherer, John. *Work and the Human Spirit*. Spokane, WA: JS&A, 1993.

Sherer contributes his conviction that work is not just about things, but also about the spirit. Spirituality is not religiosity, but a reverent view of all life.

Myers-Briggs Type Inventory

Hirsh, Sandra Krebs and Jean M. Kummerow. *Introduction to Type in Organizations*. Palo Alto, CA: Consulting Psychologists Press, 1990.

Isachsen, Olaf and Linda V. Berens. *Working Together*. San Juan Capistrano, CA: Institute for Management Development, 1988.

Keirsey, David and Marilyn Bates. *Please Understand Me*. Del Mar, CA: Prometheus Nemesis Book Company, 1984.

Kroeger, Otto with Janet M. Thuesen. *Type Talk at Work*. New York: Bantam Doubleday Dell Publishing Group Inc., 1992.

Myers, Isabel Briggs with Peter B. Myers. *Gifts Differing*. Palo Alto, CA: Consulting Psychologists Press, 1980.

Women in Organizations

Adler, Nancy J. and Dafna N. Izraeli, Eds. *Competitive Frontiers: Women Managers in a Global Economy*. Oxford, UK & Cambridge, MA: Blackwell Publishing, 1994.

Brook, Paula. *Work Less, Live More: A Woman's Guide*. Toronto, ON: Doubleday Canada, 1997.

Carter, Mae R., Beth Haslett and Florence L. Geis. *The Organizational Women: Power and Paradox*. Westport, CT: Ablex Publishing Corporation, 1992.

Colwill, Nina L. and Susan Vinnicombe. *The Essence of Women in Management*. Upper Saddle River, NJ: Prentice Hall, 1995.

Cooper, Cary L. and Marilyn J. Davidson. *Shattering the Glass Ceiling: The Woman Manager*. London, UK: Paul Chapman Publishing, 1992

Duff, Carolyn S. *When Women Work Together: Using Our Strengths to Overcome Our Challenges*. Berkeley, CA: Conari Press, 1993.

Gay, Katherine. *In the company of Women: Canadian Women Talk about What It It Takes to Create and Manage a Successful Business*. Toronto, ON: HarperBusiness: 1997.

Gerkovitch Griffith, Paulette, Judith L. MacBride-King and Bickley Townsend. *Closing the Gap: Women's Advancement in Corporate and Professional Canada*. Ottawa, ON: Conference Board of Canada, 1997.

Griffiths, Sian, ed. *Beyond the Glass Ceiling: Forty Women Whose Ideas Shape the Modern World*. Manchester, UK: Manchester University Press, 1996.

Roberts, Heather. *Taking Care of Business: Stories of Canadian Women Entrepreneurs*. Bolton, ON: Fenn Publishing, 1997.

Deloitte & Touche. *Working Our Way up: Mentoring the Next Generation*. 1997.